The Winner of the Slow Bicycle Race

THE WINNER OF THE SLOW BICYCLE RACE

The Satirical Writings of Paul Krassner

FOREWORD BY KURT VONNEGUT

SEVEN STORIES PRESS

New York

A Seven Stories Press First Edition
All rights reserved.
Copyright © 1996 by Paul Krassner
Foreword copyright © 1996 by Kurt Vonnegut

Library of Congress Cataloguing-in-Publication Data
Krassner, Paul, 1932—
    The Winner of the Slow Bicycle Race: The Satirical Writings of Paul Krassner
        p.   cm.
    ISBN: 1-888363-04-5
    1. United States—History—1960—Satire 2. Political Satire, American I. Title.

                                    95–073166
                                    CIP

10 9 8 7 6 5 4 3 2 1
Printed in the United States of America
Book design by LaBreacht Design

All the pieces in this book were originally published in *The Realist* except for the following: "Growth in Fear Stocks" and "On the 200th Anniversary of the First Amendment" were published in *The Nation*; "The Last Dan Quayle Joke," "An Interview with Nancy Reagan" and "A Letter to Dick Gregory" were published in *High Times*; "The Mime and the Pacer" and "And Whose Little Monkey Are You?" were published in *National Lampoon*; "Theologically Correct Condoms" was telecast on the *Wilton-North Report*; "Hypnotic Age Regression of a Television Addict" was published in *Whole Earth Review*; "A Sneak Preview of Richard Nixon's Memoirs" was published in *Chic*; "Thomas Eagleton Seagull" was published in *Playboy*; "I Just Got Back from an Orgy" was published in *Cavalier*.

CONTENTS

For Jerry Garcia, who will be

missed like a middle finger.

"**W**hen you are joyous, look deep into your heart, and you shall find it is only that which has given you sorrow that is giving you joy. When you are sorrowful, look again in your heart, and you shall see that in truth you are weeping for that which has been your delight."—Kahlil Gibran

"**P**eople use *The Prophet* to get laid."—Lenny Bruce

One summer, at a Field Day on the local high school athletic grounds, there was a variety of competitive events, but only one really appealed to me—the Slow Bicycle Race. You had to ride your bicycle as slowly as possible for about a hundred feet without turning or zigzagging. If your foot touched the ground, you were automatically disqualified. Whoever came in last would be declared the winner.

The starting whistle blew. Fortunately, I got off to a slow start. Now the trick was to remain behind. It was as if I had studied Zen in the Art of Slow Bicycle Riding. I *became* my bicycle. I was at one with the seat, the handlebars, the chain that drove the wheel. Pushing gently on the pedals, I gradually increased the distance between myself and the rest of the contestants until I was far enough behind them that it became obvious I would reach the finish line last. In an ordinary race, others could catch up to you, but here they would have to slow down.

Even though I hadn't crossed the finish line yet, I was so far behind now that it was inevitable that I would win.

The spectators were all cheering me on. There was no way I could lose, as long as I kept my balance. I felt absolutely exhilarated. But there was always the Unknown—that irrational, unpredictable factor—allowing you to take nothing for granted. Just when you thought you were in perfect harmony with the universe, Fate might suddenly intervene like a gigantic fist in the sky, punching at you through the clouds, as a disembodied voice boomed: *"Oh, yeah? Pow! Pow! Pow!"*

So the only thing to do was savor the experience. I was *already* the winner of the Slow Bicycle Race, whether or not I came in last.

—Paul Krassner
Confessions of a Raving, Unconfined Nut:
Misadventures in the Counter-Culture

Paul Krassner, 63 at this writing (1996), old enough to be my baby brother, in 1963 created a miracle of compressed intelligence nearly as admirable for potent simplicity, in my opinion, as Einstein's $e=mc^2$. With the Vietnam War going on, and with its critics discounted and scorned by the government and the mass media, Krassner put on sale a red, white and blue poster that said FUCK COMMUNISM.

At the beginning of the 1960s, FUCK was believed to be so full of bad magic as to be unprintable. In the most humanely influential American novel of this half century, *The Catcher in the Rye*, Holden Caulfield, it will be remembered, was shocked to see that word on a subway-station wall. He wondered what seeing it might do to the mind of a little kid. COMMUNISM was to millions the name of the most loathsome evil imaginable. To call an American a communist was like calling somebody a Jew in Nazi Germany. By having FUCK and COMMUNISM fight it out in a single sentence, Krassner wasn't merely being funny as heck. He was demonstrating how preposterous it was for so many people to be responding to both words with such cockamamie Pavlovian fear and alarm.

What hasn't been said about that poster, and surely not by Krassner, is that its author was behaving harmoniously with most of the Ten Commandments, the Bill of Rights of the Constitution of the United States and the Sermon on the Mount. So, too, were his now-dead friends Lenny Bruce and Abbie Hoffman and Jerry Rubin, roundly denounced and even arrested for bad manners and impudence, and now mourned and celebrated as heroes, which indeed they were, in this important book. They were prophets, too, at the service of humanity in jeering, like the prophets of old, at mean-spirited hypocrisies and stupidities and worse that were making their society a hell, whether there was a God or not.

And this book is emphatically not nostalgic, but raffishly responsive to the here and now. Nor are decades like chains of knockwursts, sutured off from one another at either end. To think of them as such, the 1950s, the 1960s, the 1970s and so on, is merely a mnemonic device. The only 1960s people are those who died back then. Everyone alive today has no choice but to be, like Paul Krassner, a 1990s person. Krassner does a good job of that. So should we all.

I told Krassner one time that his writings made me hopeful. He found this an odd compliment to offer a satirist. I explained that he made supposedly serious matters seem ridiculous, and that this inspired many of his readers to decide for themselves what was ridiculous and what was not. Knowing that there were people doing that, better late than never, made me optimistic.

—Kurt Vonnegut,
New York,
February 14, 1996

Introduction: The President's Penis

> Almost anything you do will be insignificant, but
> you must do it.—Gandhi

Actually, I'm quite proud of my false humility. So naturally, when Ellen Willis mentioned me in a recent *Village Voice* column—"Tell the truth, doesn't the presidential trouser-dropping, distinguishing-characteristic-in-the-genital-area scenario sound like something Paul Krassner made up?"—I immediately envisioned her readers with thought balloons saying "Who's he?" But I enjoyed serving as a relatively unknown generic reference for the absurdity of a national dick joke.

The media's great penis barrier had already been crumbling like the Berlin Wall. Anita Hill accused Clarence Thomas of comparing his penis size to that of porn star Long Dong Silver. John Wayne Bobbitt's wife sliced his penis off, went for a drive and threw it out her car window. As I recall, she was charged with littering. Michael Jackson's alleged child-molestation victim provided police with a physical description of Jackson's genitalia, and the police proceeded to videotape the King of Pop's penis. It was simply inevitable that Paula Jones would assert that Bill Clinton had once exposed his gubernatorial penis to her in a motel room.

Gennifer Flowers, whose claim to infamy is a long-time affair with Clinton, wrote in her book, *Passion and Betrayal*: "Laughter was always a big part of our relationship, so we had fun creating pet names for our private parts as well. I called mine Precious, and his penis was Willard. 'Why Willard?' I asked him. 'Because I always liked that name,' he said. 'You know, Willard for Willy!' And you know, it kind of had a Willard-like personality."

Hey, wait a minute, wasn't Willard a *rodent*? And didn't I see on TV a live rodent with a human ear growing on its back? And didn't Al Goldstein's *Screw* magazine publish the photo of a different rodent with a human hard-on growing on *its* back? Could it be that this circumcised erection is being harvested to replace Clinton's current Willard in order to fool a police camera crew who thought they were in photo-op heaven? Have I stumbled onto yet another insidious conspiracy?

All I know is that even as I write this, I'm busy making up another news story. Okay, now get this one. After four years of multiethnic cleansing in the Balkans, President Clinton, who dodged the draft during the Vietnam war, is sending American troops to Bosnia, while conservative legislators argue against such an action, feathers flying as hawks and doves switch positions. No, never mind, that's just *too* absurd. Nobody will believe me this time. I've finally gone too far. *Wolf! Wolf!*

In keeping with my false humility, when *People* referred to me as "the father of the underground press," my first response was to send a telegram: "I DEMAND A BLOOD TEST!" True, I had started publishing *The Realist* in 1958, but it was merely one link in an ongoing tradition of independent journalism in America.

One aspect of the cultural climate at that time can be illustrated by a case of television censorship in a *Playhouse 90* script. Rod Serling told me, "I was not permitted to use a line of dialogue that read as follows: 'Have you got a match?' The reason for this, advanced by the agency, was that the sponsor was the Ronson Lighter Company, and that matches were 'competitive.' " In another of his TV dramas, one that had a New York City locale, including a film clip with the usual Manhattan skyscrapers, the Chrysler Building was erased from the scene because the program was sponsored by the Ford Motor Company. On still another occasion, Serling had this line removed from a television script: "I'm an American." Reason? The sponsor was a cigarette company, one of whose competitors was the American Tobacco Company.

The closest an advertiser came to mentioning a competitive product in those days was when Kraft Deluxe Margarine referred to butter as "the expensive spread." An ad promised: "This is the margarine that tastes so good you can't tell it from 'the expensive spread.' One reason is that an extra something has been added. And yes, that extra something is 'the expensive spread' itself!"

When *The Realist* began publishing, birth control was against the law in 18 states. Now the Supreme Court has rejected a parental challenge to a school program in Massachusetts that makes condoms available free to junior and senior high school students. Also in 1958, the manufacture of munitions was a thriving industry in Israel, totaling $11 million. Exports to Germany alone during the first half of 1959 amounted to $9 million. Twenty-five years later, Israel was the fifth largest supplier of arms in the world, selling more weaponry to Latin America and Africa than either the U.S. or Russia. Munitions factories in Israel had become so busy that they functioned even on Saturdays, the Jewish Sabbath.

But that loss of Jewish tradition was later compensated for in Jerusalem by a group of 40 rabbis at a conference to discuss religious problems of space travel, including when the Sabbath should be observed on the moon, since time is so radically different there. Also, since the moon year is shorter, Jewish space travelers would face the problem of the frequency of Yom Kippur. The rabbis decided that on any trip to the moon, a good Jew should take a Hebrew calendar and a radio receiving set that would communicate the exact date of Yom Kippur.

In a similar vein, a report on the World Forum on Syphilis and Other Treponematoses stated: "The American Social Health Association warned that if the moon was to be kept free from venereal disease, prostitution must be barred there." And when I published as a Rumor of the Month that "so-called flying saucers are actually diaphragms being dropped by nuns on their way to heaven," a subscriber queried the Correspondence Organization for the Research of Aerial Phenomena and received this reply: "The explanation presented in *The Realist* is just what it was published as: a rumor. It is a rumor, not a theory. A theory would have substantial logic and data supporting it to cause the theorist to believe or support it. Do you have any idea what logic or evidence *The Realist* possesses to support their unbased rumor? Where did they get their information?"

The *Realist* became notorious for publishing satire without labeling it as such. But why deny readers the pleasure of discerning for themselves whether an article was the truth or a satirical extension of the truth? There could be a mixture of fact and fantasy within the same piece, the same paragraph, the same sentence.

When Jonathan Swift's *A Modest Proposal* was published, he didn't go around explaining, "Hey listen, folks, I was just kidding, I didn't really mean that we could solve both the overpopulation and hunger crises if only the British people could be persuaded to eat Irish babies, that was just a joke, see...." Indeed, at a recent humor conference, literature professors from different areas of the United States mentioned that when their classes were assigned to read *A Modest Proposal*, students took the satire literally, wanting only to be filled in on certain historical details.

When I published "The Parts Left Out of the Kennedy Book" in 1967, Lyndon Johnson's peculiar behavior on Air Force One was a metaphorical truth, yet it was perceived as literal truth by literate people, from an ACLU official to a Peabody Award-winning journalist to the intelligence community. Daniel Ellsberg admitted to me, "Maybe it was just because I *wanted* to believe it so badly." **21**

I also received a call from Ray Marcus, a critic of the Warren Commission Report, who had discovered a chronological flaw in my article. How could William Manchester leave something out of his book that was itself a *report* of something that he'd left out of his book? Marcus deduced that *The Realist* must have been given the excerpts by a CIA operative in order to discredit *valid* dissent on the assassination.

Merriman Smith, the UPI correspondent who always ended White House press conferences with the traditional "Thank you, Mr. President," finally felt that it was necessary to deny the incredible. "One of the filthiest printed attacks ever made on a President of the United States is now for sale on Washington newsstands," he wrote. "The target: President Johnson....It is filth attributed to someone of national stature supposedly describing something Johnson allegedly did. The incident, of course, never took place...."

Mercury Records is releasing my first comedy album, *We Have Ways of Making You Laugh*, taped before a live audience at L.A. the bookstore and containing much controversial material. But when I originally began performing in the early '50s, nightclub owners gave me a hard time for doing political humor. Specifically, they objected to my poking fun at McCarthyism. So it was with a certain sense of irony that a few decades later, I read in ABC newscaster Harry Reasoner's memoirs, *Before the Colors Fade*, the following passage:

"I've only been aware of two figures in the news during my career with whom I would not have shaken hands if called to deal with them professionally. I suppose that what Thomas Jefferson called a decent respect for the opinion of mankind requires me to identify those two. They were Senator Joseph McCarthy and a man named Paul Krassner or something like that who published a magazine called *The Realist* in the 1960s. I guess everyone knows who McCarthy was. Krassner and his *Realist* were part of a '60s fad of publications attacking the values of the establishment, which produced some very good papers and some very bad ones. Krassner not only attacked establishment values; he attacked decency in general, notably with an alleged 'lost chapter' from William Manchester's book, *The Death of a President*."

At least Reasoner had criticized me openly, under his own byline. In 1968, after *Life* magazine had published a profile of me, the FBI wrote a letter to the editor, not on FBI stationery, signing it "Howard Rasmussen, Brooklyn College" and complaining about the "aggrandizement of underground editor Paul Krassner....Am I asking the impossible by requesting that Krassner and his ilk be left in the sewers where they belong? That a national magazine of your fine reputation would waste time and effort on the cuckoo editor of an unimportant, smutty little rag is incomprehensible to me. Gentlemen, you must be aware that *The Realist* is nothing more than blatant obscenity. Your feature editor would do well to read a few back issues of *The Realist*. Try the article in 1963 [sic] following the assassination of President Kennedy, which describes disgusting necrophilism on the part of LBJ. To classify Krassner as some sort of 'social rebel' is far too cute. He's a nut, a raving, unconfined nut...."

The letter was authorized by J. Edgar Hoover's top two aides, William Sullivan and Kartha DeLoach. Their justification: "Krassner is the editor of *The Realist* and is one of the moving forces behind the Youth International Party, commonly known as the Yippies. Krassner is a spokesman for the New Left. *Life* magazine recently ran an article favorable to him. [The] proposed letter takes issue with the publishing of this article and points out that *The Realist* is obscene and that Krassner is a nut. This letter could, if printed by *Life*, call attention to the unsavory character of Krassner."

Life never published the FBI's poison-pen letter to the editor. However, they did publish *this* letter: "Regarding your article on that filthy-mouthed, dope-taking, pinko-anarchist, Pope-baiting Yippie-lover: cancel my subscription immediately! [*Signed*] Paul Krassner, *The Realist*."

The FBI's attempt at character assassination escalated to a more literal approach a year later. They anonymously printed and distributed a WANTED flyer featuring a large swastika with photos of Jerry Rubin, Abbie Hoffman, Mark Rudd of SDS (Students for a Democratic Society) and myself. The caption: "LAMPSHADES! LAMPSHADES! LAMPSHADES! LAMPSHADES!" The copy stated that "the only solution to Negro problems in America would be the *elimination* of the Jews. May we suggest the following order of elimination? After all, we've been this way before." There followed this list:

All Jews connected with the Establishment.

All Jews connected with Jews connected with the Establishment.

All Jews connected with those immediately above.

All Jews except those in the Movement.

All Jews in the Movement except those who dye their skins black.

All Jews. Look out, Jerry, Abbie, Mark and Paul!

In a letter of authorization, the FBI stated in part: "Assure that all necessary precautions are taken to protect the Bureau as the source of this leaflet [which] suggests facetiously the elimination of these leaders."

And, of course, if some militant overachiever had obtained that flyer and "eliminated" one of those "New Left leaders who are Jewish," the FBI's bureaucratic ass would be covered: "We said it was a facetious suggestion, didn't we?"

A few years later, after J. Edgar Hoover's death, his former assistant director, William Sullivan (later killed by a deer hunter), told the *Los Angeles Times* that wiretap files located by the FBI in a White House safe were kept from Hoover because he was "not of sound mind."

Talk about your raving, unconfined nuts....

Then there was the phenomenon of satirical prophecy.

I once predicted onstage that "the radical wing of the feminist movement will finally deem sexual intercourse acceptable only if the man doesn't have an erection." A dozen years later *New Republic* published

25

an article, "The New Porn Wars," by Jean Bethke Elshtain, which included this sentence: "[Andrea] Dworkin has written that it is acceptable for women to have sex with men as long as the man's penis isn't erect."

After "A Sneak Preview of Richard Nixon's Memoirs" was published, Liz Smith—who hadn't seen that piece—wrote in her syndicated column that H. R. Haldeman had been in the Oval Office with Nixon, and that his trousers were down to his ankles. Hoping to smoke out the truth, I retyped one page of the manuscript, adding a phrase (shown in italics) to this sentence: "When the incident was over, I simply returned to my desk, and although the tension of vulnerability was still in the air *and my trousers were still around my ankles*, we resumed our discussion as if nothing had occurred." I then photocopied the manuscript and sent it to Liz Smith. I had assumed she would check with her sources. Instead, she wrote in her column that she had been fooled by *me*, implying that her sources had based their revelation on my article. Somehow my hoax on Liz Smith backfired. I had become a victim of my own satirical prophecy.

In his memoirs, I had Nixon insisting that Watergate was a setup to get rid of him as President. A decade later, Nixon himself made that claim in a network television interview. Furthermore, Haldeman in his book, *The Ends of Power*, would reveal that Nixon used code words when talking about the murder of President Kennedy. Haldeman said that Nixon always referred to the assassination as "the Bay of Pigs." And, on May 5, 1977, the *Houston Post* published a UPI dispatch that stated:

26

"Watergate burglar Frank Sturgis said Wednesday that the CIA planned the break-in because high officials felt Richard Nixon was becoming too powerful and was overly interested in the assassination of John Kennedy...'Several times the President asked [CIA director] Richard Helms for the files on the Kennedy assassination but Helms refused to give them to him, refused a direct order from the President,' Sturgis said. 'I believe Nixon would have uncovered the true facts in the assassination of President Kennedy and that would have taken off the heat in Watergate. Because Nixon wanted files, the CIA felt they had to get rid of him.' Asked if Nixon ever was in danger, Sturgis replied, 'Yes, absolutely. Nixon was lucky he wasn't killed—assassinated like President Kennedy.'"

Another piece, "Sex Education for the Modern Catholic Child," turned out to have been theologically correct 26 years after I originally wrote it, when Pope John Paul II warned that the rhythm method of birth control can be "an abuse if the couple is seeking in this way to avoid children for unworthy reasons."

Likewise, five years after I wrote "Theologically Correct Condoms," I would read in *Catholic Identity in Health Care Principles and Practice*:

"Catholic moral principles rule out masturbation or withdrawal during the act of intercourse as methods of obtaining adequate samples of human sperm for analysis. Father Edwin Healy's comments on the liceity of the use of the perforated condom include the following statement: 'The perforation must be large

27

enough to permit the greater part of the ejaculation to reach the female genital tract, for otherwise the coitus would be substantially contraceptive and unnatural.'

"It should be noted, however, that distinguished theologians considered the use of the perforated condom to be immoral. In Father Arthur Vermeersch's opinion, such a means of collecting human sperm would involve 'the direct will to deposit some of the ejaculate outside of the vagina—something that makes it a *partial onanism*.' He suggested that it would not be immoral to aspirate seminal fluid from the testicles or from the epididymides by using a needle or syringe. The argument was that such methods would not involve stimulation of the generative faculty."

Not to mention stimulation of the student body.

My straight reporting in *The Realist* often became a form of participatory journalism. After publishing an anonymous interview with "a humane abortionist" (Dr. Robert Spencer), who performed the then-illegal operation for as little as $5, I acted as an underground referral service for a decade, and was called before district attorneys in two different cities, but refused to cooperate. In the course of writing about LSD researchers Timothy Leary and Richard Alpert (now Ram Dass), I became a devoted acid-head myself, distributing it free at love-ins. And while covering the antiwar movement, I began entertaining at protest demonstrations, later co-founding the Yippies with Abbie Hoffman and Jerry

28

Rubin. All I had ever really wanted to do was make people laugh, but somehow I ended up on the FBI's Roundup Index, a list of radicals to be kidnapped to Mexico in a national emergency.

This is the first anniversary of Jerry Rubin's death. A year ago, I was in New York having lunch with Steve Wasserman, who had been Jerry's gofer when he was 13 and is now editorial director of Times Books, a division of Random House. We discussed the possibility of my writing a Jerry Rubin biography. Wasserman suggested it might be a better idea for me to take an unorthodox approach.

Six months later I finished working on "Who Killed Jerry Rubin?" The story wasn't long enough to be a book, but properly nurtured, I thought it could provide the centerpiece for a collection of my satire. I gave the manuscript to my agent, who proceeded to send it to 10 publishers. They all turned him down. Even Simon & Schuster, which had just sold out 30,000 copies of my autobiography, *Confessions of a Raving, Unconfined Nut: Misadventures in the Counter-Culture*, declined. I was beginning to feel like a counter-cultural has-been. A psychedelic relic.

I withdrew the collection from my agent to see if I could place it myself. I sent it to 26 publishers. No luck. I finally decided to publish the book myself, under the Limited Appeal imprint. But then I got a call from Dan Simon, who was launching Seven Stories Press. He had read my manuscript and wanted to publish it. He was previously founder and co-publisher at Four Walls

Eight Windows, and had been the only one to respond to Abbie Hoffman's classified ad in *The Nation* seeking a publisher, so I felt a certain sense of continuity.

Dan is a thoughtful individual, and I found it a delight to work with him. It was his idea to publish my pieces in reverse chronological order. At first I thought this was just plain quirky, but then it became an experience of tracing a line back to my satirical roots, and I agreed to go along with his notion. Our collaboration was almost psychic, such as the mutual decision to include "The Mime and the Pacer" even though it's literally true, because it also works as a satiric parable.

Similarly, Dan made a marginal note above the title of "How I Spent My First Acid Trip." He wrote: "Keep this because it's a *confession* on the subject of absurdity and thus inextricably linked to your satire."

In "And Whose Little Monkey Are You?" he made a marginal note pointing to my sentence, "The bad news is, those monkeys *needed* that dirt [which they now wash off the sweet potatoes] in their diet for roughage!" He wrote, "I think dirt provides minerals, not roughage—sweet potatoes provide roughage! Oh, well..." Despite the fact that he had pulled my satirical premise right out from under me, we decided to include that story.

Dan liked my dedication of the book to Jerry Garcia, but he thought it was only a metaphor. He didn't know that Garcia was *literally* missing the middle finger of his right hand. "Maybe we should have a footnote," Dan suggested. Consider this a footnote, then. At Garcia's funeral, where his body lay in an open casket, his left hand had been placed so that it was covering his right hand. When Garcia's daughter Anabel noticed this, she changed it so that his hand with the missing finger was on top.

Later, Garcia's body was cremated. His ashes were mixed with high-grade marijuana, rolled into several joints and at a private memorial, passed around and smoked by his family, a few close friends, members of the band and one lucky Deadhead selected at random.

Of course, Dan Simon and I had our disagreements too.

He objected to the word *false* in the first sentence of this introduction: "Actually, I'm quite proud of my false humility." He argued that I'm truly humble. I disagreed. Personally, I believe that *all* humility is false. But at least false humility is better than no humility at all.

Further on, where I posed a rhetorical question—"Why deny readers the pleasure of discerning for themselves whether an article was the truth or an extension of the truth?"—Dan thought I ought to say, "Why deny readers the pleasure, *and the responsibility*, of discerning for themselves...?" But I resisted inserting that phrase. I'm just not comfortable being preachy. It probably has something to do with my false humility.

"You're not a leader," Abbie Hoffman once chastised me. "You don't urge people to do things."

When it comes to discerning truth, though, that's a totally subjective process. The other day, a massage therapist who was working on my back began to speak. He doesn't usually talk while he's working, but he wanted to respond to an interview I'd done with Jerry Garcia. It began:

Q. Does the world seem to be getting weirder and weirder to you?

A. Yeah. The weirdest thing lately for me was that thing of the Ayatollah and the mine-sweeping children. In the war between Iran and Iraq, he used kids and had them line up like a human chain, holding hands, and walk across the mine fields because it was cheaper than mine detectors.

Q. That's just unfathomable.

A. It's amazingly inhuman. People complained about the Shah—a few fingernails and stuff—but this is kids walking across mine fields. It's absolutely surreal. How could people go for that?

Q. But how do you remain optimistic? There's 48 wars going on now simultaneously, and yet the music is joyful. Even "Please don't murder me" is a joyful song.

A. Well, when things are at that level, there's kind of a beauty to the simplicity of it. I wrote that song when the Zodiac Killer was out murdering in San Francisco. Every night I was coming home from the studio, and I'd stop at an intersection and look around, and if a car pulled up, it was like, "This is it, I'm gonna die now." It became a game. Every night I was conscious of that thing, and the refrain got to be so real to me. "Please don't murder me, *please* don't murder me."

My massage therapist objected to Garcia's automatic acceptance as factual in the first place the

32

news in the mainstream press about lines of mine-sweeping children in Iran. He had a point I hadn't even considered—and I'm supposed to be a professional skeptic.

In September 1991, I heard on NPR a discussion about land mines planted by the Khmer Rouge, leaving dead and limbless victims in Cambodia. There was an interview by Mary Kay Magistod with a prosthetic specialist and Dr. Christian Oh, Red Cross chief surgeon at a hospital, who pointed out that transportation became automatic triage, because the most severely wounded died on the way. The newscaster added, "A common view in Buddhist Cambodia is that anyone unfortunate enough to have stepped on a land mine must have done something bad in a previous life to deserve it."

There are now an estimated six million land mines in Bosnia. That's one for every Jew who died of bad karma during the Holocaust. Unless, of course, that NPR newscaster had her facts wrong about how Buddhists in Cambodia commonly view reincarnation.

Postscript: The *Cambodia Daily* suggests that England ship 11 million cattle with "mad cow disease" to Cambodia to roam free and detonate the roughly 11 million "equally mad land mines."

I stopped publishing *The Realist* in 1974, but after an 11-year hiatus I re-launched it in 1985, this time in newsletter format (Box 1230, Venice CA 90294; $12 for 6 issues, $23 for 12). "The taboos may have changed," I wrote in the return issue, "but irreverence is still our only sacred cow." However, the rate of irreverence has been accelerating.

It used to be, as Steve Allen once said, that "satire is tragedy plus time." But now, between fax machines and shock jocks and online computers, there is instant irreverence. Jokes were already being spread about the fire in Waco *while* the inhabitants at Branch Davidian headquarters were being burned alive. Indeed, the process of acceleration itself has become part of the humor. In an opening monologue David Letterman said that "Dr. Jack Kevorkian has invented a suicide-fax machine, so now the suicide note gets there immediately."

In 1966 *The Realist* published "The Cybernetic Revolution" by Robert Anton Wilson. He wrote: "If the structure allows for feedback from the environment and alteration of behavior in accordance with the feedback, you have a cybernetic system. The essence of cybernetics is just that: an information flow that allows for self-correction." As if to illustrate his own point, in 1994 Wilson wrote "My Life After Death" for *The Realist*, in which he described the feedback resulting from a false report of his demise on the Internet in an obituary supposedly copied from the *Los Angeles Times*. Paranoid theories flew left and right on electronic bulletin boards.

Even though the World Wide Web is being shaped as a monopolistic vehicle of gigantic corporations, it is also becoming a vehicle for social activism. We've gone from underground to cyberspace. In response to a proposed constitutional amendment to prohibit desecrating the American flag, Warren Apel organized the first interactive political protest on the Web. He designed the Flag-Burning Page. Users could click on images of a burning flag, with comments such as, "Well, now you did it. She's blazing and Newt's not gonna like it." And "Don't stop now. Who brought the marshmallows?" A tag line indicates that "no actual flags were harmed in the production of this page." Instead, pictures of a flag were combined with flames borrowed from photos of the Aggies' annual bonfire preceding the A&M vs. University of Texas football game.

Apel explains: "I was thinking I ought to protest the amendment somehow. I could go down to the state capitol and burn a flag. But usually when people do that, they use the wrong kind of flag, so it just melts rather than burns, and they end up looking really stupid. Besides, taking a tongue-in-cheek approach to politics is a good way to make the debate a little more open. If you come out ranting and raving, people don't take you too seriously." In the dialogue that ensued, there was this challenge: "How much would you like to bet that you really don't support the idea of 'freedom of expression' and that you are really just a cultural anarchist?" As though the two were mutually exclusive. Cultural anarchy *is* freedom of expression. So here's my salute to cultural anarchy on the Web. Long may it make electronic waves. Who knows, maybe the time has come for me to start my own website, the Virtual Realist. Meanwhile, reality keeps nipping at the heels of satire, more and more often overtaking it:

America Online purged the word *breast* from profiles of women seeking to share information about breast cancer, prompting one subscriber to ask, "Must we have 'hooter cancer survivors'?"

The PBS series *Frontline* apologized to anyone at the U.S. Postal Service who saw their program about the Internet and took offense at the term *snail mail*.

The National Association of Radio Talk Show Hosts presented a Freedom of Speech Award to G. Gordon Liddy.

The E! channel blocked out the image of a scantily clad woman enveloping a peeled banana with her mouth on the Howard Stern show.

Heroic firefighters from the bombing of the federal building in Oklahoma City are featured in a 1996 beefcake calendar.

The Unabomber sent his 35,000-word treatise to *The New York Times* and the *Washington Post*, promising that if it were published he would stop mailing homemade bombs, but he proved to be a serial terrorist with high moral standards, declaring that if the less respectable *Penthouse* magazine published his manifesto, he reserved the right to make one more such killing.

During a mobile phone conversation, Prince Charles told his mistress that he wanted to be incarnated as her tampon.

When Michael Jackson collapsed while rehearsing for an HBO special, folks backstage were quoted as saying, "He looked pale."

U.S. government officials banned a shipment of Colombian chickens to Cuba because their diet consisted of American-made chicken-feed, thus technically violating the trade embargo.

The Department of Agriculture allows two pellets of rat fecal matter per two kilograms of breakfast cereal.

O. J. Simpson, having been declared not guilty, is busy producing an infomercial to prove his innocence.

A woman who was mistaken for a juror in the Simpson trial was offered $5,000 by a news organization just to talk about being mistaken for a Simpson juror.

Kidnapping has become such a way of life in the Philippines that gangs now accept checks to cover their ransom demands.

There is now available at your grocery store Spam *and* Spam-Lite.

A man doing 55 miles per hour in a 55 miles-per-hour zone on a highway was pulled over and ticketed by a police officer for going too slow, because most of the traffic was moving about 70 miles an hour. He was charged with endangering drivers and impeding traffic.

Senator Dianne Feinstein had her gun melted down into a crucifix, and then she presented it to the Pope.

Speaker of the House Newt Gingrich claimed that Susan Smith's drowning of her two children was a reason to vote for the Republicans, then topped himself when he called the slaying of a pregnant woman and two of her children in Chicago, followed by the slicing open of her abdomen and the abduction of the baby she was carrying, "a byproduct of the welfare state."

Senator Bob Dole, said on *Meet the Press*, "I think sometimes you have to do the right thing."

The director of the Richard Nixon Presidential Library and Birthplace claims that Anthony Hopkins prepared for the title role in Oliver Stone's film *Nixon* by studying videotapes of Rich Little doing his impression of Richard Nixon.

Comic-impressionist Jim Morris was a guest on CNN's *Crossfire*. He appeared in the role of President Clinton, being asked and answering serious questions about domestic issues and foreign policy. And the next day the real Bill Clinton's approval rating went up three points.

When Apollo Mission astronaut Neil Armstrong first walked on the moon, he not only said, "One small step for man, one giant step for mankind," but also, just before reentering the landing craft, he uttered enigmatically, "Good luck, Mr. Gorsky." At NASA they thought it referred to a rival Soviet cosmonaut, but there was no Gorsky in either the Russian or American space program. For 26 years Armstrong never answered questions about that remark, but finally—on July 5, 1995, in Tampa Bay, Florida—he gave in. Gorsky had died and so Armstrong felt it would not be inappropriate to respond. When he was a young boy, playing baseball in the backyard, his brother hit a fly ball that landed in front of a neighbor's bedroom window—the Gorskys. As Armstrong was retrieving the ball, he heard Mrs. Gorsky shouting: "Oral sex? You want oral sex? You'll get oral sex when the kid next door walks on the moon!"

Now I ask you, what satirist could possibly have an imagination so wild as to invent any one of the above items?

38 Speaking of satirists with wild imaginations, Harry Shearer asked me to be sure and mention in my introduction that "William Bennett is the most dangerous man in America." Done. Bennett has accused Pat Buchanan of "flirting with fascism." That's like Charlie Sheen deriding Hugh Grant because he had to pay for sex, or like Johnnie Cochran complaining that the district attorney chose to present Christopher Darden to the Simpson jury because he was black.

Now, I'm no stranger to conspiracy research, albeit through the side door.

I had once started out to gather material for a satire on the Patty Hearst case, was apprised by the FBI that I made the hit-list of a Berkeley underground group—led by an FBI provocateur, so that the right wing of the FBI was warning me about the left wing of the FBI—and I ended up believing with all my heart that the FBI and the CIA were behind Patty's kidnapping.

And I had once started out to gather material for a satire on the Charles Manson case, learned that individuals in the Los Angeles Police Department had seized home-made porno films from Sharon Tate's loft and were selling them, became a target of Scientology's Operation Dynamite—their jargon for a frame-up—and I ended up believing with all my heart that the murders had actually been orchestrated by an agent for Naval Intelligence posing as a hippie artist.

So now, when I listen to those who believe with all *their* hearts that O.J. Simpson was framed by the LAPD, or to those who believe with all *their* hearts that the federal government was behind the bombing in Oklahoma City, I can identify with President Clinton, and I want to reach out to these people and say, "I *feel* your paranoia."

Recently, I was one of four speakers at a conspiracy forum sponsored by Deep River Books.

"Remember the leg that was found in the ruins of the bombed-out federal building in Oklahoma City?" I asked. "First it was determined to have belonged to a white man. Then, on further inspection, it was determined to have belonged to a black woman. Well, now there's evidence that the leg was planted in the rubble by Detective Mark Fuhrman."

There was just a split-second hesitation before the conspiracy-oriented audience laughed, as though they had assumed that I might actually have been informing them of a journalistic fact.

But that's always the risk an investigative satirist takes.

One year after Jerry Rubin's death, his ex-wife, Mimi Leonard Fleischman, held a dinner party to celebrate his life.

My wife, Nancy, accompanied me. She had first encountered Jerry in 1969 when she was working on a pilot for CBS. She and her cohorts went to Chicago during the Conspiracy Trial. There were protests in the streets around the courthouse while they were tapping in a coffeehouse where the defendants hung out. Jerry was wearing a lady's brown wig because they had cut his hair in jail. "It looks okay, doesn't it?" he asked.

She saw him again in 1972 on the floor of the Democratic convention in Miami, which she was covering for TVTV. Jerry was sitting in the front row, the podium looming right above, and she sat next to him with her handheld camera. The shouting was so loud it was almost impossible to hear the speaker who was reading off the nominations for Vice President. Jerry's eyes were flashing wildly. "Shhhh," he said to the crowd, cupping one hand to his ear. The speaker announced, "Jerry Rubin, one vote." Jerry was bedazzled.

At the dinner, I learned that Jerry had taken to wearing old Grateful Dead T-shirts underneath his expensive new suits. Disc jockey/political activist Casey Kasem said that if he had met Jerry in the '60s "there would have been the Chicago Nine." Kasem's wife, Jean, was an Army brat during the Vietnam war and always hoped that Jerry would end the war so she and her family could come back home to America.

And Rona Elliot, my former assistant at *The Realist*, told about the time Phil Ochs was feeling particularly depressed and Jerry asked her to please fuck Phil because it would cheer him up. Rona is a good sport—once, when Ken Kesey had a severe cold and was bedded down in my home, she got dressed up in a nurse's uniform and served him chicken soup—but she graciously declined Jerry's request.

A moment of epiphany at this celebration of Jerry's life occurred for me in a conversation with

Fred Branfman, who had been present at Jerry's death. It was the first time they'd met. Branfman had had an appointment that evening at Jerry's apartment in Brentwood. After circling the block a few times, Branfman ended up parking on Wilshire Boulevard directly across the street from Jerry's building. When their meeting was over, Branfman, Jerry and his girlfriend, Stephanie, decided to have dinner out. After some discussion they chose to take Branfman's car. On the sidewalk, Jerry was hyper as usual. "Come on," he said, "let's go!" He began darting across the street. Branfman saw a car coming at Jerry and shouted to him. Jerry turned and said, "What's going on?" Those were his last words. Then, *boink*! But none of this would have happened, Branfman told me, if he, Branfman, had known more about wealthy people, their habits and privileges. If he had been aware that you can drive your car right up to the high-rise and the doorman will take it and park for you, he would have done that. Which means, in some convoluted kind of way, that Jerry Rubin was ultimately done in by his own upwardly mobile striving.

And that's the kind of cosmic irony that always helps to keep my false humility intact.

Finally, I'd like to share with you the background of a particular piece in this book, "I Snorted Cocaine with the Pope."

One Sunday afternoon I was a guest on a weekly radio program hosted by conspiracy researcher Mae Brussell, whose work I had published in *The*

42

Realist. Her first article ("Why Was Martha Mitchell Kidnapped?") delineated and documented the conspiracy behind Watergate—naming names, all the way up to Attorney General John Mitchell and President Richard Nixon—while for several months the mainstream press continued to refer to the break-in as a "caper" and a "third-rate burglary."

Theodore Charach, who investigated the assassination of Robert F. Kennedy, was also a guest on Mae's program. At one point during our conversation, Charach mentioned the autopsy report, which indicated that one of the bullets was in the back of Kennedy's neck, and I responded with a remark about how Kennedy's head must have turned around 360 degrees like Linda Blair in *The Exorcist*.

That image became a one-liner in my standup performances, and soon enough began cohabiting with another one-liner—my *National Enquirer* headline, "I Snorted Cocaine with the Pope"—evolving together, performance after performance, into a set routine about my meeting Pope John Paul II at a party, getting stoned with him in the bathroom and discussing the assassination of Bobby Kennedy.

Eventually, "I Snorted Cocaine with the Pope" was submitted in written form to *National Lampoon*. Editor-in-chief Larry "Ratso" Sloman informed me that although all the editors loved it, there was fear of an organized letter-writing campaign to the magazine's advertisers. So instead I published it in *The Realist*, which has never had any advertisers to lose.

I had told and retold that story onstage so many times that I came to believe I actually *had* snorted cocaine with the Pope. I could have passed a polygraph test. Now, whenever I see Pope John Paul II on TV, I still get a thrill remembering our brief encounter. It happened again just yesterday. I was watching the network news and there he was, standing on a balcony, waving to the crowd outside his Vatican headquarters. A newscaster reported that the Pontiff had warned against indulging in "senseless euphoria"—referring not to the Rapture as foretold in the New Testament, but merely to the last hours of 1995. It was New Year's Eve.

And so, dear reader, I hope you'll enjoy following the satirical tracks of my slow bicycle race. May your own path be strewn with countless moments of senseless euphoria.

—Paul Krassner,
Venice
January 1, 1996

Who Killed Jerry Rubin?

1995

The Abbie Hoffman Connection

In the funky, tumble-down Victorian house in Berkeley that served as the Vietnam Day Committee headquarters, 13-year-old Steve Wasserman served as a gofer for Jerry Rubin.

"Jerry had just successfully helped organize the Vietnam Day teach-ins, in May 1965," he recalls. "But he was always an *enthusiast*. One part enthusiast, one part huckster, always a hustler, and basically, always trying to do the right thing."

Kate Coleman, an organizer of the Free Speech Movement in 1964, describes Rubin as "sweet and dorky" and having "a Zen sense of excitement for whatever was going on."

But according to Frank Bardacke, another FSM organizer, "When Jerry first came to Berkeley in 1963, the word on him was that he was an FBI agent. All he ever did was ask questions. He would sit on the terrace, and some bullshit-artist would be pontificating about C. Wright Mills, and there would be Jerry taking notes. *Taking notes.* And he went from table to table and group to group doing that. For *one year*. Now wouldn't you figure he was a police spy? When we asked Jerry what he was doing, he would say, 'I am trying to figure out what I believe, what I should do.'"

What he did was to become a Paul Revere of the Vietnam war, shouting his warning: "The Americans are coming! The Americans are coming!" And when Jerry was subpoenaed to testify before the House Un-American Activities Committee, Ronnie Davis, founder of the San Francisco Mime Troupe, persuaded him to wear the uniform of a soldier in the American Revolution.

"I felt like a real asshole," Jerry told me, "but I felt compelled to do it."

When Jerry had moved to New York in 1967, Abbie Hoffman and he became partners in pranks—from throwing money in the stock exchange to exorcising the Pentagon—giving birth to the Youth International Party, the Yippies, a name I provided to describe a phenomenon that already existed, an organic coalition of stoned hippies and political activists. As editor of *The Realist*, my role in the Yippies was to serve as a media spokesperson.

In February 1968, a group of Yippie leaders attended a conference of college newspaper editors in Washington. Presidential candidate Eugene McCarthy was scheduled to hold a press conference for them. I was invited to introduce him. Then McCarthy's people chickened out, and I was disinvited.

That day, the front-page headline of the *New York Post* blared: "Reds Crack Hue Jail, Free 2000." Jerry, tripping on acid, was debating with himself whether or not to rush up to the podium with a copy of the *Post* and share this exciting Vietnam war news with McCarthy.

46

"Jerry," I said, "just do it."

Who knows, that might have been where he got the idea to title his first book, *Do it!*.

In the summer of '68 the Yippies went to Chicago to protest, by the example of their alternative value system, the Democratic National Convention, since the war had been escalating under the Democrats' watch. Although the Kerner Commission officially labeled what happened in the streets as "a police riot," eight individuals were indicted for conspiracy to cross state lines to cause a riot.

The Chicago Conspiracy Trial in 1969-70 provided a public vehicle for guerrilla theater. One day, for example, Abbie and Jerry came to court dressed in judicial robes. Judge Julius Hoffman was not amused and ordered them to remove the robes. Under Abbie's black robe was a blue-and-white Chicago Police Department shirt.

Ironically, the most startling image of that trial sprang from Judge Hoffman himself, when he ordered that Black Panther Bobby Seale's hands and feet be shackled to a chair and that a gag be put over his mouth, because Seale wanted to defend himself. Now, a quarter-century later, Colin Ferguson, an obviously insane black man who gunned down a half-dozen passengers on a Long Island Railroad train, has been permitted by a judge to defend himself. Is that progress or what?

In 1972, after the Yippies protested the Republican convention in Miami—where a group called the Zippies accused Abbie Hoffman and Jerry Rubin of being publicity-seeking has-beens—Jerry moved to San Francisco and became a health freak. He drank so much carrot juice that he turned orange. He also learned from the human potential movement how to overcome his low self-esteem for having orange skin.

Jerry met therapist Stella Resnick, and on their first date, he asked her to marry him. She declined, but they did become lovers and workshop co-leaders. "She's the female Jerry Rubin," he told me. Together, they threw balled-up slices of Wonder Bread at the audience, and Jerry lit up a joint onstage.

In 1974, he moved back to New York—and Wall Street. Meanwhile, Abbie Hoffman, who the year before was entrapped into selling cocaine to undercover cops, went on the lam to avoid a mandatory 15-years-to-life sentence. He emerged six years later and plea-bargained himself into a work-release program. In 1984 he reunited with Jerry, traveling the country in a series of debates titled "Yippie vs. Yuppie." If Abbie were to throw money in the stock exchange now, Jerry would invest it.

Jerry had become so involved in the world of finance that he announced, "Money is the long hair of the '80s." He had once written that a necktie was a hangman's noose, but now he was wearing one. He even sent out a press release requesting that the media no longer refer to him as a former Yippie leader. My headline in *The Realist*: "Former Yippie Leader Asks Not to Be Called Former Yippie Leader!"

In 1989, Abbie committed suicide. I was devastated. This was not his first suicide attempt, just his most successful one. Certain conspiracy theorists believed that he was the victim of an assassination plot, culminating with an autopsy conducted by the same coroner who had performed an autopsy on NBC news anchor Jessica Savitch, whom they also considered to be the victim of an assassination plot. But I checked it out, and came to the conclusion that Abbie had indeed taken his own life. Every year since, Johanna Lawrenson, his underground running mate, has organized a celebration on his birthday to benefit the Abbie Hoffman Activist Foundation.

In November 1994, I was in New York to speak at the fifth annual Abbie party, when I got a phone call that Jerry had died. The next morning, a front-page headline shouted, "Death of a Monster!" I was furious, under the impression that Newt Gingrich's demonizing of the counter-culture had already trickled down to the *New York Post*. But no, that headline referred to Jeffrey Dahmer, the serial killer/cannibal/necrophiliac, who had been bludgeoned to death in prison by another inmate. The *New York Daily News* headline was "Dahmer's Just Desserts." The joke was that the killer planned to hire O. J. Simpson's attorneys, and that they would have him plead self-defense: "Jeffrey Dahmer came at me with a knife—and a fork."

At the Abbie Hoffman party, attorney William Kunstler took the stage, eulogizing both Abbie and Jerry. Then he proceeded to describe my appearance as a witness at the Chicago Conspiracy Trial. True, I had ingested 300 micrograms of LSD before taking the stand, but Kunstler's account of my testimony bore no relation to the trial transcript. A reporter for the *Los Angeles Times*, Josh Getlin, who had read a completely different exchange in my autobiography, confronted Kunstler, who responded, "These are details. I mean, the man was stoned out of his mind. That's all you need to know."

The next night, I was a guest of Bob Fass on his WBAI program, *Radio Unnamable*. A listener called in to suggest that Jerry Rubin had been the victim of an assassination plot. I promised to check it out. Fass pooh-poohed the idea, but unlike with Abbie, I had reason to believe that Jerry's death could well have been the result of a conspiracy. If so, there was a certain karmic inevitability about it, stemming from his essential idealism, his widespread influence—and his various enemies.

The Phil Ochs Connection

It looked like Bob Dylan was trying to tear out his hair. This was backstage at the Newport Folk Festival in 1965. Dylan was having a fit of frustration because folks in the audience had just booed him for going electric with "Like a Rolling Stone."

"It's gonna be a hit," Phil Ochs had said to me, as people backstage were dancing euphorically. "Hey, Bob," he called out now. "It's gonna be a hit!" But Dylan couldn't hear him. "It's gotta be a hit!"

On another occasion, when Dylan played "Can You Please Crawl Out Your Window" for him, Ochs said, "I don't think it'll be a hit."

That time Dylan heard him.

"You're crazy, man," he told Ochs. "You only know protest, that's all." Then Dylan's limousine arrived and they got into it. But after a short distance,

Dylan ordered the driver to pull over. "Get out, Ochs. You're not a folk singer. You're a journalist."

Ochs had indeed started out as a journalist, rising to managing editor of the Ohio State University paper. He was dropped when he wrote a pro-Castro article in 1961. But you can't stifle a point of view. Phil then wrote his first protest song, "The Ballad of the Cuban Invasion."

And yet he was the ultimate patriot. At a Berkeley anti-war rally, somebody threw an American flag on the ground, and Phil refused to perform until it was picked up.

"If I were in China, singing the songs I sing," he said, "I would be killed. In Russia, I would be in a lot of trouble. Here, I am free. This is our strength, the power and the glory. America could become the greatest country in the world."

His song "The Power and the Glory" was later recorded by Anita Bryant.

"I want to be a noncompromising left-wing star," Phil would say. "I want to be a spokesman, not afraid to speak of Castro or Malcolm X onstage. I want to build a career in which a truly controversial song can become a hit single. I want to sing 'I Ain't Marchin' Anymore' on the Ed Sullivan show."

Although he was turned down by Sullivan, as well as by Merv Griffin and the Smothers Brothers, he did manage to sing at least the first couple of bars of "Marchin'" as part of his testimony at the Chicago Conspiracy Trial. His guitar was impounded by Judge Hoffman as an official piece of evidence.

William Kunstler had asked the witness, "Can you identify that exhibit?"

"This is the guitar I played 'I Ain't Marchin' Anymore' on."

Kunstler requested Ochs to sing it right then and there in the courtroom, the better to recapture the ambiance of the previous year's protest against the Democratic convention, but Judge Hoffman interrupted the song, and Ochs had to settle for reciting the lyrics.

"It's always the old to lead us to the war," he spoke, looking directly into the eyes of the judge. "It's always the young to fall."

But no rendition could have done justice to the memory of what had happened that summer evening at the Chicago Coliseum in 1968. At an Unbirthday party for President Lyndon Johnson, while Phil was singing "I Ain't Marchin' Anymore," an individual in the audience started burning his draft card. Then someone else did. And a third, and a fourth. It was, quite literally, spontaneous combustion.

And then, even as the war in Vietnam was continuing to escalate, Phil sang "The War is Over." When he reached the line, "But just before the end, even treason might be worth a try," the crowd of 5000 went absolutely wild, cheering him on with a combination of outrage and optimism. The ovation just wouldn't stop. It was an incredible emotional catharsis.

Backstage, we embraced. Phil was ecstatic. "That was the most exciting moment of my career," he whispered.

Seven years later, when the war finally ended in reality, he sang "The War Is Over" once again, this time for 50,000 celebrants in Central Park.

52

When Jerry Rubin originally invited me in 1965 to emcee the first Berkeley teach-in, having read *The Realist* and seen my standup performance, I suggested that he invite Phil Ochs to perform between speeches. Jerry had never heard of Phil, but he took my advice, and they ended up becoming friends. Phil introduced Jerry to musical protest, and Jerry introduced Phil to LSD.

In 1973, with Yippie stalwart Stew Albert, they went to Chile, where Phil met his Chilean equivalent, Victor Jara. They visited a newly nationalized mine, where Jara and Ochs sang for the workers. Jara did "Little Boxes" and Ochs did "The War Is Over," with Jara translating his lyrics line by line. Later on, in a public arena, soldiers of the Chilean army would break Victor Jara's fingers and force him to perform before they executed him.

The rift between Ochs and Dylan ended in 1974, when Ochs was organizing a benefit for Chilean refugees who had escaped and the underground freedom fighters they had left behind. Phil haunted the Greenwich Village folk clubs—from the Kettle of Fish to the Gaslight to the Other End—where he ran into Dylan.

"Hey, you the same Bobby Dylan who once wrote a song about Chilean miners?"

"Yeah."

"You want a job singing for those same miners now, for free?"

Dylan agreed to sing at the rally.

"I really don't see what's wrong, " Phil told the audience, "with Bob and I putting all our royalty money into chemical warfare stock."

53

Two years later, Phil Ochs committed suicide. The culture lost a rare artist, and Jerry Rubin lost a rare companion.

The Patty Hearst Connection

In the fall of 1972, when Patty Hearst was 18, she moved in with Steven Weed. They smoked pot in their Berkeley apartment and took acid in the old Hearst mansion. She had read *The Realist*, came to hear me speak on campus and borrowed my copy of *Do it!* Jerry had inscribed:

> Dear Paul—
>
> So much of you is part of this book—things we experienced together! Your spirit and life force have become part of me! Let's keep working together to destroy the government and foment riots, creating closer and closer brotherhood!
>
> With love & dope,
> Jerry

"I'm nonviolent," I told Patty, "so I am a little embarrassed by that."

"Oh," she reassured me, "it's just bullshit rhetoric."

"Yeah, but Jerry has a way of talking himself into believing his own rhetoric."

I liked Patty's wit. "I think everybody should get unemployment," she said. "They could divide them in half. One week half the people work at the unemployment office giving *other* people compensation, and they could keep switching back and forth each week, so that everybody got a chance to either wait in line or serve the people waiting in line."

I was also impressed by her insight. "When I was six years old," she said, "when Nixon was running against Kennedy, my parents were for Nixon, and actually they *reminded* me of Nixon and Pat, they had that same kind of stiffness with each other. And with me. I recall thinking as a child that it would've been nice to have Kennedy and Jackie as parents. I mean as a child I couldn't articulate it, but I could *observe* the way they related to their daughter, Caroline. You know, you adjust to your own environment because it's all you have. But aside from all the political reasons Kennedy was killed, I think there was also an unconscious rationale, because he represented a certain dynamic sexuality, you know what I mean?"

In February 1974, two weeks before her twentieth birthday, Patty was kidnapped by the Symbionese Liberation Army, a group of male and female white radicals led by black militant Donald "Cinque" (pronounced sink-you) DeFreeze. She was kept in a closet for eight weeks.

The SLA demanded $2 million in ransom for Patty. Her father, Randolph Hearst, raised $500,000 and the Hearst foundation gave a grant for the rest, but only after they got an IRS ruling that the SLA was a "charitable organization." The SLA also demanded a free food program. Patty's father arranged for such a project in Oakland. Governor Ronald Reagan watched on TV the long line of people waiting for free food and announced, "I hope they all get botulism."

Then Patty had the audacity to *join* the SLA. She renamed herself Tania and participated in a bank robbery with them. Her mother, Catherine Hearst, said that she would rather her daughter be dead than join the communists. She also observed that if only Clark Gable had been at the Berkeley apartment instead of Steven Weed, then Patty would never have been kidnapped. Probably true. In a taped communiqué to her parents, Patty stated:

Mom, Dad,

I would like to comment on your efforts to supposedly secure my safely. The food giveaway was a sham. You were playing games—stalling for time—which the FBI was using in their attempts to assassinate me and the SLA elements that guarded me. I have been given the choice of, one, being released in a safe area, or two, joining the forces of the Symbionese Liberation Army. I have chosen to stay and fight. I want you to tell the people the truth. Tell them how the law-and-order programs are just a means to remove so-called violent—meaning aware—individuals from the community in order to facilitate the controlled removal of unneeded labor forces in this country, in the same way that Hitler controlled the removal of the Jews from Germany. I should have known that if you and the rest of the corporate state were willing to do this to millions of people to maintain power and to serve your needs, you would also kill me if necessary to serve those same needs.

How long will it take before white people in this country understand that whatever happens to a black child happens sooner or later to a white child? How long will it be before we all understand that we must fight for our freedom?

Patty would later insist that the recording was made in a closet, that she had read from a script given to her by Cinque and that he threatened to kill her if she didn't read it. At the end of the tape, Cinque came on with a triple death threat, emphasizing one Colston Westbrook, whom he accused of being "a government agent now working for military intelligence while giving assistance to the FBI." This communiqué was originally sent to San Francisco radio station KSAN. News director David McQueen checked with a Justice Department source, who confirmed Westbrook's employment by the CIA.

Conspiracy researcher Mae Brussell traced Westbrook's activities from 1962, when he was CIA adviser to the South Korean CIA, through 1969, when he provided logistical support in Vietnam for the CIA's Phoenix program. His job was the indoctrination of assassination and terrorist cadres. After seven years in Asia, he was brought home in 1970, along with his war, and assigned to run the Black Cultural Association at Vacaville Prison, where he became the control officer for Donald DeFreeze, who had worked as an informer from 1967 to 1969 for the Public Disorder Intelligence Unit of the Los Angeles Police Department.

The Tim Leary Connection

Aldous Huxley once advised Timothy Leary:
"You've got to have a jingle."

Leary's jingle may have been "Turn on, tune in, drop out," but his nature was that of an activist. He met Abbie Hoffman in December 1966 at the League for Spiritual Discovery storefront in New York, he met Jerry Rubin in January 1967 at the Human Be-In held in San Francisco, and when I arranged for a meeting of all three in the spring of 1968, his alignment with the Yippies was forged.

Jerry had experimented with electoral politics. He ran for mayor of Berkeley, and when Eldridge Cleaver ran for president, he asked Jerry to be his running mate—this alliance between the Black Panthers and the Yippies was symbolized by a machine-gun crossed with a hash-pipe—but respectability is a relative quality, and Jerry's vice presidential candidacy was rejected by the alternative Peace and Freedom Party.

A couple of years later, Leary was arrested for possession of marijuana, but escaped from prison with the aid of the Weather Underground. Eldridge Cleaver was already on the lam, to avoid being tried for a shoot-out with police in Oakland. Leary and his wife, Rosemary, became Cleaver's house guests in Algeria, but then became his captives as Cleaver became increasingly paranoid. They escaped to Switzerland, which refused to extradite him to the United States.

58

Tim and Rosemary separated, and Joanna Harcourt-Smith conveniently called and took her place. Tim and Joanna went to Afghanistan where in January 1973, one month after they met, he got busted by American agents—kidnapped, actually, since the Afghans had no extradition treaty with the U.S. Leary was taken back to the States, accompanied by Joanna and her friend Dennis Martino.

At his trial in April, Leary's defense team argued unsuccessfully that when he escaped, he had been in a state of "involuntary intoxication" due to flashback effects of LSD. He was sentenced to 25 years.

In the spring of 1974, in the Scientology Club office at the California Medical Facility in Vacaville, prison psychologist Wesley Hiler was taping a conversation with Leary.

Hiler: What do you feel about the social consequence that very large numbers of young people have had psychedelic experience in our culture?

Leary: Well, that's a question I don't have enough facts to answer, because I've been quite alienated from American society for many years. What do you think?

Hiler: I feel the main effect is that it liberated people from the conditionings and imprintings of their culture. They're able to see the absurdity of certain things that their parents took for granted. So I think that's one of the reasons why there is this activism against the war in Vietnam. They are able to see beyond the blinders of patriotism.

Leary: This sounds like you're talking in the 1960s. And what has happened in the last five years since the Nixon regime took over is very different. It's hard to say anything about any positive liberating developments without being aware that a tremendously brutal repression set in to crush them. So what would have happened if we had not had the Nixon election? I think Abbie Hoffman and Jerry Rubin brought about the election of Nixon because they basically wanted to convert the neurological revolution to a political revolution. Jerry Rubin was saying in the 1960s, "Turn on, tune in, and take over." Then the occult-spiritual movement stepped in—again, totally against the continuation and acceleration of the liberation movement—and *they* wanted to co-opt it. And they made a perfect alliance with the right-wing movement in opposing the real flower of the '60s, which had to do with drugs and sexuality.

Later on, Leary had an idea:

"Why don't we try to save Patricia Hearst? I'll write a letter to the SLA about the inability of anybody to see any point of view except their own. Like with this Hearst family—everyone's very sorry for them. They don't see that the SLA and the Hearst family are in exactly the same situation as every middle-class and poor family whose children were kidnapped by armed forces and sent to Vietnam against their will, or parents of any family whose child had to go to Canada to escape the draft, or 30,000 parents in the state of California—lower-class, poor parents—whose sons and daughters are in prisons like this. It's all force and kidnapping of young people. And this is the way the SLA is thinking."

Hiler: Yeah, yeah. I hadn't thought of that.

60

Leary: All right, I'll write the letter to the SLA, you

deliver it, we'll settle the situation, get Patty Hearst released from prison, then I'll get released from prison, and you can say you were the one that did everything. (*Laughter*) All I want to do is get out of here.

Hiler: Here I've been telling everybody that Leary is a living example of a person who has his head together, happy anywhere, unbothered in prison.

Leary: And now my line is to say you can carry a good thing too far, and that I don't like the picture of me seven years from now wandering around in prison, smiling as the world continues to collapse into insanity on the outside...

Hiler: What I like to do is be like an artist here. Like today I did some really good therapy and recorded it. That's what I like, to have it recorded and good, like a work of art. Like I wish we had recorded that session with Manson. It was beautiful. Such a poetic delusional system, so beautifully expressed.

Leary: That was a terrible thing you just said—beautiful delusional system.

Hiler: It sounds awful, I know. I was integrating two points of view of schizophrenia. You have [R. D.] Laing's point of view, that schizophrenia is a beautiful thing, a person trying to find himself. The symbols he uses are often very profound, like an acid trip, a Jungian dream. I believe this, but I also believe they lose their ability to distinguish between reality and their fantasies. For instance, Manson believes he is responsible for Nixon's troubles. It's a delusion of influence.

Leary: Everything you say about Manson just blows me away, because I think exactly what Manson thinks. I think that Nixon got all his troubles because he fucked with *me*. So there's two of *us* and one of *you*. Manson's thing isn't delusional, in that he's a force, his name comes up as a symbol very regularly in the strangest places. Everyone in the Western world knows the name Manson—a kind of witch. He does have influence, right?

Hiler: Right, definitely, and he's a very beautiful person, very open. It was a very exciting session we had up there.

Leary: You were sorry you didn't have it on tape, it was such a beautiful delusion.

Hiler: Yeah.

Leary: (*Irritated*) You sound like a butterfly catcher.

Hiler: Yeah, in a sense I am. I *am* a butterfly catcher, that's right.

Leary: (*Sighing*) How do you think I'm going to get out of prison...

The Dr. Hip Connection

One morning in May 1974, just before dawn, Tim Leary was quietly taken from Vacaville to a private cell in a federal correctional institution. A state prison official said that Leary was "giving testimony about the drug culture." Panic spread from the drug culture to the radical political culture. There was fear that Leary would snitch on the folks who had arranged his original escape.

In September, an ad hoc group, PILL—People Investigating Leary's Lies—issued a statement signed by a long list of radical personalities (not including myself): "We condemn the terrible pressures brought to bear by the government on people in the prisons of this country. We also denounce Timothy Leary for turning state's evidence and marking innocent people for jail in order to get out of jail himself."

PILL held a press conference in Berkeley, with Ram Dass, Allen Ginsberg, Jerry Rubin, reporter Ken Kelley and Leary's son, Jack, all sitting on the dais. One by one they accused Leary of telling preposterous lies about a nonexistent hippie Mafia to a federal grand jury in Chicago.

Somebody was wearing a kangaroo head and costume with boxing gloves to protest symbolically the kangaroo-court nature of this press conference. I knew it was Gene Schoenfeld—whose "*Dr. Hip*-pocrates" column had been syndicated in the underground press—because he called me the previous day to ask if I wanted to wear a kangaroo costume too. Since I planned to attend as a journalist, I declined his invitation, although when Jack Leary began reading a statement denouncing his own father, it struck me as so distasteful that I impulsively bypassed my role as a reporter and blurted out, "Judge not lest ye be stoned!"

A few weeks earlier, there had been a big party at Margo St. James's place in Marin County. Margo was the founder of a prostitutes' rights organization, COYOTE (Call Off Your Old Tired Ethics). The party was on a Sunday afternoon, and Gene Schoenfeld left early to do his weekly radio call-in show on KSFO, where he answered questions, mostly about sex and drugs. But for this particular program, he decided to talk with a few of us at the party by telephone. He interviewed Margo, who talked about how prostitutes were, in effect, on the front lines of the women's movement. Alan Watts asked about the AMA's conservatism in relation to new medical procedures such as acupuncture. Someone at the party had requested me to work his frog fetish into the dialogue, so I asked Schoenfeld about the common problem of what kind of lubrication one should use when having intercourse with a frog. He said he didn't know and would have to do some research. Then it was Jerry Rubin's turn.

"Gene," he began, "your listeners should know that when you give advice about sex, you really know what you're talking about. You were great last night."

"Jerry, I know from experience in writing for newspapers and doing radio broadcasts that many people can't tell whether someone may just be making a joke."

"Joke? This is no joke. You were great last night."

Now, at the PILL press conference, Schoenfeld had stashed in the pouch of his kangaroo costume a whipped-cream pie covered by Saran Wrap. He hopped into the room, past scores of media people, preparing to smush the pie in Jerry Rubin's face. However, he was unable to remove the plastic wrapping with the boxing gloves on his hands. While he was struggling with the Saran Wrap, Ken Kelley grabbed him and pulled off the papier-mâché kangaroo head.

Later on, both Ram Dass and Allen Ginsberg were surprised to learn that the press conference had been called in the name of People Investigating Leary's Lies. Jerry Rubin proclaimed the event "a political victory" inasmuch as it stopped action on indictments that were supposed to have come down as a result of Leary's alleged snitching.

In Chicago, a U.S. Attorney said that Leary had never testified before a federal grand jury there. As far as I could determine, the only one who got hurt by Leary's testimony—before a Los Angeles grand jury—was his former attorney, George Chula. Joanna Leary had already testified that Chula smuggled hashish to Leary in prison, and Leary verified it. Chula was suspended for one month.

Joanna had taken on Leary's cause as well as his name. In June 1974, she visited Randolph Hearst with an offer from Leary to help find Patty Hearst. Prison psychologist Wesley Hiler was fired, ostensibly for an article in *Rolling Stone* that discussed how he had arranged for secret talks between Hearst and inmates associated with Patty's kidnappers.

At that point Joanna was already working with the Orange County district attorney's office and investigators for the Drug Enforcement Administration. Her companion, Dennis Martino, had also been an informant for the DEA. He was responsible for more than 30 drug busts in Santa Cruz alone, and had been spying on Leary's lawyers since 1973. He later died from an overdose of natural causes.

Either Joanna was an undercover agent from the beginning, or she had become one in order to free her "perfect love" from prison. While Tim was in jail, her mission was to gather information connecting the drug subculture with the political subculture. She conned her way into what she referred to as "the pecking order." She said Tim had given her a list of men to seduce, including Senator Ted Kennedy. When Allen Ginsberg—who was not on that list—suggested to Leary that Joanna was a double agent, Leary repeated the charge to her.

"Ginsberg just hates women," she replied.

Despite Joanna's efforts, Tim continued to reside behind bars with neighbors he described as "singing waiters in the Rathouse Café." He faced 25 years, but was released in 1976, after Jerry Brown became governor of California and pardoned him. By 1982, Leary was traveling around the country in a series of debates with G. Gordon Liddy, the man who in 1966 led a midnight raid on his research center in Millbrook, New York. If in Millbrook Leary had retroactively followed Liddy's current advice on his radio talk show about shooting agents in the head and groin when they raided your premises, Leary would now have ended up onstage debating himself.

In the summer of 1982, at a celebration of the 25th anniversary of Jack Kerouac's novel *On the Road*, a much-politicized Timothy Leary borrowed back Jerry Rubin's revised version of his own '60s slogan and proceeded to advise the audience: "Turn on, tune in, and—*please*—take over!"

The Charles Bates Connection

If Donald "Cinque" DeFreeze had in fact been a double agent, given his history as a police informer and his relationship with the CIA's Colston Westbrook, then the SLA was yet another Frankenstein monster, turning against its creator by becoming in reality what had been designed as a hollow media image. When Cinque finked on his keepers, he signed the death warrant of the SLA.

In May 1974, all but Tania and Bill and Emily Harris were killed in a confrontation with police at the SLA's Los Angeles safe-house. Tear gas and incendiary bombs ignited the SLA's supply of ammunition, turning the house into a raging bonfire. Cinque's charred remains were sent to Cleveland, where his family couldn't help but notice that he had been decapitated. Perhaps Colston Westbrook had issued an order: "Bring me the head of Donald DeFreeze!"

Consider the revelations of Wayne Lewis in August 1974. He claimed to have been an undercover agent for the FBI, a fact verified by FBI director Clarence Kelley. Surfacing at a press conference in Los Angeles, Lewis spewed forth a veritable conveyor belt of conspiratorial charges: that DeFreeze was an FBI informer; that DeFreeze was killed not by the SWAT team but by an FBI agent, because DeFreeze had become "uncontrollable"; that the FBI then asked Lewis to infiltrate the SLA; that the FBI had undercover agents in other underground guerrilla groups; that the FBI knew where Patty Hearst was but let her remain free so it could build up its files of subversives.

Virtually all of the FBI's 8500 agents were involved at some point in the hunt for Patty. A special squad interviewed 25,000 people in the San Francisco area alone. In the middle of a *Doonesbury* strip, Garry Trudeau spelled out the word *Canaan*, which was where a friend of his lived in Connecticut, but federal authorities were convinced it was actually a reference to Patty's hideout in Pennsylvania. William F. Buckley wrote that she should be sacrificed "in the name of Christ."

And who was Charles Bates, the FBI official in charge of handling the SLA investigation and the search for Patty Hearst?

A member of the Santa Clara district attorney's office testified that Bates had "categorically denied" having any of the stolen documents sought by the D.A. for an investigation of FBI-sponsored political burglaries. But after being confronted with the testimony of one of his own subordinates, Bates ultimately turned over the documents. Some of the stolen documents had ended up with Research West, a private right-wing spy organization that was purchased in October 1969 with funds provided by Catherine Hearst, Patty's mother. Their files were available to local police and sheriff departments as well as the FBI, the CIA and the IRS.

In 1969, Bates was the Special Agent at the Chicago office of the FBI when police killed Black Panthers Fred Hampton and Mark Clark while they were sleeping. Ex-FBI informer Maria Fischer told the *Chicago Daily News* that the chief of the FBI's Chicago office, Marlon Johnson, personally asked her to slip a drug to Hampton. She had infiltrated the Panther Party at the FBI's request a month before. The drug was a tasteless, colorless liquid that would put him to sleep. She refused. Hampton was killed a week later. An autopsy showed "a near-fatal dose" of secobarbitol in his system.

In 1971, Bates was transferred to Washington and later was put in charge of handling the Watergate investigation.

The only reason that Patty and the Harrises were not killed in Los Angeles was because they had gone to Inglewood the day before, where Bill Harris got caught shoplifting sweat socks at a sporting goods store, which touched off a shootout. The trio fled to Anaheim, checked into a motel, turned on the TV, and to their utter horror watched the safe-house burning and heard the newscaster say that the police believed *they* were inside.

Originally, the SLA hadn't trusted Patty's decision to join them. (Conversely, she didn't trust their offer of a choice, since they realized she'd be able to identify them if she went free.) So they made her prove herself by "fronting her off" at the bank with Cinque's gun pointed at her head. "I was doing exactly what I had to do," she would later claim. "I just wanted to get out of the bank. I was just supposed to be in there to get my picture taken, mainly." So she was only a *virtual* bank robber.

But now, having witnessed her comrades being burned alive and hearing that she was supposed to be among them, Patty's previous rhetoric was finally transmuted into reality. She was now *truly* afraid that the FBI wanted to assassinate her. She was now *truly* a member of the Symbionese Liberation Army. Bill and Emily Harris now *truly* trusted her. There would no longer be a problem leaving her alone. She would never try to escape.

Patty had become a vehicle for repressive action on the right and wishful thinking on the left.

On one occasion she was visited by Abbie Hoffman—also on the lam—and Jerry Rubin.

"She was like the patron saint of political conversion," Abbie told me. "We were *worshipping* her. I mean, I used to think she'd been brainwashed. And brainwashing does exist—built into the process is the certainty that you *haven't* been brainwashed—but Patty wasn't brainwashed, she just transcended her fuckin' *class*. And she was smart, and funny, really sarcastic. And—don't tell Jerry I told you this—we had a *menáge à trois*. The three of us are in bed, see—we had all done Quaaludes—and we're taking our clothes off, and I'm kissing Patty, and Jerry is finger-fucking her at the same time, and suddenly I could feel his *other* hand fondling my *balls*. I did a little mental double-take, but I only related to *her*, not to him. The whole thing just kind of choreographed itself. Then later we were talking about how much I missed organizing, and she convinced me to change my appearance and just go and do the same kind of work under a different name. I took it as the fuckin' gospel and did exactly what she said. That was the day I decided to become"—laughing and waving his fist in the air—"*Barry Freed, environmental activist!*"

It turned out to be a schizoid existence for him. He would call me, sometimes as Abbie, sometimes as Barry, sometimes switching from one identity to the other during the same conversation. But actually, Abbie's worst manic-depressive state came *before* he became involved as an environmental activist. Indeed, becoming an activist again helped to resolve that crisis.

The F. Lee Bailey Connection

Patty Hearst was finally captured 18 months after being kidnapped. She was so surprised that she peed in her pants—reported only in the *San Francisco Chronicle*, not the *San Francisco Examiner* (published by her father). She was permitted to change in the bathroom. The FBI inventory did *not* include "pants, wet, one pair," but there was on their list a two-foot marijuana plant and a bottle of Gallo wine—not exactly a loyal gesture to the United Farm Workers they purported to support. And there was an unidentified "rock" found in Patty's purse. A newscaster reported breathlessly: "Patti Page has been captured!"

And so the victim had become the perpetrator. Out of the closet, into the bank! And now she was in jail. Abbie Hoffman arranged for the following letter, which he wrote on the stationery of a New York hotel, to be smuggled to her:

High Patty,

I guess if our mutual friend figured out how to get this to you, she figured out how to tell you who it's from. I feel close to you since we met. Our paths have crossed in a few other ways but they have to be kept out of a letter. We went under about the same time, and everywhere I went the papers said you had been spotted. Even once when there was so much heat I had to move, I was still cheering for you to make it. Everyone was really sad when you got nailed.

I thought you were doing important work, and it was too bad you were rudely interrupted. If I were in your shoes, I'd keep real quiet and not make any statements. Play their game for a while until you get your bearings. Don't get impatient, you've got about 80 years to live.

Getting bail is your primary concern. Get out on the streets. You can be much freer then to write and say what you want. If you can't make bail and then decide to make a "showcase" trial by putting forth your views, you'll need a radical lawyer who's had experience. There are all kinds of ways to get radical testimony into a trial, but only radical lawyers understand the rules. Given the charges, it's going to be tough. Don't think you can, say, do a trial like ours. It's more complicated than it appears on the surface. If I had to choose a Bay Area attorney, I'd choose Michael Kennedy. He's one of the great radical lawyers.

If you could, you might get someone, a lay person, to survey the Bay Area attorneys for defense ideas and general strategy, that way getting a feel for their methods. I realize this is your first bust. We had a huge advantage, for between us we had over 100 previous busts. We knew the courts and more importantly enough lawyers to make knowledgeable decisions. I'll try and send more ideas as they occur—if the letters get thru—and seem helpful. Just want to let you

know you're not alone. Everyone in the underground misses you. Hope your spirits are high.

> Together in struggle,
> A.

Originally, Patty was going to be defended by the radical
team of Vincent Hallinan and his son, Kayo. Although as
Tania she had called the elder Hallinan a "clown" in a
taped communiqué, now as Patty she said of Kayo, "He's
good. Like, I really trust him politically and personally, and
I can tell him just about anything I want and he's cool."
This was, unfortunately, an attorney-client relationship
that would not be permitted to mature.

Her uncle, William Randolph Hearst Jr., editor-in-
chief of the Hearst newspaper chain, flew in from the
East Coast to warn his family that the entire corporate
image of the Hearst empire was at stake and they'd better hire an establishment attorney—fast. Enter F. Lee
Bailey. He had defended a serial killer, the Boston Stran-
gler, and a war criminal, Captain Harold Medina of My
Lai massacre infamy, but he said he would not defend
Patty Hearst if she were a revolutionary. You gotta have
standards.

So Patty had been kidnapped once again. Her obedience to the defense team paralleled her obedience to
the SLA. The survival syndrome had simply changed
hands, from Donald DeFreeze, who led the kidnappers,
to F. Lee Bailey, who led the defense. Bailey was Cinque
in whiteface. Instead of a machine gun, he owned
a helicopter (Enstrom, an anagram for Monster).

Instead of taping underground communiqués, he held public press conferences. The air reeked with show biz.

In 1976, I covered the trial for the *Berkeley Barb* and *Playboy*. There had been a rumor that Patty was pregnant by Cinque. In fact, when Patty's father met sports figure Jack Scott—who had spent time with Tania while she was on the run—the first question he asked was to ascertain if that were so. In my weekly report, I wrote in the *Barb*: "Now, with their daughter on trial, the Hearsts have hired a lawyer who wears pancake makeup to press conferences, the better to transform a racist fear into a Caucasian alibi." I received a letter by certified mail.

Dear Mr. Krassner:

You undoubtedly did not realize that the name "Pan-Cake Make-Up" is the registered trademark (U.S. Patent Office No. 350,402) of Max Factor & Co., and is not a synonym for cake make-up. The correct usage is "Pan-Cake Make-Up," capitalized and written in just that manner, or, under circumstances such as these, where you obviously did not intend to mention a particular brand, simply cake make-up. We are sure that you are aware of the legal importance of protecting a trademark and trust that you will use ours properly in any future reference to our product, or in the alternative, will use the proper generic term rather than our brand name. So that our records will be complete, we would appreciate an acknowledgment of this letter.

Very truly yours,
D. James Pekin
Corporate Counsel
Max Factor & Co.

I explained that there was a slight misunderstanding—what F. Lee Bailey had been wearing to all those press conferences was actually Aunt Jemima Pancake Mix—and I hoped that cleared up the matter.

The Willie Wolfe Connection

A three-month-old baby, whose mother wanted to expose her to the process of justice, was being breast-fed in the back of the courtroom while Patty Hearst testified that during her abduction she had been raped in a closet by the lover she once described as "the gentlest, most beautiful man I've ever known." Now prosecutor James Browning was cross-examining her.

"Did you, in fact, have a strong feeling for Willie Wolfe?"

"In a way, yes."

"As a matter of fact, were you in love with him?"

"No."

A little later, he asked if it had been "forcible rape."

"Excuse me?"

"Did you struggle or submit?"

"I didn't resist. I was afraid."

Browning walked into the trap: "I thought you said you had strong feelings for him."

"I did," Patty replied triumphantly. "I couldn't *stand* him."

It sure seemed like fake testimony. And yet, there was this letter to the *Berkeley Barb*: "Only a woman knows that the sex act, no matter how gentle, becomes rape if she is an unwilling partner. Her soul, as well as her body, is scarred. The gentleness of Willie Wolfe does not preclude rape. Rape, in this instance, was dependent upon Patricia Hearst's state of mind, not Willie Wolfe's. We must all remember that *only* Patty knows what she felt; and if we refuse to believe her, there can be no justice."

Patty also said that her intercourse with Cinque was "without affection." On the witness stand, she was asked by Bailey what Cinque had done on one occasion to show his disapproval.

"He pinched me."

"Where?"

"My breasts"—pause—"and down—"

"Your private parts as well?"

"Yes."

Browning cross-examined Patty: "Did he pinch one or both of your breasts?"

"I really don't remember."

"Was it under your clothing?"

"Yes."

"In both places?"

"Pardon me, I don't think that the other was under my clothing."

"All right, your breasts he pinched by touching your skin. The pubic area, he did not touch your skin. Is that true?"

76

Good Lord, this was supposed to be the Trial of

the Century, and the government was trying to find out whether or not Cinque got bare tit.

The Trish Tobin Connection

After Patty was arrested, she had a jailhouse conversation with her best friend since childhood, Trish Tobin—whose family, coincidentally, controlled the bank that Patty helped rob. Several times throughout the trial, Browning attempted to have the tape of that dialogue played for the jury, but the judge kept refusing until the end of the trial, when the impact of its giddiness would be especially astonishing.

Trish: I had a lot of fights at Stanford.

Patty: Oh, yeah? About what?

Trish: You.

Patty: Oh—what were *they* saying? I can just imagine—

Trish: Oh, well, "that fucking little rich bitch"—you know, on and on—and they said, "She planned her own kidnapping," and I said, "Fuck you, you don't know what the fuck you're talking about, I don't even care if she plans her kidnapping and everyone's in the world, so you know something, I don't wanna hear shit out of you!" (*Laughter*)

The gossip was that Patty had arranged her own kidnapping in order to get out of her engagement to Steven Weed in as adventurous a way as possible. "I guess I was having second thoughts," she admitted. "I wasn't sure he was somebody I could stay married to." The rumor continued that after Patty had been kidnapped, she was then double-crossed and manipulated into

77

becoming an informer. In fact, she secretly began to turn state's evidence early in her trial. Usually, defendants tell what they know before trial, so that the prosecution can decide whether or not to plea-bargain and avoid a trial. But this particular trial *had* to be held, if only to avoid giving any impression of plea-bargaining.

Patty had been gang-banged into snitching by the prosecution and the defense alike, but that jailhouse tape did appear to reveal a change in her outlook: "I'm not making any statements until I know I can get out on bail, and then if I find out that I can't for sure, then I'll issue a statement, but I'd just as soon give it myself, in person, and then it'll be a revolutionary feminist perspective totally. I mean, I never got really—I guess I'll just tell you, like, my politics are real different from, uh—way back when (*laughter*) obviously! And so this creates all kinds of problems for my defense."

An accurate forecast. Patty would later testify that her words were influenced by the presence of captured SLA member Emily Harris in the visiting room at the time Patty was talking to Trish Tobin. Bailey asked, "Was she a party to your conversation?"

"Not by any intention of ours, no."

On cross-examination, Patty continued: "Emily was also on a phone." Prisoners and visitors had to converse over telephones while they looked at each other through a thick bulletproof glass window. Patty said she knew that Emily could hear her talking simply because "I could've heard *her* if I'd stopped and listened." But jail records show that in fact Emily was not in the visiting room.

While Patty was being interviewed in jail by prosecution psychiatrist Harry Kozol, she pulled a Raskolnikov—the character in Dostoievski's *Crime and Punishment* who cannot repress the force of his own guilt—by darting from the room and complaining that Kozol had accused her of arranging her own kidnapping. Bailey asked him on the witness stand, "Did you suggest that she got herself kidnapped?" He answered, "No."

In the first interview, Kozol had questioned Patty about Willie Wolfe: "I told her that I'd heard her speak tenderly of him [on the final taped communiqué], and I asked her this question: 'Is that the way you felt about him?' She seemed to get upset and deeply moved. I felt she was almost sobbing inside—but no tears ran down her face. She said, 'I don't *know* how I feel about him.' I said, 'I'm not asking you how you feel. Is that how you *felt*?' She became very much upset, began to shake and quiver, obviously suffering. And she answered, 'I don't know why I got into this goddamn thing—*shit*.' And then got up and left the room, terribly upset."

Got into *what* goddamn thing? Patty could have been referring to her agreement to talk with psychiatrists or to her decision to join the SLA or to the kidnapping itself.

In the second interview, Kozol asked if there was anything else. He testified: "There was some delay. She was sort of thinking. She began to look very uncomfortable and I told her, 'Never mind.' And she said, 'I don't want to tell you.' And I said, 'That's okay, if it makes you uncomfortable,' and then she blurted out that she was going to tell me anyway. She told me that four days before the kidnapping, while she was sitting in class, she was suddenly struck with a terrible fear that she was going to be kidnapped. This was an overwhelming sensation. It stayed with her. I said, 'What's so surprising about a girl from a well-to-do family worrying about kidnapping?' She brushed it aside and said, 'It wasn't anything of the sort. It was different.' For four solid days, she couldn't shake the fear. She finally thought in terror of running home to her parents, where she would be safe. She somehow fought that. Then the thing she dreaded occurred."

While Kozol was testifying, Patty was writing notes to Bailey on a yellow legal pad. I diverted a marshal's attention during recess, and reporter Steve Rubinstein copied those notes, although he wasn't allowed to include them in his story for the *Los Angeles Herald Examiner*, a Hearst paper. In one of the notes, Patty described life in Berkeley with Steven Weed:

I paid the rent, bought the furniture, bought the groceries, cooked all the meals (even while working eight hours a day and carrying a full course load), and if I wasn't there to cook, Steve didn't eat.

In another note, she clearly and concisely described where her mindset really was at in the San Mateo County Jail, when she couldn't blame Emily Harris's eavesdropping as her motivation:

Dr. Kozol kept trying to equate the women's movement with violence. I repeatedly told him: 1. Violence has no place in the women's movement. 2. I didn't feel it was possible to make lasting changes in our soci-

ety unless the issue of women's rights was resolved. Kozol kept trying to say things like, "Isn't it more important to solve the poverty problem?" Any reform measures taken by the government will only be temporary.

The Donald DeFreeze Connection

Bill and Emily Harris let it be known that if called to testify, they would take the Fifth Amendment, but Emily testified in effect through the media. After Patty told the jury that Willie Wolfe had raped her, Emily was quoted in *New Times*: "Once Willie gave her a stone relic in the shape of a monkey face, and Patty wore it all the time around her neck. After the shootout, she stopped wearing it and carried it in her purse instead, but she always had it with her."

Prosecutor Browning read this in the magazine and had an *Aha!* experience, remembering that "rock" in Patty's purse from the FBI's inventory list when she was originally captured. He presented it as his final piece of evidence in the trial, slowly swinging the necklace back and forth in front of the jurors, as if to hypnotize them.

They found Patty guilty. They might just as well have found her guilty of teenage fucking—or why else would such information have been admissible as evidence? They don't allow that kind of testimony in a rape trial, but for this bank robbery case, it was apparently considered relevant. So now she faced seven years in prison.

Jerry Rubin proclaimed, "Patty Hearst is being punished in the '70s for what we did in the '60s." Her sister Anne gave Patty a T-shirt. On the back it said

Being Kidnapped Means Always Having to Say You're Sorry, and on the front it said *Pardon Me*. After serving 23 months in prison, her sentence was commuted by President Jimmy Carter.

The family of slain SLA member Willie Wolfe hired Lake Headley—an ex-police intelligence officer who was chief investigator at Wounded Knee—to find out what had really happened. He discovered, with fellow researchers Donald Freed and Rusty Rhodes, that the SLA was part of the CIA's CHAOS program. In that context they were planning to kill Black Panther Huey Newton, and succeeded in killing black school superintendent Marcus Foster *after* he agreed to meet Panther demands for educational reforms.

At Vacaville, DeFreeze was permitted to set up Unisight, a program by which convicts could get laid by visiting females. According to Headley, DeFreeze's visitors included kidnappers-to-be Nancy Ling Perry and Patricia Soltysik—and Patty Hearst, then 18, not going under her own name but using the ID of Mary Alice Siems, a student at Berkeley.

Headley's affidavit states: "That Patricia Campbell Hearst and her parents disagreed bitterly over Patricia's political and personal relations. That a love affair between a black man and Patricia Campbell Hearst did take place prior to her relationship with her fiancé Steven Weed. That Mrs. Randolph A. Hearst subjected her daughter to extreme pressure to change her personal and political relationships."

82 Patty began living with Weed in Berkeley later that year. DeFreeze was transferred to Soledad in

December 1972, where he was given the special privilege of using the trailers ordinarily reserved for married trusties. He became a leader of the SLA and renewed his affair with Patty for a brief time. The affidavit continued: "Discussions were held between Patricia Campbell Hearst and the Symbionese Liberation Army concerning a kidnapping—not her own."

Whose, then? Her sisters, Anne and Vicki. The idea of kidnapping Patty too was brought up—this was a year before it actually took place—but she didn't think it was such a great notion. However, if true, this could explain Patty's outburst at the moment of kidnapping: "Oh, no! Not *me*! Oh, God! Please let me go!"

The investigators presented their findings to the Los Angeles City Council, charging that the intelligence unit of the Police Department—the Criminal Conspiracy Section—knew of the SLA's presence but *wanted* the so-called shootout for test purposes. Headley acquired official film footage of the massacre, showing that the FBI used a pair of German shepherds to sniff out Patty's presence so she wouldn't be inside the safe-house.

And Steven Weed was told by a cop at the scene of the shootout, "Don't worry, Patty's not in there."

The Mimi Leonard Connection

As I write this, one week after the bombing of the federal building in Oklahoma City triggered such unspeakable anguish, I'm struck by the parallels of right-wing militia rhetoric with that of Jerry Rubin, starting with his dedication in *Do it!* to his girlfriend, Nancy Kurshan:

"To Nancy—Dope, Color TV and Violent Revolution!" A year later, in his next book, *We Are Everywhere*, he clarified his position: "Bombing buildings without killing people is an example of revolutionary violence."

Once, though, while we were walking around New York during a police strike, he remarked, "I'm very disappointed that nobody's doing anything."

"Jerry," I said, "I don't see *you* trashing anything."

In *We Are Everywhere*, he also wrote, "I fell in love with Charlie Manson the first time I saw his cherub face and sparkling eyes on national TV. When I was out in L.A. on a speaking gig Manson saw me giving a rap and asked his lawyers to find me and bring me to see him in jail."

Said Manson at their meeting: "Rubin, I am not of your world. I've spent all my life in prison. When I was a child I was an orphan and too ugly to be adopted. Now I am too beautiful to be let free."

In 1972, when we were hanging around with John Lennon and Yoko Ono, Jerry asked me what I thought of them. Even as I started to reply, "They're fun to be with," Jerry was already speaking his own answer: "They have a lot of power."

By 1973, he was already deep into the New Age self-help syndrome. "The irony of finding myself in a therapy to learn to love my parents tickled me," he admitted, "because it was only five years ago that the *National Enquirer* ran that fearsome front-page picture of me under the headline: Yippie Leader Tells Children to Kill Their Parents!"

In *Growing Up at Thirty-Seven*, published in 1976, he confessed, "For years I felt my cock was too small. Many American males think their cocks are not big enough. Bigness is sacred! A big cock means Big Business, and I have been overcompensating since childhood for what I thought was my small cock....For years, while making love with women, I actually tried to hide my cock from sight. It took acrobatics, but it usually worked. The government may think I am a dangerous radical, but they don't know the true size of my cock!"

Jerry argued that I had "a poverty consciousness" and needed "a success consciousness." Jerry sought success in romance as well as in business. He had never been married. Now he decided that he wanted to meet a tall blond woman who wasn't Jewish so that her neurotic tendencies would have a different frame of reference from his own.

Jerry met Mimi Leonard, a tall blond gentile whose father had written *The Transformation* and coined the phrase "human potential movement." She had written a term paper at Columbia University about Jerry and Abbie Hoffman. Jerry proposed to Mimi on their first date. He always introduced her as "George Leonard's daughter." In 1977 they started planning three huge educational festivals of consciousness on health, sexuality and success. "Like a Vietnam Day of the soul," Jerry assured me. Yet he was troubled by his new image.

"Why are the media programming me for the role of 'radical gone straight' or 'reformed radical' or 'born-again capitalist' just as heavy as they programmed me for the radical crazy role of the '60s?"

I replied, "If you live by the media, you die by the media."

"I actually don't mind it. I am happy as a pig in shit these days. I feel great, I'm in love, I've found work that I enjoy, I don't owe anybody anything. I'm getting married because I *feel* it and because I want to make a statement about commitment. Our culture doesn't understand the meaning of commitment. Yippie and gestalt are equally at fault here."

Jerry and Mimi married in April 1978. Six months later they produced a 15-hour Awareness Extravaganza with such speakers as Masters and Johnson on sexual pleasure, Werner Erhard on the experience of love, Dr. George Sheehan on jogging, Wayne Dyer on personal power, Dick Gregory on food and health, Buckminster Fuller on creativity and Arnold Schwarzenegger on body and mind control. Jerry described the event as "a kind of California event in the middle of New York City."

Jerry had gone from pot-smoking to stock-broking, from rabble-rousing to networking. He would evolve from listening to Lenny Bruce records before delivering Yippie speeches to dancing naked to Neil Diamond albums in order to psych himself up for motivating an audience of multilevel marketers. And now, not surprisingly, he found himself in a defensive mode.

"My networking salon comes out of my 1960s organizing experience," he told me in 1982, "but I really don't think that I've become the person or symbol that I preached against in the '60s. I'm not a warmonger or munitions seller or corporate pig. I am an entrepreneur, a person building an organization bringing people together in a humane way in the 1980s. Is that really so bad? Would I hate myself if I could see myself from the vantage point of the 1960s? I really don't think so. I was opinionated then, and dogmatic, but I also had my moments of sensitivity and openness. People resent me because I represent the part of themselves that is no longer radical."

By the next year, despite the small size of his cock, he had a staff of 12. Jerry and Mimi had separated, but 80,000 upwardly mobile people had attended his weekly salons, and he treasured his collection of their business cards. The next step in his plan would be franchising at $200,000 a shot. Jerry was a true workaholic, but in 1984 he decided to take several months off "to reverse the aging process." Eventually he moved to Los Angeles, where he made $750,000 a year, lived in a $5000-a-month high-rise in Brentwood, paid $15,000 monthly to Mimi for child support and began to reverse the aging process by wearing a toupee.

In the *Los Angeles Times*, columnist Al Martinez wrote about the other Jerry Rubin, a political activist with the Alliance for Survival, who was out of work and needed money. Yippie Jerry was annoyed. "They think it's me," he complained. "My landlord thinks I can't pay the rent. Girls won't go out with me because they think I'm broke." Yippie Jerry thought that out of sheer admiration, Alliance Jerry had named himself after him, and now Yippie Jerry was concerned that Alliance Jerry would become his Mark David Chapman, the fanatic who **87** killed John Lennon because he loved him so much. When they met for lunch, Yippie Jerry insisted that Alliance Jerry bring his birth certificate. When Yippie Jerry saw that Jerry Rubin was Alliance Jerry's real name, Yippie Jerry offered Alliance Jerry $10,000 to change his name—$20,000 if he would change it to Tom Hayden.

"I want you to work for me," said Yippie Jerry to Alliance Jerry. "I want every Jerry Rubin in America to work for me."

One of the Jerry Rubins who worked for him was Bobby Seale.

The Pablo Escobar Connection

In the early '90s, I was still performing standup comedy, not on the comedy-club circuit, but rather at campuses and theaters, and in odd venues, from borrowed living rooms to rented art galleries, booked by Jeannine Frank's Parlor Performances. Perhaps the oddest venue was the Brentwood Bakery. Folding chairs were set up, and everyone got a free pastry of their choice. Jerry was there—the bakery was in his neighborhood—but he asked me *not* to introduce him.

"There's someone here in the audience tonight," I began, "and he asked me not to introduce him, but I'm going to do it anyway." Jerry looked embarrassed. "Pablo Escobar," I announced, referring to the Colombian drug kingpin who had recently escaped from his palatial prison and was now on the lam. Jerry's look of embarrassment turned to one of disappointment. "Come on, Pablo," I cajoled, "don't be bashful, stand up and take a bow."

After the show, Jerry and I went for a late dinner, where he proceeded to tell me about his encounter with Patty Hearst in early 1974, verifying Abbie Hoffman's account, although in Jerry's version of the *menáge à trois* it was Abbie who had fondled Jerry's genitals. "Abbie and I had a threesome once before," he continued. "We were on a plane, and we were flirting with this girl sitting next to us. After a while she sat between us. There was a blanket covering us, and while we were feeling her up, she masturbated both of us simultaneously. But that was really impersonal. With Patty it was different—she was a dynamic *hero* and the context was totally political. I shared with her my state of acute depression. You remember how, during the antiwar movement, we felt *alive every moment*, and now I was only in my early 30s but I already felt like I was on my deathbed. Well, Patty told me to just stop feeling so fucking sorry for myself, and that I should try to bring about change by working within the system because there were *many* battlefronts. It was like a religious experience. She changed my life."

I then learned that what I had perceived earlier in the evening as Jerry's disappointment was actually his dread. He told me how he needed to keep his post-Patty agenda a secret, and in the process, took flack for hypocrisy and became a symbol for selling out. He reminisced about how difficult it had been to debate Abbie Hoffman when he actually agreed with him, how hurt he had been when he wasn't invited to a Chicago+20 reunion in 1988, and how awful it felt a year later to be booed at a memorial for Abbie at the Palladium in New York, 89 the same concert hall where he and Mimi had organized so many successful networking parties.

But now he had become an activist again, fighting the FDA's intended ban of vitamins. He called bad food "a terrorist attack on your stomach." And he described to me his latest plan, to have the members of youth gangs market Wow—a powdered energy drink containing caffeine— instead of crack cocaine. Jerry had already met with leaders from the Crips and the Bloods. While he was waiting for their answer, he got a phone call from Pablo Escobar himself.

"We had something very strange in common. Although we were both wealthy—but he's a *billion*aire— we both wanted to destroy capitalism from within by its own excesses. It was the most thrilling conversation I've had since Berkeley, when there was a group of us discussing Mao Tse-Tung's several levels of opportunism. Except that Escobar was unhappy about the competition that my project meant for him. Somehow the word had filtered up to him. He insisted that South Central and all the inner cities were his territory, and that he would arrange to have me killed if I didn't pull out of there. I was scared shitless. I told him that if I were murdered, it would only make me a martyr. He took that as a challenge and guaranteed my death would be made to look like an accident."

The Stephanie Ratner Connection

At a three-day conference in the summer of 1988, cele-

brating the twentieth anniversary of the mass protest against the Democratic convention—and held in the very same Amphitheater—Abbie Hoffman took the stage and spoke with passion:

"I believe that what happened here in the streets of Chicago energized the left and went beyond the left, cracked the barrier that the media had placed around the antiwar movement, and reached into the hearts and souls of Americans—in particular, Americans fighting in Vietnam. Of all the people I've met in the past twenty years that would come up and talk to me, the most touching is to hear from soldiers who were in Vietnam, who were not privileged to attend all the conferences where the *isms* debated the *wasms* about whether we should go this way or that way in terms of revolutionary theory as defined by Marx or Mao or Bakunin or Avakian or J. Edgar Hoover, but had seen with their own eyes their contemporaries, young people from their generation, taking risks to go against the war machine."

A young female student had a question for Abbie:

"In terms of the powers-that-be, in terms of operating within the system or outside of the system, isn't it just a little nutty to let people know that you're working against them if they have all the power? Isn't that just a little bit crazy? I mean, the problem I have with people taking pictures here is that like I'm starting to get really paranoid. I guess there are enough things against each person if the government really does have all this power that we're talking about, and people individually don't have specific ways to go against that themselves. I couldn't afford to hire a lawyer if I needed to. What I'm saying is, everyone who goes against the government, all those different people, are the people they pick out first to get rid of when there's a problem. Those are the people who get imprisoned."

Abbie answered:

"There's no way that change will come about without people taking risks—with their careers, their marriage plans, their status in the community and their lives. There's no way change will come about. You can buy the albums, you can wear the T-shirt, you can listen to classic rock 'n' roll all you want, you can go to a U2 concert, you can hold hands in a stupid pageantry like Hands Across America and think you're doing something about poverty, but that's New Age nonsense, that's being *concerned* about issues, that's not *caring* about issues. Hands Across America should've been Hands *Up*, America! That's the way it goes. Robin Hood was *right*. Steal from the rich! Give to the poor!"

Abbie killed himself eight months later. Nicole Hollander's comic-strip character, Sylvia, sat at her typewriter tapping out this letter: "Dear Network Creeps: I imagine you're working feverishly to develop Abbie Hoffman's life into an incredibly bland but offensive made-for-TV movie. Well, stop it or you'll feel my wrath."

So now two of Jerry Rubin's closest friends had committed suicide. And his marriage had broken up. At least Mimi had also moved to Los Angeles with their two children. But he was a lonely and insecure man hiding inside the healthy body of a super-achiever.

Leslie Meyers lived in the same building as Jerry, and they met for the first time in a corridor.

Speaking for the other tenants, she said, "We know about you, but you're new and you haven't given a party, which is traditional here, so we've been ignoring you. We hide in stairways when we see you coming." Jerry took her joke literally and gave a party, where he proposed to Leslie. She declined, but they remained friends.

Although he refrained from talking about his '60s past with her, she saw his books and asked which had sold the most copies. He said, "*Do it!*—but you can't read it." Leslie took a copy anyway. The next day she told him, "I can't believe that a man with so many suits hanging in the closet wrote this."

Soon after, at a screening, Jerry met actress Stephanie Ratner and told her, "I'm gonna marry you." Stephanie's mother was a guest on *Leeza*, an afternoon TV talk show, where the topic was "Women Who Marry Men for Their Money," and Stephanie was in the audience. She moved in with Jerry, then she moved out, then in again and out again. Their relationship was rather stormy.

In October 1994, Jerry and Leslie went to a movie. The next night, at four a.m., she was the recipient of a conference call from Stephanie, her mother, her brother and Jerry. Leslie hung up on such foolishness.

On the evening of November 14, Jerry, Stephanie and Fred Branfman, of the Making a Difference project to help inner-city youths learn how to start their own businesses, were leaving Jerry's apartment on their way to dinner. Branfman's car was parked across the street. Jerry was a chronic jaywalker, and he got hit by a 1991

Volkswagen GTI on Wilshire Boulevard, knocking him several yards straight into unconsciousness.

(Ironically, he had revealed in *Growing Up at Thirty-Seven* the things he shouted at his parents during a psychic therapy session, including this: "Every woman I see is no good—too tall, too short, not Jewish, not smart, not this, not that. I have a million excuses because I am scared of women. When I find one I like, I drive her crazy with my neediness, anxiety, possessiveness. You taught me to hate women, Mommy. You—sexless, lifeless, castrating, energy-draining—are my model for all women! I am doing to all women what I would like to do to you. I make them pay for my hatred toward you. I want to fail with women to prove to you that NO OTHER WOMAN WILL TAKE YOUR PLACE! Now will you love me? If I am happy, I will be betraying your teachings. And then you will be jealous, and you won't love me. Well, fuck you, Mommy, fuck you in the ass with a red-hot poker and let your arms and legs fall off and leave you in the middle of the road run over by the meanest car I ever saw.")

Paramedics found no neurological function in Jerry's body, no vital signs of life. His injuries were massive—severe abdominal and head injuries, a scattering of blood around the base of the brain, a detached aorta, a shattered leg and a collapsed lung. Emergency surgery was performed at UCLA Medical Center for 14 hours.

Jerry remained in a coma for two weeks. Family and friends maintained a bedside vigil, talking to him, holding his hand, playing music for him—but nothing by Phil Ochs because that might depress Jerry. Leslie, knowing of his love for celebrities, described her lunch with Jack Nicholson. Stew Albert asked Jerry if he remembered Judge Hoffman, and Jerry rolled his eyes. "Wake up, Jerry," Stew told him, "you'll get a big book contract for coming back from the dead. Your coma is a real opportunity." Eldridge Cleaver managed to gain access to the hospital room by claiming to be Jerry's half-brother. He shook hands with his former prisoner, Tim Leary, and suggested that they form a third party with a female candidate for president. Eldridge was entranced by Leslie and informed her, "You unleash the lightning in the souls of men." Stephanie's mother saw Leslie and wondered aloud, "What does she think *she's* doing here?"

It was, finally, the other Jerry Rubin who called to tell me the news. "This is Jerry Rubin. Jerry Rubin is dead." Tragedy and absurdity were two sides of the same coin. And so it came to pass that the other Jerry Rubin became the living Jerry Rubin.

"It's like losing a brother," he said. "We both wanted peace. I've been getting calls all day from people thinking I died."

The dead Jerry Rubin had once predicted that he would live to the age of 140, but his poor heart gave out when he was only 56. I was angry as well as sad. How could somebody who had spent the entire decade of the '70s expanding his consciousness forget the simple lesson he had been taught in kindergarten: "Cross at the green and not in between!" Jerry had committed suicide with his false sense of invincibility as surely as Abbie Hoffman did with his pills and Phil Ochs did with his noose.

Of course, on the surface Jerry seemed to be the victim of a simple automobile accident—after all, he had been dodging through six lanes of traffic—but then I remembered that threat to him from Pablo Escobar. The driver of the car that struck Jerry was neither held nor charged, and he was not named in the newspapers, but I was able to track him down by way of the police report. He smugly admitted that there had been a swarm of 36 cars, 18 in each direction, six per lane, and that his car just happened to be the one nearest to Jerry at that instant, but he refused to tell me how all the drivers knew exactly *when* Jerry would be scurrying across Wilshire.

The William Kunstler Connection

In my autobiography, although I confessed to ingesting 300 micrograms of LSD in a restaurant before testifying at the Chicago Conspiracy Trial in January 1970, I restrained myself from mentioning the fact that at the same lunch attorney Bill Kunstler joined defendants Abbie Hoffman and Jerry Rubin in eating hashish. I wrote only that "while the others were passing around a chunk of hash, I took a tab of LSD." But now that Kunstler has arrived at that Great Courtroom in the Sky just in time to defend Abbie and Jerry, who had been busted for trying to organize the angels, I feel free to share that touch of gossip.

In 1976 I was invited to deliver a keynote speech at "The American Hero: Myths & Media," a five-day symposium and deodorant pad held in Sun Valley,

Idaho, a vacation resort that resembled the locale of a TV series, *The Prisoner*, where members of the intelligence community were let out to pasture on an inescapable island. For me it was the setting for an uncomfortable situation where two participants, Bill Kunstler and Tim Leary—both friends of mine—were at odds with each other.

Kunstler had smuggled in to the conference a "real-life hero," a native American woman who deliberately shot a white man, a known child molester who had raped a seven-year-old girl. Who knows *what* Leary smuggled in? But Kunstler refused to acknowledge Leary's greeting, referring to him as "a traitor" because he had supposedly told federal authorities how the Weather Underground had helped him escape from prison.

"I wouldn't be surprised, " Kunstler whispered to me, "if somebody assassinated Leary."

And now, Leary, just turning 75, has announced that he has inoperable prostate cancer. He told me that he has "two to five years" to live, but he was enthusiastic about orchestrating a death that will serve as an appropriate conclusion to his adventurous life. "That's the biggest decision you can make," he said. "You couldn't choose how and when and with whom you were *born*."

One of Leary's options is to have his disembodied head frozen and preserved after his death for possible cloning in the future. "It's a better idea than to go belly-up and get eaten by worms," he insists. His head will be stored in liquid nitrogen in a cryogenic container— a device similar to a high-tech stainless steel thermos bottle. And if that doesn't work out, I suggested, they can always use his frozen head for *Celebrity Bowling*.

At one point in our conversation, Leary said that the O. J. Simpson trial has revealed how "evil" lawyers are. I asked if he meant defense and prosecution. "Yes," he answered, but I refrained from challenging his generalization because I was in a journalistic mode, just like Laura Hart McKinny, who didn't object when Detective Mark Fuhrman used the word *nigger* over and over again.

Anyway, I asked Leary, "What do you want your epitaph to be?"

"What do *you* think? You write it."

"Here lies Timothy Leary. A pioneer of inner space. And an Irish leprechaun to the end."

"Irish leprechaun? You're being racist! Can't it be a Jewish leprechaun? What is this Irish leprechaun shit?"

"Okay. Here lies Timothy Leary. A pioneer of inner space. And a Jewish leprechaun to the end."

And my headline in *The Realist*: "Kunstler Gone, Leary Next."

The George Demmerle Connection

Lou Salzburg and George Demmerle were both infiltrators of the Youth International Party. I was suspicious of Salzburg—a photographer, he would call to ask about our next demonstration, and I would tell him to examine the *Village Voice* classified ads under Riots—but I was fooled by Demmerle, a factory welder, older than the other Yippies, who called himself Prince Crazy, and instead of trying to keep a low profile, mimicked the penchant of Abbie and Jerry for outlandish costumes and guerrilla theater.

Demmerle had started out with the reactionary John Birch Society, switched to an ultra-right-wing militia, the Minutemen, then tried to join the FBI, which took him on as a volunteer—and later a paid—informant. Recently he confessed to *Dallas Observer* reporter Ann Zimmerman, "The government was committing more crimes than the people were. They were framing people, planting drugs on antiwar activists, breaking and entering."

When the Yippies held a pre-Chicago event on a Hudson River pier, nominating a pig for president, Demmerle played the role of a stereotypical anarchist, using for his prop-bomb a black bowling ball complete with fuse. Before he could carry out his mission to assassinate Pigasus, he was thrown into the water.

After a while, the role began to play him. Yippie archivist Sam Leff recalls how "Demmerle used to stand up at the end of meetings and say, 'Who wants to go out and get arrested?'—enticing young kids to go out and throw rocks and break windows. He wouldn't get arrested, but he'd get others arrested." Demmerle tried to convince Abbie to receive Navy weapons and explosives, and he attempted to persuade Jerry to blow up the Brooklyn Bridge. But now he claims to have been influenced by the very people he spied on and tried to set up.

"I loved Jerry and Abbie," he insists. "I don't want the ideals they stood for—love and freedom—to die with them. The ideals of the Yippies are the last hope for America."

At the memorial for Jerry, attended by 200 mourners—several were actually giving out free samples of Wow—I spotted George Demmerle. He was weeping while Stew Albert, with great difficulty, delivered a eulogy.

"To most everyone here, the key word is Wow," Albert said, "but I come from the era when the key word was Yippie. Jerry was always a rebel, but then he was always a rebel within the rebellion. He was always sort of rebelling against the norms of the rebellion. That was a constant characteristic. He always wanted things to be exciting, and he saw excitement as a form of communication. The biggest influence he had on me was to stimulate a sense that more was possible than I thought. My tendency was to say, 'Now look, Jerry, objective conditions say this, and objective conditions say that, and so you can't really do that.' And he would always find a way of saying, 'Well, look, we *could* do it.' He was always broadening the sense of what was possible. In our relationship, my function was *occasionally* convincing him that something really was impossible. That was our dynamic. Jerry changed costumes, and he changed rhetoric, but he never changed his heart."

Jerry's ex-wife, Mimi declared: "Jerry realized that America is the greatest country on earth. He realized that capitalism is the greatest system on earth. He helped many, many people make money and have good lives."

One individual, who was trying to raise funds for a *yahrzeit* candle ceremony for Jerry, declined to ask Mimi because she isn't Jewish.

Actress Sally Kirkland confided to everyone: "Jerry taught me to stand up for what I believe in. He was my lover, he was my friend, he was my teacher, he was my revolutionary mentor."

And Stephanie Ratner announced: "Jerry always wanted to get there quicker. He was the love of my life. He turned out to be my hero."

She was wearing an engagement ring that Jerry never gave her, and she claimed that he had asked her to marry him shortly before the accident, although Jerry had been telling friends *the day before* that Stephanie was "the worst relationship of my life" and he wanted out. Stew Albert called him, and when Jerry put Stephanie on the phone, she described herself only as "Jerry's sidekick."

"That's funny," Stew responded. "*I* used to be his sidekick."

Later on, when he heard that Stephanie was planning a $150-million palimony suit against Jerry's estate, Stew remarked, "She gave him the best few months of her life."

I also saw Patty Hearst at the memorial, incognito, just as she had been at Abbie's memorial. I mentioned that F. Lee Bailey would be one of the attorneys defending O. J. Simpson, and she chuckled. Patty had sought a new trial on the grounds that Bailey had represented her inadequately and kept taking "hangover medicine" during the trial.

"He wasn't *totally* incompetent," she told me now. "Before my trial, Browning [the prosecutor] had admitted that it was clear from photographs of the bank robbery that I might have been acting under duress, **101** and during the trial, with only fifteen minutes to go before a weekend recess, Bailey brought out the government's suppression of photos showing Camilla Hall [one of the kidnappers] pointing her gun at me."

"Well, look at it this way—if you hadn't been kidnapped, you wouldn't be in show business today."

"Yeah, right. And I never would've met Roseanne. She and I have something in common, by the way. We both married our bodyguards."

"Listen, if your trial were held today, what do you think the jury—"

"Oh, I would be found not guilty, there's no question about it. A dozen lawyers have told me that, because the climate is so different now."

As I was leaving the cemetery, George Demmerle approached me hesitantly, and we talked briefly.

"I guess I must still be a spy," he remarked with a smirk.

"What do you mean?"

"You see that girl?" He pointed to Stephanie. "I was skulking around, and I overheard her arguing with him." He pointed to a man I recognized as the driver of the car that had struck Jerry. "She said to him, 'You've got a lot of nerve coming here.' And he answered, 'Hey, you wanna know something, if you hadn't called us when you guys were leaving the apartment, Jerry would be alive today.' I don't know what they meant, but I wanted to tell you, because I figure I owe that much to Jerry's memory."

 A week later, I visited Stephanie at Jerry's apartment. It was devoid of all furniture, which she had appropriated, except for a pair of junior mattresses that the kids had slept on whenever they stayed over. Stephanie was sitting on the floor in a corner, looking desolate. I told her everything I had learned, and now I only wanted to understand her motivation.

"Jerry betrayed me," she sobbed. "He set Mimi up on a high level in the business, above all the others, but I have to build my *own* downline and work my way *up* his precious pyramid scheme."

She was holding onto a collage that she had constructed from photographs of Jerry and her. It had hung on the wall of his hospital room. But now I noticed that in the photos, Jerry's head was larger than hers. It made no sense visually. Upon closer examination, I realized that Stephanie's head had been glued on to the photos. I asked her about that.

"These were photos of Jerry and Leslie," she said. "But Leslie was Jerry's *former* girlfriend. So I just cut out her head with a scissors and glued *mine* on instead."

"That's really incredible."

"Oh, don't worry, I kept all of Leslie's heads in a box. So if she wants them, she can have them."

In a perverted sort of way, Jerry would have been proud of her.

In my capacity as a standup comic I always encourage questions from the audience. So in the middle of one performance, while I was talking about paranoia, somebody called out, "What do *you* fear?"

"Endless pain" was the first thing that came to mind.

After another show, a woman thanked me for making her laugh, because the last time she had gone to see a comedian he made her cry.

"He yelled at me," she explained. "And I was afraid to come here tonight."

What does it mean when even the sharing of humor, which is supposed to be the *antidote* to fear, has become a cause of it? Fear so permeates the culture that it's taken for granted. Now, when kids go trick-or-treating on Halloween, you can get free X-rays of their candy and apples to make sure there are no razor blades inside. And that's considered the *good* news.

On an economic level employees fear the loss of their jobs and security while stockholders fear that those same companies won't downsize *enough* to ensure high dividends. A recent *Money*/ABC Consumer Comfort Poll indicates that "consumers we surveyed have turned sharply sour on the state of the U.S. economy." People fear the banks more than they fear the Mafia. They fear a recession more than they fear a drive-by shooting.

Since fear has become the name of the merchandising game it's no great surprise that this trend should be exploited in the stock market itself as reflected by these top 10 growth stocks in the fear industry:

Cash and Carry
(NYSE/CAC/$23.84 PER SHARE)

This chain of combination check-cashing and pawnshops, which began modestly by filling the void left by bank branches deserting the inner cities, now boasts 60,000 outlets and has expanded to serve the needs of middle-class and upscale borrowers with cash-flow problems. Despite charges of legalized usury—interest rates reach 200%—an aura of respectability is a byproduct of TV commercials featuring actor Rod Steiger pitching the personal touch in his cinematic *Pawnbroker* persona.

Disposables 'R' Us
(NYSE/DRU/$19.93 PER SHARE)

Capitalizing on the acceleration of built-in obsolescence, this corporation built its way up from a one-product wonder—disposable contact lenses that brought in $700 annually from each wearer—into a virtual monopoly, manufacturing and distributing, to the utter dismay of environmentalists, disposable toothbrushes, disposable combs, disposable diapers, disposable diaphragms, disposable bras, disposable shoes, disposable watches, disposable camcorders, disposable microwave ovens and disposable garbage cans.

Free Enterprise Prisons
(NYSE/FEP/$52.09 PER SHARE)

Over a million individuals are already behind bars, and recidivism rates are rapidly rising, so it's an unquestionably bullish market for FEP with their emphasis on computerized systems that track prisoners' whereabouts by imprinting bar codes on their bodies. The most powerful lobby behind the "three strikes and you're out" legislation was the prison guards' union, an ironic twist inasmuch as the aggressively expanding private prison business employs nonunion guards to man the scanners of those bar codes.

Latex Industries Group
(NYSE/LIG/$49.57 PER SHARE)

It was the fear of pregnancy compounded by the fear of AIDS that led to the safe sex syndrome that now accounts for LIG's global dominance in the sale of latex condoms. The American market is currently being targeted, whereas India's 900 million population remains a dream market yet to be tapped. Plus, by the beginning of the 21st century there will be two billion teenagers in the world eager to surrender to the siren call of their glands. A failure rate of only 1.5% in slippage and breakage tests has enhanced the image of an industry that was once derisively labeled "a scumbag business" by the *Wall Street Journal*, not to mention the ever-increasing demand for latex gloves by doctors, nurses, dentists, police and Secret Service agents protecting the White House.

Organ Transplants International
(NYSE/OTI/$31.76 PER SHARE)

It may seem like moral role reversal, but despite friction over human rights, President Bill Clinton has renewed most-favored-nation trade privileges for China whereas Senator Jesse Helms advocates rescinding that status. Clinton's kowtowing to pressure from business interests such as AT&T (in 1993 they sold over $1 billion worth of cellular phones and pagers in China alone) has opened the door for OTI to take total advantage of the Chinese practice of selling organ transplants from executed political prisoners. And the AMA's concomitant support for the use of anencephalic babies (born with most of their brains missing) as organ donors is the American icing on that Chinese misfortune cookie.

Pharmaceuticals United
(NYSE/PU/$29.63 PER SHARE)

Realizing that the disappearance of the Amazon and other rain forests would also mean the loss of innumerable plants with natural medicinal qualities and healing agents, PU has capitalized on a tragedy—preventing any further destruction of those rain forests by purchasing them outright, thus enabling them to own the vines and herbs that their research & development staff finds

 so valuable. ("Doing the right thing for the wrong

reason," contends one leading ecologist.) In addition, by merging with Lintel Labs Corp., they have projected $12 billion in revenues this year thanks to a heavy diversification of projects ranging from extremely competitive HMO plans to a controversial new line of artificial endorphins.

Super Security Services
(NYSE/SSS/$61.25 PER SHARE)

The Board of Directors at Triple-S undoubtedly experienced mixed feelings about the April bombing in Oklahoma: distressed by homegrown terrorism, yet exhilarated by the sales potential of security-related products—a $28 billion industry—particularly their cement barriers that protect buildings from kamikaze-truck attacks. But the need for increased security was already obvious. Threats against members of Congress through March of this year jumped by 43% over that same period in 1994. The demand for metal detectors and surveillance equipment rose accordingly, not just on Capitol Hill but at office buildings, public schools and abortion clinics across the nation. Moreover, with its sudden acquisition of Wackenhut, SSS is now the country's largest provider of armed guards and trained dogs alike. Shareholders find no conflict of interest in their manufacture of, on the one hand, camouflage uniforms for the militia movement, and on the other hand, computerized fertilizer detectors for bomb-searching by the Bureau of Alcohol, Tobacco and Firearms. Business, we might add, is booming.

Temporary Substitutes, Inc.
(NYSE/TSI/$27.86 PER SHARE)

According to *Kiplinger's*, the underlying catalyst that will shape global economies in years to come is the extension of technology to every society on earth. But the chickens have already come home to roost here. As the *Washington Post* reports, after foreign competitors forced the U.S. to turn to technology to boost productivity in the 1970s, substituting machines for people wherever possible, companies have been trimming thousands from their payrolls, sometimes more than half of their permanent work force, 25% of which now consists of temporary employees. TSI eagerly supplies personnel to fill that demand, and workers fearful of being two paychecks away from homelessness are eager to rent their labor to corporations without any of the benefits accorded full-timers. "They're happy just to have shit-jobs," CEO Harold Levridge observes, "and that in turn makes our stockholders even happier."

Tranquility Guaranteed Insurance
(NYSE/TGI/$40.15 PER SHARE)

A friend of ours buys a lottery ticket every day and fills in the same set of numbers each time, not because he ever expects to win, but simply as insurance against the possibility that his numbers might be the winning ones on a day he *didn't* buy a ticket. That's a parable for all insurance. You buy it as a gamble that you won't need it. TGI has acquired its way into 52 major markets in 43 states by specializing in offbeat accounts, such as ebola insurance for those who are afraid that the fatal disease would spread beyond Zaire, tariff insurance for American distributors of Japanese cars, and PC insurance for universities and other institutions where acts of political incorrectness can result in expensive lawsuits.

X Spots the Mark

(NYSE/XSM/$33.28 PER SHARE)

If not for this upstart company the paranoia market might never have been mined so profitably. And with the use of skillful Amway-style traveling salespeople, what a fine variety of products and services they offer: special shields to block microwave radiation from electrical transmitters; the neutralization of microchip implants from alien abductors; deprogramming from government mind control experiments. Little wonder that the value of XSM's initial public stock offering has increased more than any other issued this year. Their official brochure sums it up by paraphrasing Franklin D. Roosevelt's most famous maxim: "The only thing we have to invest in is fear itself."

The Last Dan Quayle Joke

1992

My friend Stanley Young told me that at the Republican convention, while George Bush was giving his acceptance speech, Dan Quayle was overheard chanting, "Three more years! Three more years!" I borrowed this line to use onstage, it was repeated in Lyle Stuart's newsletter, *Hot News*, crediting me, and then Tony Scaduto of *New York Newsday* called to ask if I had actually heard Quayle chanting that. I was shocked that even a seasoned reporter believed Quayle could have been *that* dumb.

Of course, I'm partly to blame. I participated in a conspiracy by the Standup Comedians Union to associate Quayle with dumbness. Or to use Steve Allen's word, *dumbth*. So, to maintain good standing with the union, I am required to do at least one Dan Quayle joke every performance. Quayle thinks Roe versus Wade refers to alternative ways of crossing the Potomac River. Quayle saw *Teenage Mutant Ninja Turtles* and thought it was a documentary about Earth Day. Quayle thinks "quid pro quo" is a seafood lunch special.

Perpetuating Quayle's dumb image is how I pay my union dues, but to tell the truth, I'm more concerned about his arrogance. For example, when he went river-rafting with his family, Dan Quayle arranged for the Army Corps of Engineers to *lower the fucking river!* I mean, wasn't that an old Jerry Lewis movie, *Don't Raise the Bridge, Lower the River*?

Now that Bill Clinton and Al Gore have won the election, it's time for me to tell the last Dan Quayle joke, but first I have to lead up to it, starting with an awful tragedy that occurred in Egypt. After the recent earthquake there, an entire family was trapped under rubble. The man survived only by drinking his own urine, but his mother, his wife and his daughter all refused to drink their own urine—the taboo was that powerful—and so he had to watch them die, one by one. His daughter's last words were, "I want a Pepsi."

And yet in Japan there is a Buddhist monk who drinks his own urine for his health and he has a huge cult following. In India there are Hindus who drink their own urine in order to reach a higher plateau in their spiritual quest. The Prime Minister of India proudly told Barbara Walters—on *my* TV set in *my* living room—that he drank his own urine. I finally decided to try it myself and I'll be glad to share with you what I learned.

Drinking your own urine does *not* raise you to a higher plateau in your spiritual quest. It's the *decision* to drink your own urine that does the trick. Once you decide to drink your own piss, you're halfway there. If you're able to transcend that taboo in your mind—a taboo that you learned in the crib before you ever learned the English language—then it's merely a matter of taste. Mmmmm, a little salty perhaps. So that's the secret: Transcending a taboo frees you from a lifetime of conditioning and unleashes your psyche to other possibilities.

Now the scene flashes back to a hotel room where then-Mayor Marion Barry is buying crack cocaine from his former mistress. Standing in front of a one-way mirror so the camera on the other side can get a good angle, he lights up the pipe, simultaneously getting high and busted. What can his defense possibly be? "I'm one elected official who's not on the take. The videotape clearly shows me paying *cash* for that crack. I don't owe *nobody* no favors."

Before going to prison Barry was put on probation and he had to take a drug test every week. So he sent away to Byrd Laboratories in Austin, Texas, for a large supply of drug-free powdered urine. Then each week he would simply pour the yellow powder into a glass and add warm water, stirring it with a teaspoon, and use that to pass his drug test.

When there was a strong rumor that all federal employees would be required to take random drug tests, Dan Quayle panicked. He didn't know whether any traces of the marijuana he had smoked in college still remained in his system. But Marion Barry had told him about that drug-free powdered urine, so Quayle sent away for some. When it arrived, he poured the yellow powder into a glass—and then he *peed* in it. And then he *drank* it. And nothing happened.

1992

It wasn't only the sad state of the American economy that forced the Democratic and Republican parties to combine their conventions in 1992. It was also the popularity of Oliver Stone's film *JFK,* which began with a quote from the farewell speech of Dwight Eisenhower—a former general as well as a retiring president—warning against the dangers of a military-industrial complex. If there really was such an invisible government running things all along, then why pretend any longer that it made any difference which rubber stamp was elected Commander in Chief?

Since the public seemed to relish the dirty tricks of a campaign more than intelligent discussion of the real issues, this convention was run by a pair of professional pranksters: Alan Abel, who had once hired actors to play members of the audience at a Phil Donahue taping and faint, one after another; and Dick Tuck, who during the Nixon campaign had arranged for every Chinese fortune cookie at a rally to contain the same message: *What about the Howard Hughes loan?* Their goal now was to pull off the dirtiest trick of all—to maneuver all the candidates into speaking the truth.

Alan Abel had learned the value of a simple bribe when for only $500 in cash, a teacher at the school where Dan Quayle was scheduled to judge a spelling bee added an *e* to the word *potato* on the flash card the Vice President would use to determine the student's accuracy. Moreover, Abel won back $1000 when he bet Dick Tuck that Quayle would automatically assume the misspelling was correct. That was the beginning of their partnership.

But neither Abel nor Tuck could have predicted the behavior of the Act Up demonstrators when the convention opened with a screening of *JFK*. These were the same folks who had protested the negative stereotyping of gays in *Basic Instinct* by revealing how the movie ended to people waiting in line outside the theater. Now they were at Madison Square Garden doing the same thing, objecting to the negative stereotyping of gays in *JFK* by revealing how it ended.

"The CIA got away with it!" they shouted to the delegates. "The Mafia got away with it!"

A spirit of reconciliation permeated the convention, as indicated by the musical presentations.

For the Democrats, Fleetwood Mac reunited and sang "Don't Stop Thinking About Tomorrow."

For the Republicans, the remaining Beatles reunited and sang "Yesterday."

For Ross Perot, Sonny and Cher were supposed to reunite and sing "I've Got You, Babe," but then something unforeseen happened.

Perot had learned that political commercials were not subject to the same scrutiny as were regular commercials. By law, they could not be censored. He was screening a TV commercial for his political advisers, Ed Rollins and Hamilton Jordan. It featured a close-up of Perot himself speaking directly to viewers in his nasal twang:

"My investigators have uncovered some disturbing facts about the other candidates that I'd like to share with you people. Bill Clinton's father did *not* die before he was born. Actually, he abandoned the family and ignored his responsibility to send payments for child support. Clinton's stepfather was *not* an abusive alcoholic, and his mother *never* had breast cancer. That's just a ploy for sympathy. This is just stuff the spin doctors made up. The same with Gore. My investigators have learned that his son *faked* that automobile accident in order to give his father an excuse to drop out of a presidential race he knew he couldn't win. I think that's disgusting...."

Upon seeing this, Jordan said, "Ross, that commercial could really backfire. I mean, remember what happened when Gray Davis merely tried to compare Dianne Feinstein with Leona Helmsley?"

But Rollins refused to dignify the commercial with any discussion.

"I'm through with this shit," he blurted. "I would never want to be associated with a commercial like that. As of this moment, I resign!"

"Okay, go on ahead and quit," Perot snarled at Rollins as he was walking out of the screening room. "I never liked your damn beard anyway."

The next day, Ross Perot dropped out of the campaign himself, and all of a sudden the presidential race was up for grabs.

A strange phenomenon developed in the course of news coverage of this campaign. Whereas it used to be that comedians wanted to be serious actors, now all the network newscasters wanted to be standup comics. In fact, during convention week, the comedy club Catch a Rising Star featured a special Anchor Night.

Tom Brokaw was there, spouting one-liners like, "Since Bill Clinton *didn't* inhale marijuana and Al Gore *did* inhale, it shows that the Democrats are presenting a balanced ticket."

Peter Jennings did a routine about the food being served at the convention: "French-fried sound bites" got a big laugh.

Bernard Shaw and Catherine Crier took suggestions from the audience and improvised a dialogue between Clarence Thomas and Anita Hill that brought the house down.

Dan Rather was a hit with his description of Murphy Brown having a father of the week for her child. One time it would be Jesse Jackson; another time it would be Jerry Brown. Rather repeated that bit on the CBS Evening News, and instead of ending each newscast with a phrase like "That's part of our world tonight" or "Courage," he began to sign off with "You guys have been a lot of fun."

Alan Abel and Dick Tuck had worked with a group of ex-CIA chemists who were able to combine DMSO with sodium pentothal and other drugs, so that the resulting compound could be transmitted into the bloodstream through the skin almost instantly by a simple handshake. The plan was to shake hands with each candidate immediately before he delivered his speech.

Of course, the perpetrator had to tell the truth too. So when Abel shook hands with Dan Quayle as he approached the podium, he couldn't stop himself from saying, "Mr. Quayle, I've just given you a drug that will force you to tell the truth."

"Thank you very much," Quayle answered automatically, and by the time the cheering stopped, the drug had already kicked in.

"There was a lot of pressure by dupes of the cultural elite to get me off the ticket this time," Quayle's voice boomed through the public address system. "But let me remind you how I became Vice President in the first place. You may recall that during the Iran/*contra* hearings, Oliver North's courier, Rob Owen, testified that he had worked out of my senatorial office. So I had already proven myself to be a player in the game. And by the grace of implied blackmail, nobody—not Jim Baker, not Jack Kemp—nobody could get George Bush to consider replacing me. And I will continue to represent the religious right until Armageddon comes, and everyone who is not a born-again Christian shall be consigned to eternal brimstone and fire...."

Then Quayle's opponent, Al Gore, spoke.

"As you all know, I am dedicated to improving the environment. But when I voted for the war in Iraq, I helped set in motion an inevitable process by which Saddam Hussein set fire to oil wells and caused the worst environmental disaster in global history. Oh, my God, what am I saying? Is there a spin doctor in the house? Everybody repeat after me, *Is there a spin doctor in the house?*" And the delegates repeated over and over, as if with a single voice, "*Is there a spin doctor in the house? Is there a spin doctor in the house?*" Then Gore said, "I'll be honest with you. The secret of this convention is that it gives you all a chance to get high by hooting and cheering—a political equivalent to the kind of chanting that goes on at rock concerts, football games, spiritual cults...."

George Bush was next.

"You know, I've publicly blamed the legislative branch for hindering my plans, but actually they've been quite cooperative. So we are equally to blame for the lack of funds for the education thing and the health thing, and all those things that a humane civilization would naturally support. For example, let me just share with you how the funding for the Stealth Bomber got through, even though it is a total waste of money and manpower and technology. They're not built all in one place, you know. Components of the Stealth Bomber were delegated and parceled out to manufacturers in—get this, now—two hundred and eighty-six separate congressional districts, each of which would be affected by the loss of jobs if the program were killed. Very shrewd program, don't you think?"

Suddenly the president began to barf. Just a little gurgle at first, and then, as though a dam had been broken, it poured out—red, white and blue vomit—thanks to yet another chemical hoax by Dick Tuck.

Alan Abel almost missed shaking hands with Bill

Clinton—it was difficult to get past the entire casts of *Designing Women* and *Evening Shade*—but he managed to get through to him just in time.

"First of all," Clinton began, "I'd like to thank Gennifer Flowers for providing a wonderful diversion from the real reason that, as governor, I fired Larry Nichols from the State Development and Finance Authority. He had been very active in providing the propaganda that convinced Congress to renew military aid to the *contras*. Now, although I'm running against George Bush, it was in my own domain, Mena, Arkansas, that the CIA carried out most of their smuggling in cocaine for Americans and smuggling out weapons for the *contras*. My security guards even used to refer to me as Mr. Snowman. But Bush could never say a word about this because it was a Reagan-Bush operation. While Nancy was saying 'Just say no,' the CIA was saying 'Just fly low.' So, you see, I had George Bush by the snowballs...."

Clinton went on and on until finally the balloons were released from the ceiling. Only they weren't balloons, they were fetuses—thousands upon thousands of little human fetuses, provided by the anti-abortion people because of the candidate's pro-choice stance. Delegates screamed in horror as these fetuses continued to rain upon them like some kind of Biblical curse.

Pollsters had become such an integral part of the campaign that a new system of selecting a president was to be instituted for Election Day. A voter would walk into the booth, close the curtain, and there would be the choices—the Gallup Poll, the Roper Poll, the Harris Poll, the CNN Poll, the *USA Today* Poll, plus a few minor polls, with a lever next to each one. You would simply choose that organization whose poll you trusted the most.

In a hotel suite, Hillary Clinton and Tipper Gore were waiting for the results while relaxing over herbal tea and homemade cookies.

"You know," said Hillary, "if we get elected, it would be the first time in history that there'd be two bleached blondes in the White House."

Tipper smiled and blinked twice, her blue eye-shadow flashing in the light. She was busy making notes on which gospel records should be required to have warning labels.

"Now, this one is totally obscene," she said. "Just listen to these lyrics: *Go down, Moses....*"

1991

I shall identify myself only as a female aide to a Republican senator. It is also relevant that I have long nurtured a keen interest in psychohistory, the process by which a nation's direction is interpreted as an extension of the psychological makeup of those individuals who govern it.

Without going into specific detail, let me simply state that on October 5, 1991, I happened to hear part of a conversation among Judge—now Supreme Court Justice—Clarence Thomas, Senator Orrin Hatch and Senator Alan Simpson. The three were meeting informally one week after the Judiciary Committee voted, first 7-7, then 13-1, to recommend the confirmation of Judge Thomas and one day after the full Senate indicated that he *would* be confirmed.

The conversation I happened to hear had to do with those charges brought by Anita Hill and ignored by the members of the committee, both Democratic and Republican. At that point in time I still thought this was an appropriate response, because the alternative would have been to hold an executive session, and Judge Thomas would then have had no practical choice but to resort to heavy denial. Now, however, these men were, in a jocular fashion, acknowledging the truth of Professor Hill's allegations.

Senator Simpson was saying, "Y'know, Clarence, I've seen some pretty raunchy porno movies in my time, but

I never did see one where a lady was having sex with an *animal*."

"I'll never forget it," Judge Thomas replied. "They were in a barn. Except that the inside of the barn was like a theater."

Senator Hatch interjected, "Summer stock, eh?"

"There was a stage at one end," Judge Thomas continued, "and the stage was facing rows and rows of wooden folding chairs. There were haystacks piled up on the stage, and in front of the haystacks there was a beautiful, buxom, blond woman—and a donkey. Well, the woman began disrobing and she started stroking the donkey to arousal."

"Doesn't sound at all sleazy to me," Senator Simpson said.

"Probably had Beethoven playing in the background," Senator Hatch added.

Judge Thomas went on with his description. "When the woman was fully disrobed and the donkey was fully aroused they began copulating, right there in front of those haystacks on the stage of that barn. Bumping and grinding away. You've never seen a sight like this, I promise. And then the camera panned slowly toward the audience—and the audience consisted entirely of *donkeys*."

The Senate office shook with raucous laughter, especially that of Judge Thomas. His booming guffaws rang like huge gongs in a church belfry. And, I must admit, I had to suppress my own laughter. I had been totally caught by surprise, but I appreciated the insight. Homo sapiens i, in reality, the only species that has a need for pornography.

When the group's laughter finally began to simmer down, Senator Hatch said, "I suppose that movie was one of the demands of the animal rights people."

"That's right," Senator Simpson added. "Saving animals' lives is no longer enough. They need *culture*."

I felt like I was imprisoned in the boys' locker room, but I was getting ready to force myself to leave anyway and it would have ended right there for me if the subject hadn't returned to Anita Hill.

"I'm glad nobody considered calling *her* to testify against me, even for a closed-door session," Judge Thomas said. "But you fellas will really love this. Anita Hill was a very opinionated young lady. Actually, she and I once had an *extremely* animated discussion on the decriminalization of abortion. Can you imagine what the Democrats would've done with *that*?"

And that was the precise instant I made the decision to leak Professor Hill's statement to the press. Although I have constantly been sexually *hassled*, I have never really been harassed in the *legal* sense of the word. However, I *have* had an abortion, and I was totally outraged by the blatant hypocrisy I'd overheard. I had never leaked a document before, but my anger overshadowed my fear.

I chose Nina Totenberg because I had come to trust her reporting on National Public Radio. I honestly had no idea what leaking the affidavit would accomplish. I certainly did not envision that it would actually **127** embarrass the Senate into delaying the vote until public hearings were held, although that was my secret desire.

Judge Thomas *testified under oath* that he had never discussed the subject of abortion. However, in response to a question by Senator Hank Brown, Professor Hill testified that she had disagreed with Judge Thomas in a discussion about Roe v. Wade. Unfortunately, Senator Joseph Biden quickly interrupted her.

"That is not the subject of these hearings," he said.

Personally, I feel quite disappointed about that particular aspect of the testimony, but I have not the slightest regret over leaking Anita Hill's affidavit, and I would gladly do it all over again.

I certainly set a higher moral standard for myself than did the staffer for Senator John Danforth who wrote Judge Thomas's statement that began, "Nobody helped me with this."

1991

The first time I interviewed Nancy Reagan was in 1983, for an article titled "Reefer Madness II" in the *Los Angeles Times*. She had just appeared on *Diff'rent Strokes* in her role as a one-person drug-rehabilitation traveling encounter group.

The script—with the aid of White House input and approval—called for her to go to Gary Coleman's class and when a student said he heard that "pot won't hurt you," she responded with the case of a 14-year-old boy who was "burned out" from smoking pot all the time. When he finally ran out of it, he told his younger sister to go steal some money so he could buy more pot, and when she refused, "he brutally beat her."

In Kitty Kelley's unauthorized biography of Nancy Reagan, however, there is a scene where she and her then-governor husband smoked marijuana at a dinner party. We began this interview on that note of discrepancy.

Q. Do you think that your famous "Just Say No" campaign has taken on a certain air of hypocrisy in retrospect?

A. I wouldn't call it hypocrisy. I would say political necessity. You know, when George Bush was running against Ronnie in the 1980 primaries, he was *for* the ERA and *for* abortion. But when he became Ronnie's running mate, he was *against* the ERA and *against* abortion. That was simply a political necessity. In the primaries, Bush said that Ronnie was practicing "voodoo economics," but it's just plain ridiculous to think he could have continued to say that as Vice President. What would you *expect* him to do? And what would you expect *me* to do?

It's funny, when that book first came out—I was so upset and Ronnie kept trying to cheer me up—he told me I should complain that I originally got quoted out of context, that what I *actually* said was, "If anybody tries to sell you an ounce of marijuana for $500, that's way too expensive, so just say no." But seriously, what was I *supposed* to say? "All right, now, boys and girls, just say no even though I once said yes to Alfred Bloomingdale when he passed a joint to me." Besides, it was harmless curiosity, and I was an *adult*.

Q. *So I guess then that you would also call it a "political necessity" for you to have been publicly against abortion, and yet when it came to your own daughter Patti—*

A. Well, yes, of course, that was too close to home. She was unmarried—and the guy was *such* a creep—there really was no choice.

Q. *Except to be pro-choice?*

A. Exactly. But I'll tell you, what hurt me more than almost anything else in that book was where some *nameless* director reveals that Patti confided in him that she had had a hysterectomy "in order to kill the gene pool." What an incredible insult to her father! Maybe *I'm* the one who should've had an abortion—when I was pregnant with Patti!

You know, I saw on *Sixty Minutes*, they had a segment about the offspring of Nazi war criminals, and the son of Martin Bormann was one of them, and *he* said the same thing, that he wouldn't have any children because he didn't want to propagate his father's seed. I mean, how *dare* she say a thing like that?

Q. Are you referring to Patti or Kitty Kelley?

A. Both, I suppose. I call her Kitty Litter, by the way. I am still so furious. The whole world has become a tabloid. What was it that Jimmy Durante always said?

Q. "Goodnight, Mrs. Calabash?"

A. No, no. "Everybody wants to get into the act." I became a total media object. Did you catch what's-his-name, Terry Sweeney? Remember he used to play me on *Saturday Night Live*? Well, on one of the local news shows, they put him in his fright wig and red dress again, and they had him inside a bookstore, frantically gathering up a whole bunch of copies. That was cute, I must admit. But Simon & Schuster even leaked an advance copy of the book to Garry Trudeau, and he was quoting from it in *Doonesbury*—a comic strip, for goodness sake. I mean, how cynical can you get? And that editorial cartoon in the *Times*, with Ronnie holding the phone and saying to this really *cruel* caricature of me, "If it's Frank Sinatra, just say no!" God, that was vicious.

Q. Sinatra hasn't actually denied that you had an affair with him, as the book implies so strongly—he merely said that the book was degrading to you—

A. And inaccurate.

Q. How? What does she write that's inaccurate, specifically?

A. No, I'm not talking about the book—the *cartoon* is inaccurate, because Ronnie *approved* of my relationship with Frank. It took a lot of pressure off him. And don't forget, Ronnie and Frank were *friends*—unlike the Kennedy brothers who dropped Frank because of his so-called mob connections. I've met those connections— they're Ronnie's friends too. But no, the *book* is accurate about that, even though she only presents circumstantial evidence. Ah, if she only knew.

Q. If she only knew what?

A. If she only knew what we used to do. Frank would (*laughing*) handcuff me to the bed that Abraham Lincoln slept in, and I would say, "Oh, please, Master, I'm your slave, oh, please, free me"—and he would say, "Never, you WASP bitch!" At the same time he's on the stereo singing "I did it *my* way...." And if Kitty Litter only knew who *else*. She didn't do enough research, that's her trouble. And if she thinks I have piano legs, then *she's* the whole *piano*.

Q. Can you tell me who else you slept with?

A. Of course not. That would put me in real danger.

Q. Would you tell me off the record?

A. You know, I think I might *already* be in danger. If I speak on the record, would you agree to hold off publishing this for a while?

Q. For how long?

A. Until I get out of the country. Or if something happens to me here before I get out.

Q. What kind of danger are you in?

A. Remember Martha Mitchell right after the Watergate break-in? Five men threw her on the bed and injected her with something-or-other. They treated

132

her like a political prisoner to keep her quiet—they pulled her phone right off the wall. I don't want anything like that to happen to me. I really do know too much.

Q. But don't you think it could protect you if this is published before something happens to you, maybe even help prevent it, instead of waiting till it's too late?

A. All right, I'll tell you who it was. Do you remember a couple of years ago, that time I accompanied Chief Gates on a drug raid in the ghetto? There was loads of publicity on that one.

Q. You made it with Daryl Gates?

A. Nothing romantic, the way it was with Frank. Chief Gates did have a sweet side—I mean, it was thoughtful of him to give me that LAPD jacket with my name embroidered—but the sex was more like a power thing. I think maybe we both got turned on by the raid and by the media coverage. After we got our sound bites in, I left with Chief Gates in his red Acura Legend. He took me home and I smoked pot for the *second* time in my life. His stuff was a lot stronger than Alfred Bloomingdale's, though. The Chief told me that it was from the evidence locker.

Q. So, did he put handcuffs on you too?

A. No, silly, I never do that on the first date. In fact (*giggling*) we didn't even have intercourse. He just wanted me to perform fellatio on him. But I'll tell you something, his weenie veers to the right more than any weenie I've ever seen.

Q. And if anybody's seen a lot of weenies, you certainly fit the bill.

A. Now stop that. Anyhow, when we finished, suddenly his mood seemed to change, and he

said, "Little lady, that was the best blow job I've ever had."
I thought that was quite crude.

Q. What, for him to say blow job?

A. No, to call me little lady—in that context—because
the next time I saw him he said it again, in a different context, but with the same condescension. "Now, little lady,"
he said, "I've got a problem maybe you can help me with."
And he started going into detail about an incident that had
happened back in 1967, when Ronnie and I were living
in Sacramento.

He was governor at the time, and a couple of his
aides had been involved in a scandal. He finally fired them
both, and we thought that nobody would find out, but later
on Drew Pearson wrote in his column that "a homosexual ring had been operating out of Governor Reagan's
office" for six months with his full knowledge. That's when
I first learned the meaning of "political necessity." Ronnie and I had gay friends—we could make fun of them
right to their faces—but for the public we had to adopt a
militantly anti-gay stance

I asked Chief Gates why he was bringing that old
scandal up now, and he said, "Have you ever read one
of those stories in the newspaper about a raid on a house
of prostitution? There's usually a mention of how vice
squad officers seized the hookers' address books and
videotapes, and then it's all forgotten about—by everybody except the police." He didn't actually use the word
blackmail but that's what I inferred from his demeanor.

134

And you know, after that recent videotaped beat-
ing of Rodney King, when the City Council didn't

call for Chief Gates's resignation, I wondered what does he have on *them*?

Anyway, the Chief continued to "refresh my memory," as he put it, about how, in the wake of that homosexual public relations nightmare, I turned to Alfred Bloomingdale as a sort of daily adviser. He was my best friend Betsy's husband. I consulted him every single day— much, *much* more often than I was ever in contact with any astrologer or psychic, believe me. Alfred was one of those extremely wealthy men in Ronnie's so-called Kitchen Cabinet.

Alfred had a very kinky thing going with his mistress, Vicki Morgan. Whips and playing horsy and all that. And he was paying her $18,000 a month. When he died, Betsy cut off that money, and Vicki sued for it to continue. How do you like that—the mistress was suing the widow. Then the kinkiness became public knowledge, and as George Bush would say, the doodoo hit the fan.

Q. So then who could be blackmailed? Bloomingdale was dead.

A. Yes, but Ronnie had been to a couple of Alfred's orgies. A few months after he died, Vicki Morgan was murdered by her roommate, who was a homosexual. He beat her to death with a baseball bat. Chief Gates told me that this guy was part of the Gay Mafia, and that it was a contract killing (*sobbing*) and that my Ronnie was the one who had *hired* him, to prevent Vicki from blabbing about his participation in the orgy. And now the Chief wanted to blackmail *me* or else he would leak those tapes to the press.

Q. How did he express that?

A. He didn't use the word but he *implied* blackmail when I asked for the tapes. He said, "Don't worry, little lady, they're perfectly safe. Nobody will get their hands on 'em, I can guarantee you that." Again, he didn't use the word *money* but he did speak of a "financial problem" I could help him with. I told him I wasn't in a position to give him anything.

The Chief looked at me like he had *ice* in his blood, and he said, "What about those funds you took back from Phoenix House?" My heart jumped. "Remember," he continued, "that 3.8 million from King Fahd and the others that swayed your husband the President to reconsider selling surveillance planes to Saudi Arabia? Sort of like a dress rehearsal for the Iran/*contra* conduit, wouldn't you think?"

He was literally walking around me in circles, like a vulture or a movie detective or something. "Remember that 3.8 million you transferred from Phoenix House to the Nancy Reagan Drug Abuse Foundation? So now you have your own private and personal bank right here in L.A., and you aren't accountable to *any*one, right?" And then he shouted: *"Well, you are accountable to me!"* Then, in almost a whisper, he said, "I understand you've already accumulated nearly five million dollars, and distributed less than ten percent." I was so frightened.

Q. What did you do?

A. Well, I *didn't* just say no. What did I do? I've only been giving him $10,000 every month, that's all.

Q. That's your choice, though. You could've just said, "Fuck you, Daryl." So he leaks those tapes—

so what? Ronald Reagan's image would go down the toilet, that's all. Worse things have happened.

A. But that's my point. Worse things really *could* happen. I don't think I'm being paranoid. Last week I told Ronnie I wanted to stop making those payments to Chief Gates, and you should've seen the way he lost his temper. I'm beginning to fear for my life. You know, they can make it look like an accident or a suicide or even like an ordinary burglary. I mean John Mitchell loved Martha Mitchell but—

Q. Wait, who do you mean by "they"—Daryl Gates or your husband?

A. Either one. It doesn't make any difference. They both work for the same people, ultimately. The Alfred Bloomingdales of the world. I'm expendable. I mean, Kitty Litter may think that I was the co-President just because I had enough power to get a few people fired, but it wasn't *me* who told Ronnie which people to appoint as federal judges. Can you understand this? More than half the federal judges in this country were appointed by my husband, and he never even had the slightest idea....

Nancy Reagan suddenly stopped in mid-sentence when there was a knock on the door. It was her Secret Service guard. Time to go. The thought suddenly occurred to me that this room could have been bugged and that I might not get out alive. But I walked away easily, carrying my tape recorder. Apparently, nobody else there was aware of our conversation. Until now.

I can only hope and pray that Nancy is safe in some other country by the time you read this. Saudi Arabia, perhaps, or Jordan—any one of those Middle Eastern cultures where men will truly appreciate her infamous steady gaze of adoration—unless, as Calvin Trillin wrote in *The Nation*, that gaze sets back progress and prompts a lead editorial in their official newspaper describing it as "the best argument we in the Muslim world have seen for the reinstitution of the veil."

Progress is, after all, a subjective kind of thing.

1991

A gynecologist at the reproductive center is talking to his client, a poor African-American woman who is pregnant but can't afford to raise another child.

"This is absurd," he tells her. "The Supreme Court gives me the right to burn that American flag, but takes away my right to give you medical advice. Well," he says with a fiendish grin, "I've had it." He gets the flag in the corner of his office and brings it to his desk. "Sometimes," he says, "an act of civil disobedience can be the highest form of patriotism." And he proceeds to write on the flag with a marker—*Abortion. Dr. Burnhill's Clinic. 555-9143*—then hands the flag to his patient and says, "Here, bring this home with you. And after you read what I've written, burn the flag. Don't worry, it's perfectly legal."

However, the woman decides to save the flag for the next Welcome Home Troops parade, where, unfortunately, a police officer happens to notice the message on it. He calls in a handwriting expert, federal funds are held back, and the reproductive center is finally forced to close down.

And the moral of this story is: "You can wrap yourself in the American flag, but it doesn't mean your ass is covered."

1991

January 5, 1991

Dear Butcher of Baghdad:

In view of our previous relationship, I feel I owe you an explanation for why we are preparing to attack Iraq. We already have the blessing of the UN Security Council, and I am sure the U.S. Congress will grant me the power to make war, although I will do what must be done no matter how they vote. I have many lawyers.

I suspect that Tariq Aziz will not accept this letter because I refuse to consider your demand that negotiation include linkage with the Israeli-Palestinian conflict. Since you cannot obtain linkage through diplomacy, you threaten to get it through bombs. However, we have dissuaded Israel from carrying out a preemptive strike, for such imprudent action would merely help unravel our coalition.

Please understand that there is nothing personal about this. But when the Cold War ended, there was panic at the Pentagon. Their budget would have been cut by $243 billion. We needed an evil demon, and you fit the bill. Did you see the *New Republic* cover photo of you with your mustache cut to resemble Adolf Hitler? To put it bluntly, Saddam, you became the international equivalent of Willie Horton.

Of course, in order to be sure that you *would* invade Kuwait, we had to pretend that we didn't care. Senator Bob Dole assured you that there would be no sanctions. Assistant Secretary of State John Kelly promised we would remain neutral. Secretary of Defense Dick Cheney almost screwed things up when he told reporters we were committed to defend Kuwait militarily if you attacked, but Pentagon spokesperson Pete Williams straightened that out quickly.

It wasn't just our *men* who fooled you, either. State Department spokesperson Margaret Tutwiler announced that we had no treaty with Kuwait. And then our ambassador, April Glaspie, actually *encouraged* you to cross their border. Jim Baker even sent a cable instructing her to tell you that I only wanted better relations with Iraq, but when questioned he said he couldn't be responsible because as Secretary of State he signs a lot of cables.

Let me give you a historic parallel to this situation. At the end of World War II, when Japan was making peace overtures, we proceeded to drop the atomic bomb on Hiroshima and Nagasaki. We simply had to test it in a real-life situation. So when CIA director William Webster told me of *your* plan, I knew it would provide the perfect excuse for us to test our high-tech weaponry. I must say, you've sparked our military-industrial complex with new life. Ironically enough, the stockholders from Kuwait who share in those profits are grateful too.

I will amend that to our military-industrial-*media* complex. Not only are we going to kick your Arabian ass on the battlefield, but media-wise we're so much more sophisticated than you. The news anchors will serve as our cheerleaders, the retired generals will serve as their experts, and the standup comedians will make you the butt of their jokes.

When it comes to media, you are quite naive—your version of Tokyo Rose, broadcasting: "Why are you Americans here? Don't you know you will die in the desert? While you are here, your wives and girlfriends are dating American movie stars like Tom Selleck, Paul Newman and Bart Simpson." You fool! Didn't you realize that Tom Selleck is merely an animated cartoon character?

During World War II, novelty shops were marketing toilet paper with pictures of Hitler, Mussolini and Hirohito with the slogan "Wipe Out the Axis!" Now there will be toilet paper with pictures of you and the slogan "Wipe Out Saddam!" Our national attention span has been so conditioned by television that the public can concentrate on only one villain at a time.

Admit it, you played right into our hands. I forced myself to read the Amnesty International Report on your vicious behavior. It made me nauseous. I had never read an Amnesty International report before, and I pray that I never have to read another. Yet now while our kids in the service are reduced to masturbating over their copies of *The Rape of Kuwait*—being careful not to get sand in their hands—I feel totally justified in our impending action.

We may be a debtor nation, but we are also a loyal nation. King Fahd donated so much to the Iran/*contra* cause that we now willingly bow to his culture.

But believe me, it sticks in my craw that Americans have been tortured in Saudi Arabia. One gentleman had six toenails pulled out because he was watching a videotape of *The Love Boat* that showed in the background a girl wearing a bikini. And I certainly didn't appreciate being there on Thanksgiving. As you know, I'm left-handed, but I had to eat that darned turkey dinner trying to hold a fork in my *right* hand after I was briefed on how the left hand is traditionally reserved for sanitary functions.

Well, now we are going to create a New World Order—and it won't include you. We learned our lesson from World War II. Japan was prohibited from having a military force, their fighting energy was sublimated into business, and now they can *buy* Pearl Harbor. Manuel Noriega was about to convert from the dollar to the yen, and we would no longer have been able to launder drug money through Panama.

We expected to kill Noriega, but who could have predicted that he would hide out in the Vatican mission? We will not allow any such escape for you. Oh, sure, there was a time when all we wanted to do was take you out to dinner and a movie. But now we just want to take you out.

So long, sucker!
George

Spike Lee Meets Tom Wolfe

1990

Recently black filmmaker Spike Lee and white novelist Tom Wolfe participated in a fundraising event for the sixth annual Coro Foundation leadership dinner at the Pierre Hotel in New York City. The following is excerpted from a transcript of their debate.

Wolfe: It seems to me that *Do the Right Thing* is somewhat idealized. That is to say, you give the impression that drugs and crime don't even exist among the inhabitants of Bensonhurst. They're guilty only of wanting music in their ghetto blasters, pizza on the table and photographs of black heroes on the wall.

Lee: That's a racist attitude you're revealing. I mean, does this give you the right to go to the opposite extreme in *Bonfire of the Vanities*? The South Bronx has to be a drug-infested, crime-ridden sewer? You know, the residents there are very unhappy about that.

Wolfe: You're talking about the movie. But I don't know if there are a lot of people in the Bronx who feel slighted by the book. I don't think you can go through life as a writer worrying about public relations. You either write what you see, honestly and frankly and candidly, or you should get out of the business and go into something else.

Lee: What, it's not public relations for Warner Brothers to agree to put a disclaimer at the end, reassuring the audience that the story is only fiction and any resemblance between the characters and real life is purely coincidental?

Wolfe: I think the whole business of disclaimers has gotten to be a joke. There's no one naive enough to believe them, so why tack them on? It's an empty ritual to avoid lawsuits.

Lee: Everybody cares about how they're portrayed in the media. It has to do with the truth, not lawsuits. Black people are upset about the way they've been portrayed in films ever since *Birth of a Nation*. Because it's from TV and movies that a lot of white Americans get their opinions on blacks, especially whites who don't live anywhere near black people. That's exactly what's happening with *Bonfire of the Vanities*.

Wolfe: Look, I wrote about a white Wall Street bond trader who accidentally runs over a black teenager. The trial becomes a media circus, and the victim lapses into a coma and dies. Now how can you say my book is causing racism?

Lee: No, not your book, but the *movie* that's being made out of it. They've changed the ending into a racist conclusion.

Wolfe: I haven't even seen the script.

Lee: Well, I have. And now, in the last image, in the hospital room, the black kid looks around, sees that nobody's looking, he takes the tubes out of his nose and stuff, and he runs smiling out of the hospital. Like the whole thing was just a nigger *scam*. I mean, how do you feel about that?

Wolfe: That's news to me. Maybe I better read the script. If the idea is that it's just been a shuck and he's been pretending, that would be a pretty startling change. But I'm wondering about your double standard. In *Do the Right Thing*, it's perfectly acceptable for the black youths to let a fire hydrant drench the inside of a convertible being driven by a white man—after assuring him that they won't—but then there's a sudden buildup of racial tension on the block when a white man is walking his bicycle on the sidewalk and the wheel *inadvertently* goes over a black's sneaker. Incidentally, you have a terrible moment of inconsistency there, because the white man walks *behind* the black youth, and yet he complains about a mark across the *front* of this sneaker. But don't get me wrong—I love Hollywood.

Lee: Oh, boy, now that's really nit-picking. Listen, I saw *Total Recall*—and that's a multi-multi-fuckin'-*multi*-million-dollar film—and there's this crucial scene where Arnold Schwarzenegger's girlfriend spits right in the face of the Bad Guy, but there's *no saliva* on his face. So let's not use America's Wackiest Movie Bloopers as a diversion from my point. I mean, you can write a great book, but don't you care what they do with it?

Wolfe: Of course I care, but if I sell the rights I lose control. Which would happen even if I were hired to write the script. But I write books, not screenplays. The book is my art, and the movie is Warner Brothers' commerce. So don't confuse their water with my pump.

Lee: So you just take the money and say, "Go on, do with it what you want."

147

Wolfe: Isn't that what you do with your TV commercials for Nike sneakers? Just take the money and run? There are black kids getting killed for their sneakers. Don't you bear any responsibility? After all, you're helping to attach the status to those sneakers. I would never pay $125 for a pair of sneakers, and I can afford it. But you *personally* participate in that commercial, you *personally* participate in creating that false value, for which black kids have been killing each other.

Lee: What are you talking about? *Society* creates false values, not me. Only when black entertainers or athletes attain a certain level of visibility are they suddenly expected to be the moral conscience of America. That commercial has never gotten anyone killed. I challenge you or anybody to prove that connection. *You* have to understand what a pair of Air Jordans means to a poor black kid, but what do you want *me* to do, make a special announcement that they should always buy their own and never kill anybody for them?

Wolfe: Just do the right sneaker....

1990

Dear Greg,

You and I have been friends for 30 years now. We've marched for civil rights. We've fasted to protest the war. We've demonstrated against one injustice after another, and we've shared the stage at many a benefit.

I have always been inspired by your personal evolution. You were the first black standup comic to break through the comedy ghetto. Then you were on the front lines demonstrating for peace and human rights. You brought frozen turkeys to Mississippi on Thanksgiving and you went fishing with native Americans to publicize the plight of Indians. Then you became a health activist, and again broke through the color line of the New Age industry.

All along, you've preached nonviolence while practicing civil disobedience. There were those who began to think of you as an American equivalent to Gandhi. And so I feel a bit petty writing this letter, but the alternative is to keep silent, and I'm sure that you would want me to speak out.

There was this small news item in the business section of the newspaper:

"Kroger Company agreed to change its policy on the sale of cigarette papers after anti-drug activists led by former comedian Dick Gregory threatened a nationwide boycott of the supermarket chain. Gregory and the other activists said the rolling papers are used to smoke marijuana. Marnette Perry, vice president of merchandising for Kroger's Delta division in Memphis, said the company has decided it will 'require the purchase of tobacco with the purchase of tobacco papers.' The policy change will affect 103 stores in Arkansas, Tennessee, Kentucky, Missouri, Mississippi and Alabama, she said."

Hey, Greg, what have you been smoking—your own Bahamian Diet powder?

I'm not questioning your motivation, just your judgment. And your priorities. You must remember how marijuana-smoking was not exactly an unknown pleasure in the civil rights and antiwar movements. It's a mellow weed. Folks can grow it in their backyard or their window box or even their closet.

On the other hand, listen to what investigative journalist Linda Feldman reports:

"Think about cocaine—a $150 billion business leaving in its wake murder, addicted babies, jail time, robberies, ruined lives and billions of dollars spent on punishment, protection and treatment. And a few minutes of personal power. But the big crime, 'the national shame,' as President Bush so aptly called it, starts with the accessory to the crime. The American chemical companies. Exxon Chemical and Shell Chemical are the leading suppliers of an ordinary chemical called methyl ethyl ketone—the chemical of choice for Colombian businessmen to process cocaine base into cocaine.

150

"In the case of Exxon, a million-pound shipment of MEK from Dallas to Cartegena is not an unusual day's business. During the 'Just Say No' years from 1982-1988, exports of MEK doubled while no comparable industrial expansion existed in Colombia to meet the new imports. According to the *Los Angeles Times*, U.S. experts in Colombia were quoted as saying that as much as 90% of the 13 million pounds of American-made MEK imported by Colombia winds up being diverted for use in cocaine manufacturing."

So why not boycott Exxon and Shell? These greedy chemical companies are certainly a much more relevant target. Ironically, because of the government crackdown on marijuana and the resulting shortage, the sale of rolling papers has been decreasing anyway. More ironically, the shortage of pot has led to an increase in the use of crack cocaine.

Besides, Greg, yours is really a rather silly protest. I mean why not ban toilet tissue and Reynolds Wrap too because marijuana smokers can use the inner cardboard roll and a piece of aluminum foil to make a pipe.

And finally, isn't it just plain *bizarre* for Kroger's to require the purchase of tobacco with the purchase of tobacco papers? Marijuana might drive somebody to raid their neighbor's refrigerator, but tobacco kills more than a thousand people every day in this country alone. So I look forward to seeing you on the picket line in front of Kroger's, protesting their sale of tobacco.

Requiring a pot-smoker to buy tobacco is like saying it's okay for Pee Wee Herman to play with himself at a porno movie as long as he participates in a drive-by shooting on the way home.

Love,
Paul

I Snorted Cocaine with the Pope

1988

This year will mark the 20th anniversary of the assassination of Robert Kennedy. The myth of a conspiracy behind Sirhan Sirhan will continue to be perpetuated. But now that Pope John Paul II is visiting the United States again, it behooves me to tell about the time I snorted cocaine with him and finally came to understand the mystery behind the shooting of Bobby Kennedy. It was on the occasion of the Pope's earlier visit to America.

When he arrived at JFK Airport, a band was waiting there to welcome him, and they played "Hello, Dolly." They didn't even do that for the Dalai Lama when he came here from Tibet, and it certainly would've been more appropriate for *him*.

The Pope was touring the country, speaking to young people in different cities. It was in Chicago that we met. There was a big reception. I was representing the alternative press. Cardinal Cody strode up to me. I knew it was Cody because money kept dropping from his vestment.

"That's all right," he said, picking up the cash. "It's for my sister."

The Cardinal drew me aside and said, "Listen, the Pope is really tired. He's been on this whirlwind tour, and he still has to speak to the youth of America on TV tonight.

He needs a little *lift*, if you know what I mean. And you were pointed out as someone who might have some cocaine you would be willing to share."

Now, I don't ordinarily do coke. It's like red meat—I never buy it myself, but if somebody serves it I'll partake—and it just so happened that a friend had given me a small baggie of cocaine as a birthday gift.

So I said to the Cardinal, "Look, I'm going to walk to that bathroom over there. You tell the Pope to wait three minutes and then follow me in. We've got to be very discreet about this. It would look really suspicious if the Pope and I went into the bathroom together."

Okay, so now I'm in the bathroom, chopping up the coke with a razor blade on this little hand mirror, and the Pope walks in, rolling up a thousand-lira bill. He looks just like himself, with rosy cheeks and a skull cap and his collar flowing in the breeze, even though there is no breeze.

I hand him the mirror with four lines of cocaine on it. This happens to be one of Heloise's Hints: "Always let the Pope snort first."

Well, Pope John Paul speaks 23 languages, and he is reacting in each one. Sniff. Sniff. "*Magnifique!*" Sniff. Sniff. "*Wunderbar!*"

In between snorts, we make small talk. For example, I ask, "What is Lech Walesa really like?"

The Pope answers, "Very nice!"

His brain gets more and more frozen. He begins spouting these *pronunciamentos* that they would never let him do back at the Vatican: "In the matter of abortion, life may now be considered to begin at the moment of foreplay." And: "Henceforth, fellatio shall be deemed an acceptable form of birth control."

I suddenly realize that I cannot let this opportunity go by without asking him a question that has long been on my mind. "Excuse me, your Royal Pontiff, but tell me the truth, do you really believe in God and the devil and all that theology, or is it really just for the tourists?"

"Oh, no," he says, "I absolutely do believe it. In fact, your whole American government has been possessed by Satan."

"Really? I didn't know that. Here, have another snort."

"For instance"—sniff, sniff—"*Muy bueno!* When your President Ronald Reagan was shot by—what was his name again?"

"John Hinckley. I remember that Hinckley came out for gun control and Reagan came out against it. That was a sure sign of senility, or maybe just a combination of plaque and smegma between the lobes of his brain."

"Well," the Pope continues, "an orderly at Bethesda Hospital noticed that there were three little sixes behind the President's left ear. That is the mark of the Beast— the Antichrist—as stated in Revelations in the New Testament. Naturally, the hospital orderly got kicked upstairs to keep him quiet."

It all began to fit together. I remembered that there was another guy who followed Hinckley to New Haven, stayed at the same hotel, also wrote letters to Jodie Foster and was prepared to kill the President, but his personal plot was nipped in the proverbial bud. There was even that line in the lyrics of the Eagles song, "Hotel California": "You just can't kill the beast...."

"But wait," I said. "Is it only the Republican Party that's possessed by Satan, or is it a bipartisan policy?"

"Oh, both," replied the Pope. "The Democrats too. Even Bobby Kennedy, that great hero of young people, was possessed by Satan."

"Jeez, I didn't know *that*. Here, have another snort."

You may recall that Senator Kennedy was shot in June, 1968, at the Ambassador Hotel in Los Angeles. He had just won the California primary in the presidential race, and he declared, "On to Chicago!" Then he went into the hotel kitchen, where Sirhan Sirhan was waiting for him.

So there was Bobby Kennedy standing there, and there was Sirhan shooting at him. And although his gun could hold only eight bullets, they found a total of 10 in Kennedy's body, in others who got hit, and in the doorway jamb. Enough to make a conspiracy theorist out of even the most naive person.

Not only that, but one of the bullets was in the *back* of Bobby Kennedy's neck, which would certainly seem to indicate that there was a second gunperson. Bear in mind that this was according to the official autopsy report by Thomas Noguchi.

Noguchi has since been fired from the L.A. County Coroner's Office for dancing on the graves of his celebrity clients. However, he continues to perform autopsies on a freelance basis. Because he loves to work with people.

Anyway, as the Pope explained it to me, "At the precise moment that Sirhan Sirhan was shooting at him, Bobby Kennedy's head turned 360 degrees—just like Linda Blair in *The Exorcist*."

And that cleared up the strange and puzzling autopsy report. I felt so much better knowing that there had not been a conspiracy after all.

Just then, Cardinal Cody knocked on the bathroom door. "Five minutes," he called out.

The Pope said to me, "Hey, listen, I really want to thank you for this—what is it, Peruvian flake? We have a secret war in Peru."

"Oh, I'm very glad you enjoyed it."

"Is there anything I can do for you in return?"

"No, please, just consider this an ecumenical gesture."

"But I insist," said the Pope. "I have lots of power. Kindly let me exercise it on your behalf."

"No, really, reciprocation is not expected."

"But I have loads of connections."

Then I recalled how, during the Inquisition, the Catholic Church had excommunicated the great astronomer Galileo because he had claimed that the earth revolved around the sun.

"Do you think you could possibly arrange a pardon for Galileo, the way Gerald Ford did for Richard Nixon?"

"Well," the Pope replied, "I would have to go through channels, but I think it can be accomplished."

Cardinal Cody knocked on the bathroom door again. It was time for the Pope to speak.

You may have seen him on TV that night: "I want to say, to the youth of America, *wooooo-wooooo...wooooo-wooooo....*" Remember how the Pope kept going *wooooo-wooooo*? That was because his brain was still frozen from all that cocaine.

But sure enough, just a few months later, Galileo was pardoned, posthumously, by the Church. John Paul II had definitely proven to be a Pontiff of his word.

Theologically Correct Condoms

1987

I was a writer and on-air commentator for the Fox network's short-lived Wilton-North Report. *On Christmas Eve I delivered the following commentary, in a plain brown wrapper:*

If you haven't done all your Christmas shopping yet, it's not too late. Just find an all-night drugstore. For only $3.50 you can buy a handsome, suede-like carrying case holding four condoms made with industrial-strength latex.

For the kiddies, you can get Condom Mints—chocolate candy in the shape of condoms. Each silver box contains 12 chocolate mints individually wrapped in foil. The package reads: "For internal use only. Application of Condom Mints to body parts will result in a sticky mess."

Indeed, this has been the year of the condom. Now that Gary Hart is back in the presidential race, I'm not concerned that he committed adultery—that's his own business—but I would like to know that he practiced *safe* sex. We want a *responsible* leader of the Western world.

We've all seen that public service announcement warning, "Any time you sleep with somebody, you're also sleeping with everybody they've ever slept with, and everybody *they've* ever slept with." Malthusian paranoia, back unto Adam and Eve.

But there's still a lot of ignorance in this era of high-tech communication. According to the *Dallas Times Herald*, in a recent survey about AIDS, 65% of teenagers thought they didn't need to use a condom if the girl was taking birth control pills; 60% believed they wouldn't get AIDS if they had sex with somebody they loved. Who says romance is dead? They need Dr. Ruth: "Today I have some reservoir tips for teenagers."

When I was an adolescent, purchasing condoms was a traumatic experience. I'd buy other stuff to avoid being embarrassed. "I'd like a *Batman and Robin* comic book, and gimme this candy bar, and [*whispering*] a pack of prophylactics—and a tube of toothpaste, please." But now there are huge *billboards*: "If you can't say no, use condoms." However, an executive of the Gannett Outdoor Advertising Company confirms that they held off putting up these signs until after the Pope's recent visit.

The Church is faced with an interesting dilemma here. On one hand, they are opposed to condoms as an artificial method of birth control. On the other hand, they're aware that condoms can serve as a protection against AIDS. A group of bishops has issued a statement that educational programs that include information about condoms should also stress that they are morally incorrect. That's sort of like Richard Nixon saying, "We could get the million dollars—but it would be wrong."

A compromise is possible, of course. They could manufacture theologically correct condoms—with teeny tiny holes in them—just to give those spermatozoa a fighting chance. That's fair enough. But the problem then is that if the sperm can get out, the AIDS virus can get in, so it's back to the Vatican drawing board.

Now, theologically correct condoms would have those same teeny tiny holes, but on the outside there would be little feather repellers with the message "Wrong Way—Do Not Enter—Severe Tire Damage." And so, when Santa Claus comes tonight, what's hanging by the fireplace may not necessarily be socks.

The Mime and the Pacer

1987

I found myself walking around and around in a counter-clockwise circle on the stage of the Wallenboyd Theater in downtown Los Angeles, just as a young man known as the Pacer does for several hours every day, always in the same direction, at the exact same spot in the middle of the boardwalk in Venice Beach. He is an inspiration to me and I sometimes talk about him in my performances.

The boardwalk in Venice is both literally and figuratively on the edge of this country. Here a grungy wino, who needed a shave long before Don Johnson made stubble fashionable, is wearing a T-shirt that says "Yes, I Am a Model." There a nerdy tourist is trying not to let the pizza drip on his T-shirt that says "I Choked Linda Lovelace." T-shirts are the hieroglyphics of our time.

The boardwalk resembles one of those double-page-spread montages in a children's book showing many different modes of transportation being used simultaneously. Airplanes fly by, trailing printed messages such as "The New Dating Game Wants You" and "Scientology, Give Us Our Money Back," while below, rollerskaters and skateboarders mingle with cops riding bicycles and Hare Krishnas preparing for their annual parade featuring an elephant nourished entirely on trail mix.

A lone Jesus freak walks along and yells at them—"Antichrist! Antichrist! Antichrist!"—trying to drown out their chant. "Repent, Krishna! People are starving in India every day because these foolish Krishnas refuse to eat the cow! Eat the cow and believe in Jesus Christ! Repent, Krishna!"

You can buy all types of stuff along the boardwalk—rainbow sunglasses and fake Rolex watches and falafel-shaped yo-yo's. But, complains a flower vendor who pays over $600 a month for a ten-by-two-foot space, "rent will be going up to $800 and then to $1200 by summer. Venice will eventually be inhabited by a bunch of wealthy lot owners and a population of slaves who work for them."

However, the performers pay no rent, dependent on voluntary donations. There is a poet who speaks professional gibberish; an artist who draws on the ground with colored chalk; a fellow who juggles an electric chainsaw, a bowling ball and an apple, for which strangers put money in his hat because they're grateful to God that *they* don't have to do such a bizarre thing to earn a living.

There is a woman who plays the violin while standing on her head. And a man who has a table covered with wineglasses of different sizes filled to varying heights with water, and he plays this musical instrument by rubbing his fingers around the tops. Audiences gather spontaneously to hear his rendition of a Mozart sonata or a ragtime melody or the theme from *Chariots of Fire*.

There are breakdancers who bring their own personal linoleum-floor sections, and a jogger who jumps hurdles over the endless row of garbage cans lined

164

up along the boardwalk. He has to avoid one garbage can because a homeless person is foraging for lunch.

If I had to choose my favorite moment on the boardwalk, it would have to be the time a Rastafarian yogi was standing on the very top of a wooden chair, preparing to jump barefoot onto a pile of freshly broken bottles. "This is serious shit," he reminded the large semicircle of onlookers. And then, during the anticipatory silence, along came that Jesus freak. Upon seeing this crowd, he edged his way in. Now the Rastafarian yogi was poised upon that unseen edge between "Look before you leap" and "He who hesitates is lost." Suddenly the Jesus freak called out, "Hey, wait, before you commit suicide there, how do you feel about abortion?"

In front of the Sidewalk Cafe on the boardwalk, the Mime, a black man wearing white gloves along with a tuxedo and top hat, just stands still—often for hours. He is listening to a stereo headset. One might think he was playing music to counteract the boredom, but it is really a tape loop reminding him, "Don't move, stay still, it doesn't matter if your back itches, people are paying you not to scratch...."

Passersby do indeed put cash in the cardboard box at his feet after they have gaped at him long enough to get their money's worth. Standing still is his job. People pay him not to move. When he goes to the unemployment office, a clerk asks, "Did you look for work this week?" He answers simply, "Yes, I stood on the corner of Hollywood and Vine, and then I stood on the corner of Beverly Boulevard and Sierra Bonita, and then I stood...."

In contrast to the Mime is the Pacer, who intrigues me most. He doesn't call himself the Pacer. He may not even know that others do. But the circle he walks around and around in is his turf. Even an occasional police car respects the force field he creates, and the cops drive around him.

Obviously he originally started this strange stint as a matter of choice. "I think I'll walk around in circles on the boardwalk today." And the next day. And the next. But somewhere along the way, walking around in circles became a compulsion, and *it* started doing *him*. When you play a role long enough, the role can begin playing you if you're not careful.

I've been out at six o'clock in the morning and there was the Pacer walking in circles. I've been out at six o'clock in the evening and there was the Pacer walking in circles. He does stop to eat—which indicates that at some level he is still acting voluntarily. He walks in a straight line to a greasy-spoon diner and sits at the counter, but he does not twirl on his stool, nor stir his coffee, nor roll his eyes.

Once he talked about his obsessive activity. "I'm in control of walking, but out of control too. When I walk I'm in a trance. If I slow down at night I see colors. I see millions of faces—some with Pilgrim hats, some with cowboy hats—modern faces and prehistoric faces."

There must be some kind of spiritual path that the Pacer keeps treading, even if it's circular, some unique relationship with the universe by which he justifies his existence to himself. Everybody has to feel they're making *some* contribution to society, if only to maintain self-esteem. Even those who work in a missile factory need to rationalize, "Well, the United States needs to have a strong defense."

It's an absurd age we live in. *Future Shock* is already an outdated book. Children whose shoes stay on their feet by the grace of Velcro may never experience the thrill of tying their shoelaces in the dark. They have developed a fast-food approach to perceiving time because all they know is digital clocks. Time goes click, click, click, and if the power goes off they think that 12:00-12:00-12:00 is appliance language for "Help! Help! Help! Turn me back to the right time! Help! Help! Help!"

Kids have lost that certain sense of time in motion, going around and around, eternally. That concept is endangered, just like the whooping crane. But we can all be grateful to the Pacer, for he is the Keeper of the Counter-Clockwise. That is his spiritual calling. But the Pacer does not have a cardboard box for people to drop money into—he walks around in circles out of the goodness of his heart.

The Mime and the Pacer provide a perfect metaphor for the two-party system in America. The Republicans are like the Mime, standing absolutely still while the world passes them by—Iran, Iraq, Nicaragua, El Salvador—and they get paid for it, just like the Mime.

The Democrats are like the Pacer, walking around in circles while the world passes them by—Israel, Libya, Cuba, Honduras—and they *don't* get paid for it, just like the Pacer.

But recently the Pacer did something that hurled such a comparison right into the metaphor graveyard, along with "that's like bringing coals to Newcastle" (for Newcastle finally did run out of coal) and "good as gold" (since the government now prints money without the benefit of the gold standard). The Pacer put a cardboard box down on the ground and started walking around it. And people began giving him money.

By the mere presence of that cardboard box, the Pacer had transformed his personal perversion into a marketable talent. Just like so many of us. And I could no longer feel superior to him. He was not just some nut walking around in circles. Now he was earning a living.

I still "do" the Pacer in my act, but with increased respect. "His job is no less dignified than anything we do," I tell the audience. "He works hard all day, and then, just like you and me, he goes home and unwinds." And I walk around and around in a circle onstage, only now in a clockwise direction.

1986

There are no numbers on the campus clock. Instead, letters spell out ARIZONA STATE in a circle. The time was exactly N after R. I had 35 minutes before the first plenary session began. To be honest, I didn't know the difference between a plenary session and a breakout session, but there are always plenty of both at the annual WHIM (Western Humor and Irony Membership) conference.

In 1981, a dream began to turn into reality for Don Nilsen of ASU's English Department. Art Buchwald was coming to consult with the planning committee. However, when he got there, he tried to discourage them: "A humor conference can't possibly succeed because people would come expecting to laugh for three days—which of course is impossible—and disappointment would be the inevitable result."

Assistant Dean Alleen Nilsen recalls: "His advice wasn't as important as the fact that he lent credibility to the whole project. And with forty of the most important people at the university having witnessed our public commitment to proving Buchwald wrong—that such a conference *could* be a success—we were off and running."

The first national humor conference took place in 1982. Now I was attending the fifth WHIM humor conference, but the first to be combined with TAASP (The

Association for the Anthropological Study of Play). Presentations undulated along an invisible divide between the scholarly and the silly.

From "Humor in Alice Walker's *The Color Purple*" to "The Humor of Popeye, the Proletariat's Sir Walter Raleigh." From "Environmental Factors That Affect Black and White Basketball Performance and Style" to "Psychological Services in the American Shopping Center: Or, Can I Get a Refund Within 7 Days If I Haven't Used the Insight?" From "Incongruity-Based Humor as an Index of the Child's Understanding of Quantity and the Investigator's Misunderstanding of Compensation" to "Joke Analysis Analysis." From "The Humor of Sign Language Used by Deaf Children" to "How to Stamp Out Rape from U.S. Campuses and Balance the Budget." From "The Limits of the Transgressive Behavior of the Vidusaka in Sanskrit Drama" to "Mystic Secret From Pakistan Offers Cure for Cancer, Loneliness, Acne, Poverty and Religious Doubt." From "The Status of Muslim Women in Sport: Conflict Between Cultural Tradition and Modernization" to "Play, Fun, Comedy and Dead Seriousness in Minnesota Queen Pageants." From "The American Indians' Attempt to Get the Last Laugh" to "Computer Recognition of Situational Ironies." From "The Trickster/Clown Dichotomy and the Problem of Individual Freedom vs. Social Propriety" to "American Humor and the Death Event."

At this conference, you could learn new euphemisms: In a Pentagon document, peace is "permanent prehostility." Civilian casualties are "collateral damage." The invasion of Grenada by paratroopers was a "pre-dawn vertical insertion." At Expo 87, vomit is a "protein spill."

Or you could hear examples of Maine humor:

Gramp Wiley says, "I see in the paper that even the people who keep building these nuclear plants don't know what to do with the waste. And I certainly don't know what to do about the waste. But if my barn was fillin' up with cow manure faster than I could shovel it out, I'd learn to live without cows."

And: "It was about two years ago that Gramp Wiley fulfilled one of his lifelong ambitions—streakin'. Took off all his clothes, and had nothin' on but Nike sneakers and ran right through the vestry of the Baptist church where the ladies was holdin' their flower show. There warn't one of them Baptist ladies that raised an eye. Think of that control. But one of them did say to the lady next to her, 'Martha, what was that?' Martha never looked up either, and she said, 'I don't know, but it sure needed pressin'.'"

I had the pleasure of emceeing a Saturday luncheon. The speaker was Gene Perrett, who has written for Bob Hope, Carol Burnett and more recently, "I worked with a gentleman who's the youngest at heart of anybody you'd ever want to meet. That's George Burns, who just celebrated his 90th birthday. Last year, he had more love affairs than Burt Reynolds. The only difference is, Burt remembers his."

"It's amazing," I announced, "that George Burns makes out better than Burt Reynolds. I think it may be because women think he's aroused when it's merely rigor mortis on the installment plan."

Later, a linguistics professor cornered me: "Your rigor mortis line was a most appropriate vehicle to point out that sex and death are actually two sides of the same coin...."

The keynote address that afternoon was given by Gershon Legman, a cantankerous gargoyle whose nemesis is respectability and whose delight is pricking the prudery of academic virtue. The 69-year-old folklorist coined the phrase "Make love, not war"—and then, as if to aid in that process, co-invented the vibrating dildo.

His talk, "Erotic Folk Elements in the Humor and Play of Adolescents," overflowed with raunchy references:

"When I was waiting for the plane to take me to this conference, my wife told me she was very embarrassed because our twelve-year-old daughter asked, 'Does semen taste sweet or sour?' Now who would have been embarrassed if the question had been, 'What is the taste of human blood?' "

He told of a bar in Tijuana where "stripteasers performed on tables. Students and sailors were all sitting around chugging beer, and they would move forward, their friends slapping them on the back, to perform cunnilingus on the girl dancing—while she danced. And if the girl could be made to have an orgasm, or pretend to, he would give her $10 and be a hero to his friends. It reminded me of the time I'd gone to communion.

I remembered seeing the same look on people's faces. Sort of a gone, happy look of being lost in a ceremonial reunion with something. And these kids were sitting there with exactly the same expression, waiting for their turn...."

Later on, in the hallway, Legman got into a shouting match with a literature professor. They were arguing over whether a philosophical maxim—"I laugh so that I will not weep"—came from Lord Byron or *The Marriage of Figaro*.

What do you do at a humor conference for serious relief?

The schedule for Saturday evening called for a trip to Rawhide with Cowboy Dan. Instead, Scot Morris, "Games" columnist for *Omni* magazine, Peter London, standup comedian, and I decided to watch the first *Comic Relief*, an all-star comedy special to benefit the nation's homeless, hosted by Robin Williams, Whoopi Goldberg and Billy Crystal. After much hassle, we found a hotel on the outskirts of town that carried HBO.

There we were, three men without luggage, explaining to the desk clerk that we only wanted to rent a room for a few hours so we could watch a certain TV show. He gave us a look of bemused skepticism and said, "That must be some flick."

As it turned out, there had been a misunderstanding about broadcast time, and at first it appeared as though we might have missed the show altogether. We simply collapsed into uncontrollable, high-pitched, rolling-around, fist-thumping belly laughter at the sheer futility of our quest.

Then *Comic Relief* finally did come on. But nothing in those three hours was able to evoke an encore of that laugh.

We gave our key and fast-food leftovers to a couple of street people to spend the night in luxury, in keeping with the spirit of the show, and we went back to our own hotel rooms.

Perhaps the most bizarre intellectual pursuit of the humor conference took place on Sunday morning: a study of laughter itself, "Acoustic Correlates of Young Adult Laughter."

Don Mowrer reasoned that "laughter is an acoustic event and therefore can be subjected to the same sophisticated empirical scrutiny speech scientists have employed successfully in analyzing speech sound for over four decades."

He defined a laugh as "any nonverbal vocal behavior that occurred beginning at the onset of the vocal behavior to the termination of the vocal behavior as marked by a 250-millisecond or longer unfilled pause."

His associate, James Case, described the machinery that "gave us an intensity readout of the laugh burst." Also, "Pitch measurement analyzes fundamental frequency of the voice signal up to every burst in the lar- ynx." Conversation samples were "compared with measurement of the actual laugh signal."

They concluded that "we laugh at around the same burst rate as we speak," and similarly that "we laugh and speak at about the same pitch level." However, "the chief departure from speech behavior was the lack of phonemic variation in laughter."

Specifically, "Laughter usually contains only reduplicated neutral vowels and glottal-stop consonants." Consequently, "Laugh syllables are devoid of consonants typically used in speech." Of course, *h* is the most popular consonant. Thus, "You'll probably seldom hear people laughing using a consonant reduplication such as ka-ka-ka-ka-ka-ka or fa-fa-fa-fa-fa-fa. You will *never* have mixed consonants with vowels in a laugh such as ta-ha-ka-sa-fa-ka."

Nor was the official nerd laugh ignored: "Some laughs occur on inhalation, but we never speak on inhalations in speech."

There has been developing in the humor movement a slight conflict between the theoreticians and the practitioners.

In 1982, Des McHale proposed a humor conference in Ireland in which "all of the papers would have to be funny to be accepted." The academics protested loudly.

At the 1984 WHIM conference, joke-collector Larry Wilde proposed a requirement that all papers delivered at a humor conference should be at least 15% funny. He was 100% serious.

At the 1985 conference, academician Larry Mintz gave a presentation lamenting that increasingly, "The scholarly, intellectual component of the humor conference has been taking a back seat to the activities of humorists, humor aficionados, humor hucksters and people who use humor in various forms of social, 'human potential' activities. None of this leads to arguing that a paper dealing with humor *cannot* be funny; the point is that it *need not* be funny. Our purpose is to inform, not to entertain; to learn rather than be amused."

Wilde disagreed: "I think academia often ruins the very essence of humor by overanalysis. Humor is spontaneous, gleeful, fun. Putting it under a microscope so that it can be categorized, analyzed and subjected to scrutiny beyond reason actually defeats its very purpose. There is no question that some studies should be made, but unfortunately I find that most of the people making them are humorless, poorly trained and ill-equipped to make the necessary judgments.

"If you had agile comedic minds like Art Buchwald, Russell Baker, Woody Allen, Steve Allen, Shelley Berman et al. doing the proper research and writing the subsequent papers, you'd have brilliant analysis that would stand the test of time, but they're too involved in the business of making people laugh. I suppose the business of understanding the whys and hows must be left to academics. I only wish they had more firsthand practical experience in the field to guide them."

Mintz responded: "I guess we just come from different traditions. Well-researched papers that deal with interesting, important issues just don't bore me, even when read in a monotone by a little old guy in a wrinkled brown suit. Ironically, the collecting of jokes you've done is worth more in the long run than the scholarly work of most of us, since we can't do much without a data-base, and yours is probably the best in the world."

It was one year later, at the 1986 TAASP/WHIM humor conference, that mutual respect seemed to break down.

Louis Androes was reading his paper, "Test Patterns for Living: The Rajneesh Approach to Play." It triggered an antagonistic, anti-cult reaction in Gershon Legman, who in the '50s had written in *Neurotica* an exposé of Epizootics, a satirical takeoff on Dianetics, which later became Scientology.

At one point, Legman knocked over a chair and walked out blustering, then came back to heckle.

Legman: What was the purpose? Why did you give us all this? Are you a member of that cult? Have you got money invested in it?

Androes: Let me answer you in about three different ways.

Legman: That's too many. One way.

Androes: Okay, one for *you*, one for *you*, and one for *you*. [*The mounting rage could now be heard in his voice.*] I'm *not* enlightened. I'm *not* a Rajneeshian. I'm *not* a supporter or a detractor—

Legman:—not a detractor, that's for sure.

Androes: This is one thing I want to make clear. What I'm interested in is what *happened*. The first thing that happened is, I submitted an abstract that got in WHIM's hands instead of TAASP's. Don't ask me why.

Legman: Very appropriate.

Androes: Obviously my interest lies somewhere outside of—what would you call it—humor?

Legman: You pretend to be studying play, but we're talking about a con game, we're not talking about play.

Androes: But they don't feel that way.

Legman: Because they were hypnotized.

Androes: No, no. You talk about con games—the street people conned the Rajneesh.

Legman: What about Jonestown? I don't see the difference.

Androes: Why do *you* think the way you do? Who brainwashed *you*?

Legman: I don't have any victims.

Androes: How do you know you don't have any victims? How do you know I don't feel like a victim right now?

Legman: I believe you do.

Androes: I just made my point.

Legman: Are you writing a book about this?

Androes: No. My interest in Rajneesh is pretty well completed. I've got three articles out there in publication right now, and that'll be the end of it.

A woman in the audience asked, "Does it bother you that you were included in a WHIM breakout session as opposed to a TAASP breakout session? Does there have to be that much division between humor and play, when they're integral?"

Androes replied, "Yes, it bothers me to this extent: I prepared for a TAASP presentation, and I find myself in a WHIM situation. I might add [*his voice shaking*] I think what's going on in WHIM is very typical of the Rajneesh. They [*sarcastically*] laugh an awful lot. They are the most *exuberant*—and I can't think of a better word, unless you want to give me ecstasy and all that kind of stuff you get from meditation—but they are the most exuberant group of people, *five thousand* of 'em, that I have ever seen, not just now and then, but all the time. And I say to myself, are *you* people real? Those of you here in this room [*bordering on the edge of hostility*]—you're playing with jokes, and *you* write 'em for people to get up and *perform* and make their living. Is *this* real? I don't know. For those people, it is very real. I made three trips there...."

There was something utterly poignant about this confrontation. Androes had begun his presentation with a question: "How long has it been since anyone knocked on your door or called you on the phone and asked, 'Can you come over to my place and play?' "

The humor conference had indeed invited him to play, and now he found himself being attacked instead.

On Monday, I deliberately sat next to Louis Androes at "A Study of Empathy for Victims of Practical Jokes, Pranks and Hoaxes." He was still quite upset: "I just wanted to show how Rajneesh was able to tap the ritual power of many religions."

179

Mary Ann Rishel was describing various prank situations that test-students had to rank on a horizontal line from Least Offensive to Most Offensive.

Ranked as "Not Offensive At All":

The niece and nephew of an elderly couple put the couple's names in a magazine ad for couple-swapping.

Someone let greased pigs loose at three a.m. in the middle of a sorority house.

Students planted corn in a field in back of the Cornell Student Union, and when the corn sprouted it spelled out FUCK.

McDonald's sponsored a $50,000 sweepstakes that offered a year's free groceries and a Datsun as top prizes. Three Cal Tech students took literally the contest rules in fine print that read "Enter as often as you wish." Helped by a computer, they printed over a million entries, deposited them at 98 McDonald restaurants across southern California, and won 20 of the top prizes, including a Datsun station wagon, $3000 in cash and $1500 worth of McDonald's gift certificates.

Ranked as "Somewhat Offensive":

Stanford's humor magazine floated the hoax that the university's bowling team had been killed in a plane crash.

The U.S. Military Academy at West Point had female cadets bite the necks of chickens as an initiation prank.

 Young adults sunbathed in a cemetery on Memorial Day.

Students in a junior high school in Canada used stink bombs to explode the school's toilets.

Ranked as "Very Highly Offensive":

On Halloween outside New York City, a 16-year-old boy sprayed a synagogue with shaving cream, forming a swastika, a large X, an obscenity and the word *Jew*.

College students pledging to a fraternity were forced to consume large quantities of wine and spaghetti, vomit, then consume more, then eat garbage, sit in a chair that jolted them with a car battery, lie soaking wet in the snow, get paddled and be branded on the buttocks with a coat-hanger shaped into Greek letters.

Residents of an upstate New York county received phony reports that a young boy was castrated in the restroom of a local department store, and that he was either in a coma or dead.

A group of students got dressed up as the Ku Klux Klan, with a white student in blackface as a slave crawling at the end of a rope, and walked into a black caucus meeting.

Rishel proceeded to examine the varieties of misunderstanding in empathy.

Sometimes preconceived values couldn't be shaken. During a welcome-back party, a 55-year-old teacher returning after cancer surgery was served marijuana-laced brownies by her tenth-grade students. Testees found this only "Slightly Offensive"—they didn't find marijuana-laced brownies per se as something to be criticized and overlooked that the victim of the prank was a cancer patient.

Other times there was a failure in cognition. Several members of a rugby team rolled seven human skulls they had stolen from a dental school onto a playing field in an attempt to intimidate opponents. This was rated "Not Offensive At All," and the testees didn't think the victims would find it offensive. All they thought was that one team was scaring another, merely a discourtesy since it interrupted the start of the game. They overlooked the fact that the skulls were stolen and that they were *human* skulls.

Suddenly a man dressed as a clown appeared onstage.

We had seen him—or at least someone in that costume and makeup—at a previous session, "The Limits of Comedy: How Far Can a Circus Clown Go?," and now we were laughing at his antics again. He took the wooden pointer from the ledge of the green blackboard and pranced into the audience. He stopped in front of Gershon Legman, then *lunged* at him. The clown and Legman shrieked simultaneously. We thought they were laughing. Nobody did anything. The clown ran out. We all assumed this was some kind of April Fool's joke, perfectly timed to coincide with the session on pranks. And what better "victim" than Legman?

But now he was bleeding. Somehow we still expected him to stand up and shout, "What is the taste of human blood?" But instead he just kind of melted onto the floor.

As a group, we had been conditioned by the conference in general—and by this session in particular—to accept what was happening as an educational hoax.

While the conference continued, Legman was taken to a hospital, where he died of a hemorrhage. Police investigators were led to believe that Louis Androes was the most likely suspect, but I assured them that he had been sitting next to me when the incident took place. I'm ashamed to admit that even though I knew the cops were doing their job, I somehow resented the fact that their questioning had prevented me from attending a session on "Training College Students to Utilize Laughter as a Means of Reducing Stress." I had really been looking forward to that session.

Although Legman had offended and irritated countless of his colleagues, a sense of shocked confusion engulfed the entire conference, since it now appeared that somebody's rage toward him had resulted in fatal violence. The Tempe Police Department didn't have a clue. The identity of the clown remained a mystery.

That evening, a feeling of subdued hysteria permeated the Holiday Inn ballroom as we watched the "Humor in Flamenco Dancing" demonstration.

There was even an element of violence in the Joke-Telling Competition. The first-place winner:

"Once upon a time there was a lion. And the lion was in the jungle. And he said to the monkey in a tree, 'Hey, monkey, who's the king of the jungle?' And the monkey said, 'You are, oh great one, king of the jungle, your majesty.' Then the lion turned to the giraffe and said, 'Hey, giraffe, who's the king of the jungle?' And the giraffe said, 'You are, oh great one, king of the jungle.' Then he turned to the elephant and he asked, 'Hey, elephant, who's the king of the jungle?' And the elephant picked the lion up, smashed him against a tree and then threw him down on the ground, *kerplunk*! The lion picked himself up, brushed himself off and said, 'Hey, listen, just because you don't know the right answer, you don't have to get sore!' "

Ah, well. How strange I felt, having come innocently to a humor conference, only to end up serving as the alibi for an angry anthropologist accused of murder. I could only chortle quietly to myself: fa-fa-fa-fa-fa-fa....

1985

Sometimes I think I'm dreaming when I read the news.

But there are places where the inhabitants have never seen a magazine or a newspaper, and it is simply not a part of their psyche to dream about lines of type.

In a spurt of generosity, the United States shipped surplus battery-operated TV sets across the sea to one group of islands in the Pacific Ocean so that those natives could pass directly from a preliterate society to a post-literate society without having to read a single book in the process.

They watched in amazement as so-called psychic Uri Geller bent forks on the Merv Griffin show.

The strange thing was that even though Geller accomplished this feat by trickery, there were young children back in America who hadn't yet been taught about the self-fulfilling rules of twentieth-century physics, and to their parents' dismay, *they* were able to bend various kitchen utensils by means of sheer willpower.

As more and more deadly conflicts around the world continue to escalate, more and more people are saying, "Boy, the shit's really gonna hit the fan now." That phrase, incidentally, did not come into the language until after there was electricity. People who say that are not referring to a lovely Japanese lithograph showing a kimono-clad woman whose long shiny black hair is twisted up into a bun, and who is coquettishly providing her own personal breeze with a colorful rice-paper fan. Then *splat!*—right in her porcelain-like face. No, it has to be an *electric* fan, which revolves so fast it protects you from the shit—or spreads it, depending which side you're on—or what's a fan *for*?

Meanwhile, even as all that shit is hitting all those fans, the laxative industry continues to blossom. New brand names are constantly competing in the open marketplace. Ex-Lax has even come out with a "milder" version for women—certainly an indication of rampant male chauvinism in their research & development section. What is the implication of this trend? Do females have different digestive systems? Is it perfectly acceptable for macho men to have chocolate-covered sandpaper coursing through their intestinal tracts?

And yet credit must also be given to those friendly folks at Ex-Lax. They were the very first sponsor on television to include a sign-language translation of a commercial—a long-overdue service for the constipated hearing-impaired. Indeed, this had been an early demand of the Deaf Liberation Front. You've probably seen their frontline members on the street and in airports, selling little cards with the sign-language alphabet. Some have been getting arrested for being deaf without a license. Naturally, the police recite their Miranda rights, shouting, "You have the right to remain silent!"

Anyway, this particular Ex-Lax commercial features a pleasant, matronly woman reminiscing through her family photo album while a young fellow in the corner of the screen ostensibly translates the message into sign language. Actually, he can say whatever he wants. Nobody monitors the translation. He can indulge in private jokes for all the deaf viewers and only they will know.

The matronly woman in the Ex-Lax commercial says: "Thank God my family is *normal*."

The young fellow shifts the emphasis slightly in his translation: "Thank God *her* family is normal."

She continues: "Of course, once in a while somebody in our family will be troubled by irregularity."

He translates: "No shit."

She concludes: "So then we do what we've done in our family for generations—we turn to an old friend, Ex-Lax."

He translates: "Jimmy Hoffa knows too much."

And while the hearing-impaired viewers at home giggle at this mistranslation, all over the globe the shit continues to hit the fans.

These are rough times, but it's extremely important to develop a sense of optimism. The *Bulletin of Atomic Scientists* periodically updates a clock on their cover to indicate how close we are moving toward nuclear war. Recently they moved it from four minutes to midnight to three minutes to midnight, with midnight representing total annihilation. I don't know exactly what their time scale is—whether one minute represents a month or a year or a decade—but, whichever, they are saying that we are all now only three minutes away from the ultimate holocaust.

That's the bad news.

The good news is that atomic scientists are just as fucked-up as the rest of us. They overeat, they forget to floss, they suffer from premature ejaculations, they don't have time for serial orgasms, and they set their clocks 15 minutes ahead so that if they need to mail a letter by six o'clock and their clock says it's ten after six, it means they still have five minutes to get to the mail-box.

So that clock on the cover of the *Bulletin of Atomic Scientists* is 15 minutes fast. We don't have just three minutes till doomsday, we have 18 minutes.

And that's the good news.

Life remains peaceful on a certain island off the coast of Japan. Here, humans and animals live in peace and harmony.

There are monkeys who for eons have subsisted entirely on sweet potatoes. They would pick the sweet potatoes right out of the dirt in which they grow—eating them, dirt and all. This is the way they have always done it. But one day, for whatever mysterious reason, an individual young female monkey carried her sweet potato to the shore, washed the dirt off in the ocean and proceeded to eat the sweet potato.

Who knows why it was this particular monkey. Any explanation will suffice. Maybe she was an Aries, with a strong pioneer spirit. At any rate, once this monkey broke the ice, other monkeys began to wash the dirt off their sweet potatoes before they ate them. But only the young monkeys.

It was not until the hundredth young monkey had washed the dirt off a sweet potato in the ocean—not specifically number 100; it could've been the 93rd monkey or the 108th monkey; the hundredth monkey is merely a metaphor for reaching critical mass—not until then did the first *adult* monkey wash the dirt off a sweet potato. This was a case of reverse generational influence.

And then other adult monkeys started to imitate this behavior. Washing the dirt off sweet potatoes even began to occur on adjoining islands, indicating that there was some kind of psychic communication in the air.

Now, how can this living New Age parable be applied to *human* behavior? Well, whatever you do personally to help further the cause of justice and the pursuit of ecstasy, even though you might get discouraged, you must always remember that you might be the one who turns the tide—you have to act as though you are the hundredth monkey—and this gives us reason to hope.

That's the good news.

The bad news is, those monkeys *needed* that dirt in their diet!

So now there were all these monkeys on this island who weren't able to shit.

But it just so happened that this was one of the islands where we shipped our surplus TV sets. Across the island, monkeys were gathered around those TV sets, all watching a program that was sponsored by Ex-Lax. Moreover, here was that commercial with the sign-language translation. And fortuitously enough, these monkeys had relatives trained at Stanford University, where they learned how to communicate in sign language, and had been returned to the island to teach others of their species how to sign.

That's the good news.

The bad news is that this was the Ex-Lax commercial where the brand name of the product was not translated. The message in sign language was "Jimmy Hoffa knows too much."

These monkeys—serving as shock troops of the Deaf Liberation Front—took that private joke to be their marching orders. So, even though you may have heard the propaganda that Hoffa was killed because he was prepared to speak out about the alliance between military intelligence and organized crime, the truth is that he was eaten to death by hordes of constipated monkeys.

That's the bad news.

The good news is, they washed the dirt off him first.

It is several years later now. Things have returned to normalcy.

190   The monkeys on those islands off the coast of Japan still watch TV, but they no longer wash the

dirt off their sweet potatoes, and they are just as regular in their defecation as they used to be.

But in America, those children who once bent kitchen utensils to the dismay of their parents have grown up.

One such young man now works on the assembly line in a missile factory, and he is able to bend certain working parts out of shape through the use of sheer willpower.

Soon others will follow suit.

Already the intelligence agencies are training their operatives in methods to counteract this psychic sabotage.

Hypnotic Age Regression of a Television Addict

1978

Recently there was an intriguing little news item about a Palo Alto mother who shot her television set. She was arrested for disturbing the peace. The judge gave her a suspended sentence on condition that she undergo immediate psychotherapy.

A routine check of court records led us to psychiatrist Thomas R. Burnhill who, together with colleagues at Stanford Research Institute, developed a technique of hypnotic age regression in conjunction with Ketamine, an anesthetic that leaves a patient feeling numb but fully conscious.

This process enables one to verbalize sense-memories with unusual objectivity. Moreover, an individual can articulate even pre-speech childhood experiences.

The subject in this case was a 27-year-old Caucasian female identified only as Jessica. She works as a graphic designer at home in order to take care of her infant daughter, Ariadne. Jessica agreed that excerpts from the tapes of her sessions with Dr. Burnhill could be quoted in the present context.

After a preliminary meeting to establish rapport and determine Jessica's susceptibility to hypnotic induction, Dr. Burnhill entered into an exploration of her behavioral roots, beginning with the day of the incident:

Now, as you approach your TV set for the first time today, tell me, what emotion do you feel?

Mixed. Mixed emotions. I feel annoyance, a slight annoyance.

At your television set?

No, at my clock-radio. It gets me up at seven o'clock in the morning. But I also feel anticipation. I like to watch the TV news in the morning. It puts my own problems in perspective. And I think David Hartman is kind of cute. But there's a touch of guilt I also feel.

Why? What makes you feel guilty?

Disloyalty to CBS. I used to watch their morning news. But now I watch ABC instead. They have *Face-Off*, plus Jack Anderson with the inside scoop, plus Rona Barrett with the gossip. Then, around five minutes before the hour, when they do the national weather report on *Good Morning, America*, I switch to CBS just in time to catch Hughes Rudd and his final witty story. This is my morning ritual, which I adhere to religiously.

Is there anything in particular on the news this morning that stirs you emotionally?

Not really. It all just sort of goes by, like on a conveyor belt. Although, I do get a little bothered by their reminder to watch the CBS evening news with Walter Cronkite. Every program is always telling you to be sure to watch all these *other* programs. If they had their way I would be watching TV all the time—except when I'm supposed to be out buying all the sponsors' products.

Indeed, a pair of TV-commercial-oriented encounters would occur later that same morning. Here, Jessica is shopping at a local supermarket:

I'm in the aisle where they have kitchen supplies. And I notice this, what you might call a mini-adrenaline rush, just as I'm putting a box of Ajax into Ariadne's stroller. She reaches out as though it's a prize. And the exact instant I give it to her to hold, that's when I have this reaction. My heart gives a little thump.

What do you feel?

As though I am handing over something *evil* to her.

Why? Why does it feel evil?

Because of their commercial. The Ajax commercial is evil.

Tell me about it.

They show a housewife in the kitchen. She's worried because her in-laws are coming to dinner, and they might despise her because they can't see their faces shine in her dishes. Then this handyman or plumber magically appears in the kitchen. And he does her dishes with Ajax. Then he rubs his finger along the plate to show her how clean it is, and you hear this godawful *screech*. Like when you rub your fingernails on the blackboard, you get an actual physical reaction. I mean this commercial borders on sadism. And there I am buying a box of Ajax. I guess that makes me a masochist, huh?

Afterward, she finds herself standing "slightly perplexed" in front of a McDonald's restaurant:

Can you pinpoint precisely what it is that perplexes you?

Well, I'm trying to be a vegetarian. But I'm *so* tempted to have a Big Mac. It's like I'm *almost* not in control of myself. So I just stand there. I'm aware of a certain feeling of excitement.

Could this be due to a forbidden aspect of eating meat for you?

More than that. It's the commercial again. There is something evil about their commercial.

Describe it, please.

I can't. I mean, it isn't the commercial itself. This has to do with the *placement* of the commercial. I associate McDonald's with the relief of tension. But the tension is not from hunger. There's something else.

Tell me what you feel. Pluck it gently from your subconscious.

There is a connection with the excitement, the vicarious excitement that a crime show builds up to immediately before the commercial. And then *the commercial itself* relieves that tension. So now I am in front of McDonald's and I realize that I have been programmed with a sense of *adventure* about eating there. I feel like Pavlov's dog standing there on an invisible leash.

Do you go inside? Do you have a Big Mac?

Yes. But only because I already bought the box

of Ajax.

Dr. Burnhill proceeds to take Jessica through her viewing day. At three o'clock she watches Dinah Shore. From four to five-thirty she alternates between Merv Griffin and Mike Douglas:

It's like going to a party every day with all these different show business personalities, without having to participate. And sometimes there's an interesting fact you learn. At least it's more intelligent than all that kaka-doodoo shit they have, like on *The Newlywed Game*—that's really insulting—but I'll admit, I watch it. I'm a true TV junkie.

You believe you are addicted to television?

Oh, for sure. I watch an average of nine hours a day. And it doesn't even give me *pleasure*. It's just a way of avoiding pain. Isn't that how you judge addiction?

What pain are you avoiding?

The pain of not watching. I told you I was hooked. After Merv Griffin and Mike Douglas I watch reruns of the Mary Tyler Moore show on afternoon prime time. Or if I remember the episode, I'll watch a Carol Burnett rerun instead. It's like my TV is always *on* something, and it constantly tries to entice me to get on it too. Then comes the local news at six o'clock, then the CBS evening news, then the NBC evening news.

Why do you watch them both?

My rationalization is that I like to compare their news. What they emphasize. One time, remember when that sleazoid Henry Kissinger was touring China, and he was in Hong Kong? The CBS correspondent said he was visiting the Garden of Paradise, but the NBC correspondent showed him walking in the same place and *he* called it the Garden of Fools. Maybe the world is actually being run by professional translators.

Why do you call Henry Kissinger a sleazoid?

Well, because he *is* a sleazoid. He's a war criminal. I mean that's what is so, well, schizophrenic, about my TV set. One day John Chancellor tells me that the former CIA director, Richard Helms, threatened to implicate Henry Kissinger in the whole Chilean coup if he went to prison, that Helms would bring Kissinger down with him, and then another day David Brinkley sits down and has a civilized *chat* with Kissinger because the sleazoid happens to be a *special adviser* to NBC news. That's sick, it really is.

On this particular evening, Jessica has refused a dinner invitation because there is a Richard Pryor special on television:

I can see those friends any time, but if I miss Richard Pryor, that's it. I felt bad when I missed the Lily Tomlin special. That was also on one-time-only. It's creative obsolescence. Plus, my TV forces me to be right there at a specific time on a specific day.

Do you resent this?

I adapt to it. I talk to my TV set. I tell Richard Pryor, "Massa, I am your slave. I am at your beck and call." No matter how excellent a program may be, this is still slavery. Voluntary slavery.

Later that evening, Jessica watches the Dick Cavett show. He is interviewing actress Louise Lasser:

I used to watch *Mary Hartman, Mary Hartman* every night. So I have been looking forward to this interview. But I feel a certain restlessness while it is on. My boyfriend, Gary—he's a musician—he's supposed to call me long-distance tonight. I find myself secretly hoping that the telephone won't ring while the TV is on. I feel as if I am psychically conspiring with the TV set against the phone. Also, I am waiting for a commercial break so that I can get up and pee, but there are no commercials on PBS.

Do you get up to pee?

No. Not even when the interview gets boring. Instead, I switch to *Fernwood Forever.* Tom Hartman is saying how much he misses Mary. I say out loud, "Turn on Channel Nine and you'll see her." Then I ask myself, "What the hell are you doing? This is crazy."

What is crazy?

I don't even enjoy the company of these assholes and yet I'm all involved with their nonexistent problems. But when a commercial comes on *this* channel, then I get up and pee.

Finally, Jessica watches the *Tonight* show with Johnny Carson. It is during this program, shortly past midnight, that she shoots her television set:

I am rolling a joint as Johnny is delivering his opening monologue. I smoke a little weed and after a while I just lay back and start playing with myself. But I've never masturbated in front of Gary. Isn't that strange? I can be more intimate with my TV set than with my lover.

Do you masturbate to a climax?

Absolutely. I am floating in this sweet post-orgasmic haze. Suddenly I hear a voice say, "Stay where you are." At first I think there's a burglar in my bedroom. Then I realize it's only Johnny Carson, concerned that I might leave during the commercials. And I suddenly understand. My TV set is afraid of me. It is even more insecure than it tries to make *me* feel.

How does your TV set try to make you feel insecure?

It is constantly bombarding me with fears couched behind smiles. Fear that I don't have enough iron in my blood. Fear that my oven cleaner will fill my kitchen with deadly fumes. Fear of indigestion, fear of stinko breath, fear that my headache won't disappear fast enough. But the moment I realize that my TV set is afraid of me, I start crying. Uncontrollably. It wakes the baby up. Ariadne says her first word when I go to pick her up. She says, "Meow meow meow meow." And we don't even have a cat. I'm horrified. She has gotten her first word from a TV commercial for cat food. I hug my baby. "Sweetie, you're a human being, not a cat. Jesus, you can't even speak *English* yet. What have they been *doing* to you?" And this is the instant. Very calmly I put her back in her crib. "Excuse me just a minute." And I simply walk back to the bedroom to get my gun. Surprised at how centered I feel.

Now wait. Try to stretch out this moment, as if you are pulling taffy. What are your exact thoughts?

Rape. They are raping Ariadne's soul. Gary gave me a gun to protect us while he's on the road. To protect us from burglars and rapists. Well, this TV set is a burglar. It has been stealing my time. And it is an electronic rapist that I have *allowed* into my home.

What are you thinking as you go to the TV set with the gun in your hand?

This is self-defense.

Do you have any doubts over what you are about to do?

For a few seconds I hesitate. I have an urge to check my copy of *TV Guide* to see who the guest is on the Tom Snyder show. Then I aim. I don't shoot yet. Paul Ehrlich is the guest. He always says important stuff about ecology. Maybe I'm making a mistake. Then a commercial comes on. "Nestlé's real chocolate Morsels—my family's worth it!" And I pull the trigger. My TV set explodes.

What is your feeling at this moment?

Exhilaration. I have been boycotting all Nestlé's products because they keep selling infant formula to Third World mothers who don't have sterilizing equipment or refrigerators, and who could breast-feed their babies just the way I breast-feed Ariadne. Their babies keep dying. I have killed my TV set to avenge those murdered Third World babies. I have committed a political assassination. I have liberated myself from my TV set. I have protected my helpless daughter from this stationary marauder. I have done the right thing. I am sobbing with pride.

Dr. Burnhill remarked to this reporter that "Jessica's relationship with her television set paralleled that of a subject toward a hypnotist." In order to test this hypothesis, he regressed her all the way back to her own infancy. Here she is at the age of two:

My parents are watching television. I am waiting for my favorite lady in the box. Her name is Betty Furness.
    Why is she your favorite?
    I get a feeling of security from her. I like the friendly way she always opens the refrigerator door. I wish my mother was like her, smiling all the time and never yelling.

Jessica at the age of 18 months:

I am crawling into my parents' bedroom. They are wrestling like those men on TV they watch. But they don't want me to watch them. I get picked up and put in my playpen.
    How does this make you feel?
    Confused. Because they start wrestling again. I can tell because I can hear them grunting. But then the telephone rings. They stop grunting. I hear my father say hello. I feel he loves the telephone more than he loves me.

Jessica at the age of one year:

202   I observe my parents in order to learn how I should

behave as a human being. When the alarm clock buzzes, they wake up. When the toaster pops up bread, they go and fetch it. When the teakettle whistles, they obey it immediately. When the doorbell rings, they go and answer it. When the TV gets sick, they bring in a doctor to examine it.

How do you feel when your TV gets sick?

I want it to get better. I miss looking at it. I like to watch the TV people tell my parents to go get this and go get that, and then later they go out and get it.

Why do you like that?

Because it's fun to learn. It just feels good.

What does your TV teach you?

That the purpose of life is for machines to tell people what to do.

Epilogue

Dr. Burnhill is expounding his new theory of Video Hypnosis on the Phil Donahue show:

"I realize the irony of discussing this *on* television," he states, "but actually it's a way of reaching a great many more people than, say, an article in a professional journal. I have a duty to warn the public about my findings. For example, the latest trend I have noted in my research has to do with the nature of passivity as influenced by the two-part situation comedy. During the interim week the viewer's attention remains, on some level of consciousness, focused on an artificial crisis. So far I have personally monitored this trend with *All in the Family*, *Good Times, Welcome Back, Kotter, Maude, One*   **203**

Day at a Time, Busting Loose, Laverne and Shirley, M*A*S*H, Barney Miller, Eight Is Enough, Rhoda, Happy Days...."

1976

An old friend approached us with a thick sheaf of what was purported to be a photocopy of the autobiographical manuscript on which former President Richard M. Nixon was still at work. Our first reaction was skepticism. While most of the contents dealt predictably with contemporary history as it has already been recorded, there were enough surprises to shock even our own jaded psyche.

Just to be sure, we employed the services of a reputable private investigative firm. Their report verified that our source did indeed know an individual inside the San Clemente hideaway. The next step was to hire a professional graphologist, who determined the authenticity of Mr. Nixon's handwritten notes on the typed transcript. Finally, our attorneys assured us that there was no violation of copyright laws involved, because it was unlikely that Nixon had submitted such unfinished material for copyright protection.

The book, as yet untitled, is dedicated "To Patricia Ryan Nixon, who has been named the most admired woman in the country, and deservedly so, for your loyalty has been a continuing inspiration, not only to your husband and family, but to Americans everywhere." Here then are several excerpts from this preliminary draft of the memoirs of the only United States president ever to resign from office.

Although President Dwight David Eisenhower encouraged me to call him Ike during the years I served as Vice President, it was a superficial form of intimacy. I regretted his failure to share decision-making responsibility with me at the White House. That privilege he reserved for his special assistant, Sherman Adams.

When media coverage of a minor scandal in 1958 involving a rug and a vicuña coat pressured him into letting Adams go, Ike at last revealed a facet of his humanity to me. "By sheer force of habit," he remarked, "I was ready to seek out Sherman's advice on whether or not I should fire him."

It was not until 1961, after Ike's farewell address, that he confided in me again, this time about a more momentous occasion. "I suppose," he began, "my reference to the dangers of the military-industrial complex in my speech came as something of a surprise to you, eh?"

"Well, sir, it did strike me as a rather incongruous position for a renowned Army general to take—"

"I had a visitation," he interrupted, "while I was in the process of composing my farewell address—now this is utterly impossible to describe—but I do believe it was some kind of extraterrestrial communication."

"In English or what?" I was dumbfounded.

"It was in English but also beyond all language. They told me that their associates had been to see Harry Truman when he was President. Now remember, Dick, he's the one who ordered the atomic bomb to be dropped on Hiroshima and Nagasaki. And yet these creatures convinced him not to turn Korea into another nuclear holocaust. That's really why he brought back General Douglas MacArthur."

Ike stared ahead with a blank expression in his eyes.

"Sir, are you all right?"

"Yes, yes, I just don't know if I can articulate this extraterrestrial experience. It was as though my body remained in the chair and my spirit was taken on a journey. All I know is that when I returned, I just had to tell the truth. There was no other choice—"

Ike stopped in mid-sentence. He never mentioned that incident again. Nor did I feel it would be proper for me to broach the subject. I dismissed it from my mind. It would not be until nearly 14 years later that my *visceral* understanding of his experience would occur.

The year 1974 was so rough on me that for a while I thought I could actually be going insane. I wondered if I was being drugged without my knowledge. I found myself wallowing in paranoid fantasies, and I gave voice to these at press conferences. I expressed the fear that my plane might crash. I resorted to using expressions like, "They can point a gun at your head." I was practically begging for mercy.

When I entered Memorial Hospital Medical Center in Long Beach on October 23 for my phlebitis condition, I brought my own jar of wheat germ, because I was afraid that poison would be put in my food.

On October 29, the doctors placed a clamp on a vein in my pelvis in order to prevent the blood clot from moving to my lungs where it could have killed me. It was then that I went into cardiovascular failure.

On October 30, Ron Ziegler announced, "We almost lost President Nixon yesterday afternoon." This was almost three months after my resignation, and he was still referring to me as President. "Poor Ron," I thought to myself. "He thinks he's still in Disneyland."

For a few hours I was considered to be clinically dead. It was an incredibly ecstatic feeling. I was conscious, but on some other plane of existence, and there was an overwhelming temptation to remain in that blissful limbo. Yet there was also something in me that kept saying "Don't give up!" It was my survival instinct speaking.

But why not give up? What was there left for me? The answer came to me by the same extraterrestrial path it had come to Ike: *Tell the truth!* That was the turning point of my life. And these memoirs are the tangible result of my transformation. No one shall be spared, least of all myself.

Those hairless creatures told me that President John F. Kennedy had also been visited by their kind. His father, old Joe Kennedy, had gotten rich off illegal booze during Prohibition, and you can be certain that the underworld bootleggers he was tied up with were not about to dissolve their silent partnership in this huge liquor industry they had built up, simply because Prohibition had been repealed. Yet there was Joe Kennedy's own son, Jack—not to mention his brother Bobby—refusing to cooperate any longer in allowing organized crime to have a comeback in Cuba, and furthermore, going after organized crime in *this* country. At best this was ingratitude; at worst it was treason.

But I finally understood the extraterrestrial force that had motivated young Kennedy.

And so now I am ready to peel away the final layers of my poker-face mask.

For example, I occasionally went too far while wearing my anti-Communist mask. When former Attorney General Nicholas Katzenbach exposed the DuBois Clubs as a Communist front organization, poison-pen letters and threatening telephone calls were received by many of the Boys Clubs from patriotic Americans who were understandably confused by the ostensibly coincidental pronunciations. But in my capacity as National Board Chairman of the Boys Clubs of America, I charged that the name choice was "an almost classic example of Communist deception and duplicity" and that the W. E. B. DuBois Clubs "are not unaware of the confusion they are causing among our supporters and among many other good citizens."

In retrospect, however, I admit that this was a slightly foolish position to espouse.

In August of 1945, while I was still serving in the Navy, stationed in Maryland, there was a Committee of 100 seeking—according to an advertisement they placed in several California newspapers—a candidate for Congress "with no previous political experience, to defeat a man who has represented the district in the House for ten years." This was a reference to Jerry Voorhis.

I did not see the ad, but destiny acted as though I had answered it, when I was contacted by Murray Chotiner for Herman Perry, vice president of the

Bank of America. Perry later became vice president of the Western Tube Corporation, a CIA front located in the Whittier Bank of America Building. But now he wanted to know only if I was a Republican and if I was available.

My responses were both affirmative.

It was Perry who brought me out for an extremely brief meeting with Howard Hughes. Hughes was handsome, dynamic, self-assured. Somehow he had seen the FBI dossier on me, which had apparently been compiled when I applied for a position with the Bureau after graduating law school. Oddly enough, I had never heard back from the FBI directly.

"Nixon," he addressed me, "you have a magnificent political future ahead. You will be able to steer your ship independently. But always keep it in a tiny compartment of your mind that you do not own the ocean. I do."

I never saw Howard Hughes face to face again.

The seeds of my distrust of the Justice Department were sown in 1948 during the Alger Hiss case. Those people just sat on each other's hands. If not for the work of our House Un-American Activities Committee, the prosecution would never have been so successful.

I refused to turn over to those bunglers the microfilms we had in evidence. When there was a possibility I might be cited for contempt, I raised the point of what a dangerous precedent could be set, since here I was, a U.S. Congressman, appearing voluntarily before a grand jury.

But the truth of the matter was that those microfilms were copies of documents forged on an old Woodstock typewriter that had been specially constructed to resemble—to have the same peculiarities as—the one that had actually belonged to Alger Hiss's wife, Priscilla.

Then Whittaker Chambers hid these "old" 1938 microfilms inside a pumpkin on his pumpkin farm. The trouble was, the Eastman Kodak people stated that the type of film we used was not manufactured by their company until after 1945.

To this day, whenever the comic strip *Peanuts* mentions that bird Woodstock or the mysterious "pumpkin papers," I suspect Charles Schulz is trying to remind me of something.

There seems to be a tradition of accusing those who fight Communism of being homosexual. This smear tactic was used against Whittaker Chambers, against Senator Joseph McCarthy and against J. Edgar Hoover. In that vein, gossips used to joke about Hoover and Clyde Tolson double-dating with Charles "Bebe" Rebozo and myself.

Neither Rebozo nor I are "gay." We have been very close friends since 1950. What we enjoy most about each other's company is the fact that small talk becomes unnecessary. We are not afraid of silence. But we have never had any kind of sexual relationship.

We were introduced by Senator George Smathers, who was infamous for supplying female company to his fellow politicians. It was Smathers who eventually sent Mary Jo Kopechne to be with Senator Edward Kennedy.

Whenever I was in Florida, I would stay with Bebe, and he would occasionally get a couple of beautiful $200-a-night girls. Or as they would be called nowadays, $200-a-night women. But when I bought my own home in Key Biscayne, then his yacht became our rendezvous site.

I was certainly not promiscuous, but I had been a virgin until marriage. I proposed to Pat Ryan the very same night I met her. She refused, but I was a determined son-of-a-gun. I even drove her to Los Angeles where she dated other men while I waited in the wings. I finally charmed her with my perseverance and self-effacement.

Once I expressed concern to Bebe that word might get out about my "affairs" in Key Biscayne. "These girls," I pointed out, "are likely to brag about going to bed with a United States Senator."

"They're professionals," Bebe reassured me. "It's just like your lawyer-client privilege. Stop worrying."

One evening in 1949, while I was still serving in Congress, I received an anonymous call at my home. A male voice said three words, "Watch Jeane Dixon," and hung up the telephone.

A week later, the psychic Jeane Dixon held a press conference. One of the reporters asked her to predict my future. She drew a blank, however, explaining that she needed time to meditate. I believe that in show business parlance this is known as "milking the audience." Finally she said it: "I predict that one day Richard Nixon will become President of the United States."

I could only conclude that the higher source from which she had received her intelligence was not necessarily supernatural.

When I lost the presidential election to John F. Kennedy in 1960, Jeane Dixon *continued* to predict that I would be President. "Destiny," she stated, "cannot be denied."

Even after I was defeated in the 1962 California gubernatorial election and announced that I was through with politics, she said, "Richard Nixon has not even *begun* his rise in politics." And then she predicted the assassination of President Kennedy in 1963.

After the Watergate affair, she stated: "God gave us Richard Nixon to divide us, to test us where our faith is concerned, to see if we could come together." A local paper published her statement ("God gave us Nixon to divide us.—Jeane Dixon") as the caption for a cartoon showing a cloud with the voice of God saying, "Don't blame me—I voted for McGovern." I had to admit it was funny, even though she had been quoted out of context.

Harry Robbins "Bob" Haldeman came into my life when I was a senator in 1951. He volunteered to work on my vice presidential campaign the next year, but that campaign was not to be for him, so he tried again in 1956, and this time we took him on. He rose to 213 be my chief advance man for the presidential race in 1960.

After my defeat, Haldeman remained loyal. He volunteered to help me with my book, *Six Crises*. I wrote the chapter on the 1960 campaign myself because it was so fresh in my mind. Al Moscow drafted four other chapters with Haldeman—this was not ghostwritten material because I rewrote what they presented—and Haldeman worked mostly on the Alger Hiss chapter.

He was apparently so eager to please, though, that he screwed up on his research. He had it that the FBI found the old Woodstock typewriter. And the book was published that way. Then the facts came out, the trial records and all, and we had to change it for the paperback edition. So now it reads that the FBI was *unable* to find the typewriter.

The truth is, Alger Hiss found it himself. But the FBI had *planted* this fake Woodstock typewriter. And then the *defense* presented it in the trial as what they *assumed* was evidence in their favor. So at least Hiss was found guilty of perjury.

That verdict added immeasurably to my political strength. I had the courage of Alger Hiss's conviction and it served as the magic carpet that transported me from the Congress to the Senate to the vice presidency. I would have had the presidency in my pocket if not for Kennedy's performance in the Great Debates—but only on television; I fared better on radio.

214 Kennedy's charisma was the variable that none of us had counted on.

How strange that the incident from the entire eight years I spent as Vice President that stands out most prominently in my memory occurred not in the White House but in Peru. There was a rioter who spat on me, and it was with great pleasure that I kicked him in the shins.

Back in the safety of our hotel that night, I recalled an early formal debate at Whittier College—"Resolved: that insects are more beneficial than harmful"—because I had been so intrigued as to how insects did not think, they just acted. Now, having myself acted totally without hesitation, I was able to identify with those insects.

As Vice President, I labored diligently behind the scenes to establish Operation 40, by which our CIA covertly trained Cuban intelligence officers in exile. Operation 40 was to serve as our link between the White House and the CIA in April of 1961. My plan was to invade Cuba.

Ironically, during the 1960 presidential campaign, Kennedy began advocating *my* plan. I could not reveal that it was already in effect because Operation 40 was a *secret* project. Further, I found myself in the schizophrenic position of attacking my own idea whenever Kennedy articulated it because it violated our treaty commitments.

Of all the professional newscasters I have met, Walter Cronkite of CBS was the most charming. He treated me with respect and dignity. After the broadcast interview, we sat in his anteroom and talked informally.

"I've always wanted to thank you," he said, "for inadvertently bringing me back to sanity that horrible weekend John Kennedy was killed."

"Oh, really—how so?"

"This followed on the heels of the televised shooting of Lee Harvey Oswald by Jack Ruby. A journalist asked for your reaction, and you replied with a slip of the tongue, 'Two rights don't make a wrong.' Before you could correct yourself, I was finally able to break through my depression with a bit of laughter."

"Yes, those were muddled times. Do you know I *forgot* where I was the day the assassination took place? I had to tell the FBI I couldn't remember, and it was not until later that I remembered I had been in Dallas, of all places. There was a convention of the American Bottlers of Carbonated Beverages, and I was there representing Pepsi-Cola. But I flew out of there at eleven o'clock that morning. Kennedy was shot around one o'clock, as I recall. Where were *you* that day?"

"In my office," Cronkite said. "When we got the word from Bethesda that he had passed, I cried openly."

"And you're supposed to be objective," I teased him. "I didn't realize you were that much of a Kennedy supporter."

"Well, by that time I was crying because it had also come over the wires that Lyndon Johnson was already preparing to be sworn in as the new President."

It was encouraging to find that in person this superstar really was just like your favorite uncle.

When Robert Kennedy was attorney general in 1962, he was busy checking out the Hiss case for some reason. Of course, he discovered that the FBI never had the Woodstock typewriter.

Then, in 1968, when he was running for President, he approached New Orleans District Attorney Jim Garrison to be his attorney general. Garrison had gotten a lot of publicity due to his investigation of the assassination of Bobby's brother.

During that campaign, Howard Hughes dispatched Robert Maheu to visit me. Hughes felt strongly that the Vietnam war should continue—he had a huge defense contract for helicopters—yet at the same time he wanted a halt to underground nuclear testing, presumably because it upset the roulette wheels in his Las Vegas casinos.

I mentioned the Bobby Kennedy information to Maheu, and he said, "Uh-oh, the boss will have to keep a sharper eye on *him.*"

It was poetic irony that while Bobby Kennedy was giving official permission to J. Edgar Hoover to spy on Martin Luther King, I was giving unofficial permission to Hoover to spy on *Kennedy.* That is to say, Robert Maheu may have been working for Howard Hughes, but he had also continued working for the FBI. So when he referred to "the boss," I asked, "Which one?"

Maheu smiled and held up his arms, two fingers from each hand extending up into the air. "Both," he

217

said. This was the exact moment I decided to use that gesture for the crowds.

Winston Churchill had used the V-sign to signify Victory. Then the antiwar protesters perverted its meaning to signify Defeat. Now I was restoring its original victorious symbolism by co-opting the co-opters. Or so I believed.

The problem was that Lyndon Johnson desperately wanted to have the Vietnam war settled before he left office. Whereas, I am ashamed to admit, we were trying to prolong it.

Anna Chennault—the Dragon Lady, as we called her—was our liaison to South Vietnamese government officials. Her task was to dissuade their ambassador, Bui Diem, from attending the Paris peace talks.

But LBJ got wise to this. I had to call and cajole him personally. He was absolutely furious. He complained bitterly at how "shit-kickin' pissed off" he was. "Thieu is *our* boy," he shouted, "and don't you fuckin' forget that!"

On November 1, 1968, only four days before the American election, President Nguyen Van Thieu announced that Saigon was pulling out of the peace talks. The Dragon Lady had obviously convinced his associates that they would obtain a juicier deal under our new administration than under Johnson or his chosen successor, Hubert Humphrey, who would surely have won if the Democrats had ended the war.

And so, because it was in the mutual interest of the South Vietnamese and the Republicans to extend the war for several more years, we became the recipients of kickbacks from our own government's aid to the Saigon government.

I do not ask for forgiveness. No, rather I must live with the memory of myself as an idealistic adolescent first reading about the Teapot Dome scandal and saying to my mother, while helping her to mash the potatoes, "I would like to become an honest lawyer who can't be bought by crooks." But my character had already been set. When I was only five years old, my mother intended to buy me a copy of *The Prince and the Pauper* but she asked a bookstore clerk for *The Prince* and so of course he gave her Machiavelli's book. My mother was a saint. Her little mistake changed my life, and I will always be grateful for what I feel must have been a touch of divine intervention.

We created a couple of Frankenstein monsters, and when I say we, I mean the administration and the media in an unintentional collaboration.

One such monster was Martha Mitchell. The first time she made one of her famous telephone calls and we saw how the press ate it up, we realized we had a political gold mine. The wife of the attorney general could serve as our mouthpiece for floating various trial balloons.

John Mitchell would get thoroughly briefed on whatever the issue was—Haiphong Harbor or Senator Fulbright or the need for increased spending—and then, without ever letting Martha know that he expected her to give a scoop to some lucky reporter that evening, John would simply smoke his pipe and just happen to engage her in casual conversation about the matter.

Martha was much too strong-willed to be *instructed* to make a call, but she could be counted on to make the call, even if it was three o'clock in the morning when the urge hit her. This was a great joke among the reporters. One little news item quoted her latest pronouncement, and after the quote the sentence was completed with, "Martha Mitchell confided to the *Washington Star* yesterday." Confided, indeed, to a newspaper!

But in the process of becoming a public character, she developed many contacts in the media. By the time her husband became my campaign manager, Martha Mitchell was already a household word. We thought she would prove to be a wonderful asset until she started blabbing about Watergate.

Another Frankenstein monster we created was Henry Kissinger. I never really wanted him in the first place. He had insulted me publicly when I received the nomination in '68. But I made an agreement with Nelson Rockefeller that if he would actively support me, I would take Kissinger onto the team, and of course I had to keep my word.

We all felt somewhat uncomfortable about his German accent. H. R. Haldeman decided that whenever Kissinger made any statement, his picture could be shown on TV but there would be no audio. And the electronic media cooperated.

Meanwhile, we built up his image, got him dates with glamorous movie stars—Jill St. John, Marlo

Thomas, Liv Ullmann—until he became known as a harmless, pudgy playboy. Then it was acceptable for his voice to be heard.

"Henry," I once remarked to him, "there's a rumor going around Washington that you're lousy in bed."

"Mr. President"—speaking very slowly and distinctly—"I can only say that...*power*... is the ultimate aphrodisiac."

And he just kept glaring at me with those worried-looking eyebrows frowning over his spectacles. This was just three days after our destabilization of the Chilean government. Kissinger wanted all the credit, but it was really a team effort.

We could not have succeeded, for example, without the invaluable aid of Teamsters Union President Frank Fitzsimmons and his Bob Hope-like timing in manipulating the truckers' strike in Chile. It is possible to bring about the collapse of an entire economy by shutting down one integral aspect, especially communications or transportation.

Moreover, the Soviet Union was trying to cut off the United States' supply of a metal vital to jet engine production, by their support of the Allende government in Chile and also by backing guerrilla actions in Angola. In order to maintain the war in Vietnam, we needed Chilean copper as well as the trace metal. At any rate, we were a smooth, well-oiled team, on the way to winning the whole, beautiful, global game.

In 1968, George Wallace ran for President as the candidate of the American Independent Party. This almost lost me the election to Hubert Humphrey. In 1972, Wallace ran for President again. This almost cost him his life. I honestly have no knowledge as to how long Arthur Bremer was in our employ, but I do know that the cover story of his having stalked me before he went after Wallace was fabricated simply to defuse any suspicion that might have pointed to our role in the tragic event.

After all, my supposed public mandate that November came from a majority that included 20 million votes that would otherwise have gone to George Wallace. We had not expected him to pose so much of a threat. In fact, we had already taken certain steps to preclude any such possibility. In 1970, immediately after he became governor of Alabama again, the IRS and the Justice Department launched an investigation of Wallace and his brother Gerald for tax evasion and other forms of financial corruption.

I don't fault Wallace for family loyalty, by the way. I have carried out similar filial responsibility to my own brother, Donald. This is only natural.

In any event, John Mitchell, still attorney general at the time, came to me early in 1971 and said, "We've got to stop George Wallace. He could force the election into the House of Representatives if he runs on a third party ticket again."

In May of that year, I was in Mobile and invited Wallace to fly with me on the presidential plane to Birmingham. Enroute, we shook hands on an agreement. I promised that Mitchell would call off the investigation of Wallace and his brother—although their

222

underlings would still be subject to prosecution—and the governor in turn promised me that if he ran in '72 it would only be as a Democrat.

In August 1971, we discovered that CBS correspondent Daniel Schorr had been asking around about the possibility of such a deal. Haldeman commented, "We'd better get on *his* ass—fast."

Two years later, when Schorr reported that John Dean was afraid of going to prison because he might get raped there, we were able to find out immediately from the FBI that his source was Dean's own attorney, but there was nothing constructive we could do with that information.

However, it must be noted for posterity that John Dean was a closet queen supreme. His lovely wife, Maureen, is merely window dressing. Oh, how neatly she rolled up her blond tresses into a perfect bun and sat behind him at the Watergate hearings every day, blatantly projecting a modern-day American Gothic image. I recall how it came out that Dean had taken almost $5000 from a White House safe for a hurried honeymoon right smack in the middle of the cover-up. He was already disguising his tracks. Their marriage was purely protective coloration.

The case of John Dean does raise the question, when is a so-called leak actually convenient propaganda?

Maureen Dean was on an airplane flight when she "accidentally" dropped her purse and spilled a vial of amyl nitrite capsules on the floor. She explained to the man sitting next to her how wonderful these were for enhancing her sex life with John. Is it not possible

223

that this lady was protesting just a mite too much, particularly to someone who would just happen to let the media in on her secret?

No wonder G. Gordon Liddy said that John Dean was qualified to sing the title role in *Der Rosenkavalier*— because it is sung by a woman. Liddy once made a remark in German that I asked him to translate for me. He said, "John Dean's priorities are all screwed up. He doesn't know whether he wants to go down in history or down on a historian."

Young people might use the expression "karma returning" to describe a deal we made with Jack Anderson, who had himself exposed the corruption of so many others in his syndicated column for the *Washington Post*.

We were tipped off that Anderson was researching the Dragon Lady connection. He had learned that her late husband, General Claire Chennault, who had commanded the Flying Tigers in World War II, had in 1946 formed a private commercial airline that later merged with the CIA's Air America.

He also learned that our Dragon Lady was currently profiting from a Pepsi-Cola factory I had established in Laos, but which had never spewed forth a single drop of Pepsi. Air America had been shuttling out its actual product: heroin.

However, Anderson agreed not to publish this material. In return, we agreed not to publicize the fact that he knew about the Watergate break-in weeks before it occurred. He had warned Lawrence O'Brien at Democratic National Committee headquarters, but O'Brien remained silent because he assumed that such a scandal would provide ammunition for a Democrat coup in the '72 election. He overestimated public outrage.

Anderson held back because he did not wish to endanger his source, one of the "burglars," Frank Sturgis, whom he had known for some 20 years. Shortly after my resignation in 1974, I received a long letter from Sturgis. I shall quote here a portion of that correspondence:

> Now, I'm telling you this because I still consider you my Commander in Chief. I realize that the same faction of the CIA that masterminded the assassination of Kennedy was also behind your downfall. They thought JFK was soft on Communism in Cuba, and that you were soft on Communism in China, but that they didn't necessarily have to kill you to get rid of you.
>
> While I participated in Operation 40, our job was primarily to infiltrate foreign countries. I was a member of the Assassination Section. Orders would filter down, and our job would be to kill, say, a military official or a politician. Even in those days, unstated policy included domestic as well as foreign enemies.
>
> But I had nothing to do with the Kennedy assassination myself. The FBI came to interview me the day after it happened, and I didn't have a thing to tell them, except that I could agree

with their speculation that the motive was revenge for the Bay of Pigs failure. There's no doubt in my mind that if you had been elected in 1960, the invasion would have been completely successful....

For a while I believed that Bernard Barker was the double agent in Watergate, but I have since come to the conclusion that our leader, James McCord, was guided to do the things he did by certain officials in the CIA. We were definitely set up. They used us to eventually destroy the office of the presidency. You were just as expendable as Kennedy.

I shouldn't have been surprised. Mr. McCord was our Security Chief. I myself, as an infiltrator of Castro's inner circle, rose to Director of Security for the Cuban Air Force and Director of Intelligence. Who can you trust?...

Whereas I agree with Frank Sturgis that the Watergate burglars were "set up," I question the reason he gives. The CIA was fully aware that relations with the People's Republic of China were bound to open up sooner or later. And of course I wanted to earn credit for that in history.

Rather, I am convinced that there was a power struggle *within* the Agency. The "faction" to which Sturgis alludes—most likely led by Richard Helms—was jealous of the Special Intelligence Unit we had developed inside the White House.

Not only was the Watergate break-in deliberately bungled in order to discredit me, but the White House taping system was never part of my domain. I knew it had been installed by the Secret Service, but I lacked access to the tapes and more important, to any switch that would shut off a recording device.

I was a prisoner in the Oval Office. A mobile prisoner, to be sure—I could go to the Cabinet Room or the Lincoln Room—but it didn't make any difference; there were bugs everywhere. They even bugged my cabin at Camp David. I was under more surveillance than Larry O'Brien could ever imagine.

If I had the tapes in my possession, don't you think I would have gotten rid of them? Just the way I did with those microfilms in the Hiss case. Everybody was recommending this—from John Connally to Chuck Colson—but I simply did not have access to the system.

I should explain that "Bay of Pigs" was our code word for the assassination of President Kennedy. When we were attempting to put the brakes on the FBI investigation of Watergate, I told Haldeman to get word to Helms that otherwise, because of E. Howard Hunt's involvement, the whole Bay of Pigs thing would open up.

Hunt was the CIA station chief in Mexico when agent Lee Harvey Oswald made contact there in 1963. The whole world already knows what a fiasco the Bay of Pigs operation turned out to be—that is, the invasion of Cuba—but because Kennedy didn't keep his campaign promise to support the exiles, he then became the prime "Bay of Pigs" target.

Had the Watergate mission not been aborted, Hunt would have continued to simulate documents blaming Kennedy and Ted Sorensen for the murder of Che Guevara, just as he forged those cables blaming Kennedy for the murder of Ngo Dinh Diem.

I hasten to add that Hunt was merely *clarifying* the issues. The Kennedy Administration *was* responsible. But what we were trying to do was hurt *Ted* Kennedy's chances if he decided to run.

That is guilt by relationship, which is wrong and irrelevant.

I was convinced that Nelson Rockefeller was behind it all. He had never forgiven me for defeating him for the Republican nomination in 1968. What with that whole 25th Amendment arrangement, I figured their chronological plan was to:

1. Get Spiro Agnew out of office.

2. Replace him with Gerald Ford.

3. Get me out of office.

4. Replace me with Ford.

5. Replace Ford (as Vice President) with Rockefeller.

6. Knock off Ford before the election by Squeaky Fromme, Sara Jane Moore, whoever.

7. Replace Ford again with Rockefeller, declare martial law and cancel the election.

    Alternatively, this could be done by killing
Jimmy Carter before the inauguration.

Now I realize how naive I was. Granted, Carter is more
progressive than I am—after all, politics is the art of finding a balance between the status quo and the force of
evolution—but it became crystal-clear to me that he had
made some kind of deal. The intelligence-gathering system knew about G. Harrold Carswell's tragic gay problem. Now, *he* would have been a fine prospect for
blackmail: "We have this photo of you and a friend in the
men's room, Justice Carswell, but don't worry, we won't
leak it!" I wonder, if I had been successful in appointing
him to the Supreme Court, how would he have voted on
the constitutionality of entrapping homosexuals? Anyway,
my suspicions were aroused when it did not come out in
the media until *after* the election—immediately before
Carter's inauguration when it was too late to do us any
good—that his son Jack had been discharged from the
Navy because of marijuana.

    Our hammer over George McGovern's head in 1972
was that his daughter had been hospitalized for an LSD
freakout. We never had to resort to using that particular
bit of intelligence, however, despite the fact that it was *we*
who had arranged for her to be "dosed" in the first place.

Woodward and Bernstein were not the only ones with
reliable sources. According to one of my contacts
in the intelligence community, the Democrats' first

choice for a presidential candidate in the 1976 elections was a southern governor—Askew of Florida—but their analysts calculated that Jimmy Carter's resemblance to Howdy Doody would provide a subconscious association in the minds of voters who were weaned on that folksy puppet.

What the American public does not realize is the impact of the long-range planning that goes on in think tanks such as Stanford Research, the Rand Corporation and the Hudson Institute. They are already beginning to orchestrate the Bimillennium, the 2000th birthday of Christ. The function of Jimmy Carter—with all his religiosity and his talk about not living in sin—is to provide an opening wedge for the Christianization of the United States. The arms manufacturers would be well pleased by a repeat performance of the Crusades. After those Korean bribes via Reverend Moon's Unification Church and the brainwashing of the Moonies, they'll finally figure it's time to make Christ an *American* again.

Incidentally, Billy Graham recently tried to convert me, the same way he did with that professional gangster Mickey Cohen. "Think what it would be like," he said, "if you were to go on an evangelistic tour with Eldridge Cleaver and Colonel Sanders."

"You mean the Kentucky Fried Chicken guy?"

"Yes, he has been born again too!"

"No, thank you, Billy, I seem to have found serenity in my own way."

230 I truly have been able to gain true humility now that Chuck Colson and Susan Atkins are saying the

same things about Jesus Christ that they were once saying about myself and Charles Manson, respectively.

History is an unending conveyor belt that either perpetuates or corrects the inaccuracies of the past.

Therefore, the first thing I wish to point out, concerning that infamous eighteen-and-a-half-minute gap in the White House tape of June 20, 1972, is that it actually lasted only eighteen-and-a-quarter minutes. At ten-thirty that morning, John Ehrlichman was in my office. We did not discuss Watergate. Before leaving, however, he handed me two sealed envelopes. One contained a gram of cocaine; the other contained a preliminary report on the surveillance of Woodward and Bernstein. This task had been assigned to Tony Ulasewicz immediately after their first story on the break-in was published in the *Washington Post*.

It was strange. Ehrlichman's own first assignment had been to spy on the Nelson Rockefeller people for us during the 1960 campaign, and now he had his own chain of command. I have noticed that Ehrlichman's brow has become more knitted as he has advanced in his career. When he left, I opened the sealed envelope and read the report. It was brief:

Bernstein, Carl: Heavy pot-smoker. Living apart from his wife. Began affair with Nora Ephron, Esquire *columnist, in New York while her husband, Dan Greenburg, book author, was at Erhard Seminar Training.*

Woodward, Bob: A loner. Clean as a hound's tooth. So far.

Then I began to "chop the coke," as they say, with a razor blade. When Bob Haldeman entered, we each took a couple of snorts. Haldeman was my Sherman Adams. I had always felt I could depend on him. We were discussing whether my itinerary for an upcoming trip to the West Coast might include Ely, Nevada, which was the birthplace of Mrs. Nixon.

"That's perfect, " Haldeman said. "We need anything we can get, PR-wise."

"But you know something, Bob? It's all image."

"Well, that is precisely the *purpose* of public relations."

"No, I mean my so-called marriage is all image. Pat and I have not, you know, slept together for nearly a dozen years. My God, I'm the President of the United States, and I can't even get laid by my own wife."

"Sir, you don't really want to talk about this?"

"And I'll tell you where it started. During the Cuban Crisis in October '62. Boy, Kennedy sure won a helluva lot of points on that one. And it could've been me confronting Khrushchev. I mean a real international shootdown, not just waving my finger in Safire's goddamn makeshift kitchen."

"That would have been the logical extension of your Russian trip."

"I tell you, the unspeakable frustration of not being in a position to negotiate that missile thing, I just couldn't get it up for Pat, plus the pressure of the California campaign was going on then too. And after we lost that election, she started talking about a divorce. We compromised with separate bedrooms."

Suddenly I stood up, walked around my desk to where Haldeman was sitting, and I ran my hand back and forth across the top of his crewcut. I am not very physically demonstrative, but I had always wanted to do that. Still, this was almost a spontaneous gesture.

"You stuck by me, Bob," I said while I was rubbing his hair. "Finch dropped out, but *you*..." I suddenly began weeping uncontrollably.

"Sir—is there anything I can do?"

Between sobs I blurted out, "Oh, sure!"—and I certainly did not intend for this to be taken literally—"Why don't you try sucking my cock, maybe *that'll* help."

To my utter astonishment, Haldeman unzipped my fly and proceeded with what can only be described as extreme efficiency. The whole thing could not have taken more than five minutes from beginning to end. He must have had some practice during his old prep school days. Neither of us said a word—before, during or after.

This misunderstanding was comparable to the time that Jeb Magruder remarked how convenient it would be if we could get rid of Jack Anderson, and G. Gordon Liddy assumed that was a direct order and rushed out to accomplish the act. If Liddy had not blabbed his "assignment" to an aide in the corridor, Anderson might not be alive today.

As for my own motivation, here was an experience not of homosexuality but of power. I realized that if I could order the Pentagon to bomb Cambodia, it was of no great consequence that I was now merely permitting my chief of staff to perform fellatio. In fact,

233

I was fully cognizant of what an honor it must have been for him.

When the incident was over, I simply returned to my desk, and although the tension of vulnerability was still in the air, we resumed our discussion as if nothing had occurred.

"Now," I said in a normal tone of voice, "what's on the agenda?"

"Sir," Haldeman began, "on this Watergate problem, it would be advantageous to us if any similar activity on the part of the Democrats could be leaked to the media."

"Well, Hoover once told me—this was right after we won in '68—he said that within the previous month, LBJ had the FBI put the bug on Agnew and me. And Ramsey Clark was attorney general then, but he never authorized it, so that was an *illegal* wiretap."

"Perfect. We start with Lyndon Johnson and work our way back."

"But no, on second thought, the LBJ tap would open up the whole Dragon Lady can of beans. I mean that was the goddamn *excuse* they had for spying on us."

Then Haldeman delivered a resounding pep talk—when he lets loose he can be an emotional marvel—about the importance of launching a counterattack against our enemies.

I must say at this point that Rose Mary Woods deserves a Medal of Honor for the way she was willing to humiliate herself by taking full blame for accidentally erasing those first five minutes rather than stand by while my public image was destroyed.

Moreover, when General Alexander Haig learned from Haldeman's notes that during those additional thirteen-and-a-quarter minutes there was a discussion of how to deal with Watergate, thereby proving that I was involved in the cover-up only three days after the break-in, Haig attributed the erasure to "sinister forces." He said this under oath in Judge John Sirica's courtroom.

Now *that* is loyalty above and beyond the call of duty.

In retrospect, I realize that H. R. Haldeman was part of the plot against me all along, always trying to ingratiate himself—anything to impress me, when actually he was trying to hurt my political career. Not that he was against me personally; I was just his particular assignment as part of an overall plan "to destroy," in the words of Frank Sturgis, "the office of the presidency."

Haldeman was a saboteur in the guise of a sycophant. In 1967, when he was a vice president at the J. Walter Thompson advertising agency, he sent me a long memo on how I could use the media in my '68 campaign. I have since learned that during World War II, various corporations—Standard Oil, Wrigley Chewing Gum, Paramount Pictures—lent their executives to the Office of Strategic Services, which later became the CIA. The Thompson Agency supplied Kenneth Hinks to be chief of the OSS planning staff. One of Haldeman's predecessors, Richard de Rochemont, a vice president of J. Walter Thompson, was offered a position with the Secret Intelligence Branch of the OSS. Another Thompson official, Donald Coster, stayed on with the CIA in South Vietnam from 1959 to 1962.

That's when Haldeman really latched on to me, in the '62 campaign. And when we lost, it was Haldeman who persuaded me to make a public fool of myself with that godawful "you-won't-have-Nixon-to-kick-around-any-more" press conference. It was Haldeman in 1972 who acted as a double agent and conspired with Dick Tuck to have all those Chinese fortune cookies contain the same message: *What about the Howard Hughes loan?* And it was Haldeman who consciously sabotaged the research on the Hiss chapter in *Six Crises*.

On one occasion I was meeting with a group of blind veterans in the Oval Office. I wanted to display my empathy with them, so I began describing the Presidential Seal, which was woven into the carpet we happened to be standing on. A blind veteran got down on his knees and started feeling that design with his hands. I closed my eyes and proceeded to do the same. It was perhaps the most spontaneous gesture of my life, although I must admit I was grateful to hear the sound of cameras whirring. I was pleased that this scene of my true humanity was being recorded for posterity. But Haldeman ordered an embargo on that photograph, ostensibly to protect the dignity of my image, because the President should never be seen in a kneeling position.

Even a year after he resigned, there he was, old faithful Bob Haldeman, backstage with me at the Grand Ole Opry in Nashville. He chided Johnny

Cash for that time he refused to sing "Welfare Cadillac" at the White House, and Cash now replied, "Should I do it tonight and dedicate the song to you now that *you're* on welfare?"

Haldeman did not appreciate the humor in that. He was too preoccupied with the betrayal he had in mind. He handed me a yellow yo-yo and said, "This will really please the crowd. It's an official Roy Acuff model." I put the yo-yo in my pocket. Haldeman did not mention that the string had been loosened at the bottom, so when I was onstage and I flung that yo-yo down, it just *stayed* there. Once again, Haldeman had transformed the President into an asshole.

It was Haldeman who had urged me to install the White House taping system. It was Haldeman who hired Alexander Butterfield, who told the whole world about the tapes, and told the FBI about E. Howard Hunt. Butterfield brought in Al Wong to set up the system and check it every day. And it was Wong who brought James McCord onto the team. It's all so obvious now.

One thing about Gerald Ford, though: He keeps his promises—not only to pardon me, but also his promise to fire Alexander Butterfield, even though Ford was actually grateful to him. As for me, I should have listened to L. Patrick Gray when he warned me, "People on your staff are trying to mortally wound you."

My wife, Pat, has sworn to me that she never told anyone about our marital difficulties, and of course I believe her, so the leak to Woodward and Bernstein could *only* have come from Haldeman. On top of all his other betrayals, he must have been Deep Throat too.

There was one plan of the White House Plumbers that never came to fruition. It involved the theft of Patricia Ellsberg's dental records. This was my own idea—not Haldeman's, not Hunt's, not Liddy's—*they* were satisfied with obtaining the records of Daniel Ellsberg's psychiatrist.

But I remembered that the first time Alger Hiss confronted Whittaker Chambers, he requested to see his *teeth*. Hiss explained to me that he suspected Chambers might be someone he had known years before, and he wanted to see his teeth to make sure.

Well, that recollection inspired me. We were able to obtain the dental records of Ellsberg's wife, all right, but did not have the opportunity to use them in helping to prove that she was guilty of espionage. I could not imagine exactly how we were going to achieve this but I did know that, *whatever*, it would be accepted by the public simply because the charge itself was so "off the wall."

How odd that Whittaker Chambers, the dignified translator of *Bambi*, had been asked to publicly show his teeth as if he were some kind of stud at a horse show. I have never been able to forget that moment.

The paradox of our nation is that we turn our vices into virtues. As the truth about political assassinations—from Malcolm X to Mrs. Dorothy Hunt—finally begins to emerge, we may truthfully say, "Only in America does there exist the freedom to reveal how insidious we have been—and then to continue in our insidious way with an even more determined spirit."

I still believe that the United States is the greatest country in the world. It is also the greatest show on earth.

I once had a vision of myself leaving Washington the way Jimmy Durante used to end his TV program, standing in a spotlight and bowing gracefully to the audience, then walking back a few steps into another spotlight, bowing again and so on. Instead, I ended up sounding as helpless as Hal the Computer in the movie *2001*, unable to control my own memory banks.

My consolation for this personal tragedy is summed up in Jeane Dixon's prediction: "Historians yet unborn are going to take the facts, and Richard Nixon will go down as a great President. They're going to find that the price the world is paying for trying to discredit Nixon is going to be that we'll practically lose our freedom."

In the meantime, I am, at long last, completely at peace with myself. It has been worth all the struggle.

Thomas Eagleton Seagull

1972

This fable was inspired by its own title, a purely whimsical combination of Jonathan Livingston Seagull, *a New Age mystical book by Richard Bach about a seagull who was determined to fly, and Senator Thomas Eagleton, who was dropped by Democratic presidential candidate George McGovern as his running mate when it was discovered that Eagleton had once received electroshock treatment for depression.*

In the very earliest time, when both people and animals lived on earth, a person could become an animal if he wanted to and an animal could become a human being. Sometimes they were people and sometimes animals and there was no difference. All spoke the same language. That was the time when words were like magic. The human mind had mysterious powers. A word spoken by chance might have strange consequences. It would suddenly come alive and what people wanted to happen could happen—all you had to do was say it. Nobody could explain this: That's the way it was.

—"Magic Words" (after Nalungiaq),
from *Eskimo Shaking the Pumpkin:*
Traditional Poetry of the Indian North Americas,
anthologized by Jerome Rothenberg

Then I said to myself: 'Self, it won't be pleasant. It won't be sweet. It won't be easy, but it's got to be done.' So later that night, we decided to hold a press conference in Los Angeles the following morning, then one in Honolulu, and again today in San Francisco. I've got to win. I've got to do it for [my son] Terry. I've got to make it for Terry.

"I don't know where I'll be five years from now, but I know that I'll look back upon this experience as a positive turning point in my life. I'm stronger and wiser because of it. I've taken the heat by myself and I haven't crumbled. I'm not being smugly complacent, but I think that I have come through a tough crucible, and I feel a helluva lot stronger as a result. I feel like a man.

—Senator Thomas Eagleton
Newsweek, August 7, 1972

Chapter 1

It was evening, and the sunset beyond the county dump created a disquieting silhouette of obsolescence.

This was dinnertime for the elite flock of gulls who ate there each day. They were feasting upon a delicious spread of moldy caviar that had been discarded by a friendly neighborhood restaurant.

Down on the beach, the tide was starting to come in. Snakelike seaweed was beginning to gather in clusters along the shore. Fading jellyfish were returning home to have their bodies tie-dyed again. And

Thomas Eagleton Seagull was busy trying to build a castle in the sand.

He didn't have a pail or a shovel, but this lack merely served to increase his sense of determination. He knew only that he was going to build a sand castle even if the ocean planned to wash it away.

Waves of salt water splashed over him even as he was squeezing out the final turrets from the mud inside his beak. Yet he quickly repaired the moats, making them deeper by digging sideways with his webbed feet.

He looked at the castle he had almost completed, and a surge of pride ran through him as he shook the sand from his wings. At the precise moment he was feeling most proud of his accomplishment, however, the tide swept it away.

"Come back!" he called to the sand castle. "I'm not finished playing with you!"

"There'll be others," the sand castle called back. "Besides, I have my own life to live!" And it merged with the sea.

"There must be more to life than feeding off human garbage," mumbled Thomas Eagleton Seagull to himself. He was attempting to develop his willpower to the point where he would be able to transcend his species. "Why should I have to settle for leftovers as a seagull," he asked himself," "when I could *become a human being* and dine on the original?"

And so, as an act of faith, he moved just a little farther up the beach and began to build another sand castle.

243

Chapter 2

The idea of changing his species had originally occurred to him one afternoon while he was feeling depressed because some friends had died as a result of a baffling oil slick in the ocean.

Flying moodily past a house with a picture window in the living room, he noticed that inside, the color television set was on. It happened to be tuned to *Let's Make a Deal*.

One of the contestants, a woman wearing a seagull costume, seemed to be experiencing a fit of ecstasy. Thomas Eagleton Seagull naturally assumed that she was pretending to be a gull.

"I'll trade places with you, lady," he squawked.

That spontaneous outburst would turn into an obsession. The image of role reversal had imprinted itself indelibly on his psyche.

Each day he flew around the house with the picture window, expecting to get a glimpse of the same woman on TV again. At first he tried to glide by with a nonchalant expression on his face so that none of the inhabitants would get suspicious.

As he grew increasingly confident, he would circle slowly in front of the living room, peering in unabashedly. Smirking with hope.

He never saw the woman in the seagull costume again. But in the process, Thomas Eagleton Seagull became a regular—if intermittent—viewer of daytime television.

Soap operas especially fascinated him. Everyone always looked so perturbed. The tension of their grim demeanor was relieved only by an occasional Smiling Savior holding up a bottle of pellets or a box of flakes or maybe patting a machine or else pouring the contents of a box into a machine.

And Thomas Eagleton Seagull was going to join their species. This became his all-consuming passion.

Chapter 3

Molly Salami Seagull was his favorite companion. He could really confide in her. Although she had no desire to become human herself, at least she recognized the depth of *his* yearning.

One night they stayed up late, sitting and chatting in front of a small bonfire on the outskirts of the county dump.

"I was watching some surfers today," Thomas Eagleton Seagull began. "I was trying to imagine what it must be like to be human. And, I don't know, I mean, the ocean seems like such an impersonal thing, but when it's carrying you along like that, it must also seem like a very personal thing. Wouldn't that be a wonderful way to relate to the whole world?"

"But you can already do that as a seagull," said Molly Salami Seagull. "When humans go clamming, though, they can't catch clams the way we can. They have to get dressed in those dark rubber coveralls and then they go into the ocean and prod the mud with those big sticks or whatever."

"But it was a human who built this fire. Can a seagull build a fire?"

"A seagull can't even light a match," she admitted.

"Or play with a Frisbee. We aren't *built* for Frisbee. But wouldn't it be fun to be able to toss a Frisbee back and forth? I was watching some people on the beach with a Frisbee, and they looked so graceful you wouldn't *believe* it. And the philosophical inferences one could draw—"

"You're already beginning to *sound* human."

"Let me tell you, I stood there watching that Frisbee go back and forth, back and forth, until a message came through, and it was that *time keeps happening no matter what you do!*"

"Oh, sure, but if you can conceive of that as a sea–gull, then why do you have to be human?"

"Because as a human I could do different things all the time. As a seagull I'm limited." He gazed into the fire. "I want to open myself up to new experiences. I don't even want to say the same thing twice."

"That's exactly what you told me yesterday," said Molly Salami Seagull.

Chapter 4

One night, Thomas Eagleton Seagull had a dream. He preferred to think of it as a vision.

A pair of spirits had come to battle for his allegiance. He couldn't see them clearly. The Spirit of Permissiveness appeared as a swirl of rainbow. And the Spirit of Productivity was an ethereal crazy quilt of brand names. But he could hear their voices as distinctly as his own.

"If you wish to become human," said the Spirit of Permissiveness, "you must learn to make moral choices."

"Morality is relative," argued the Spirit of Productivity. "You must base your choices, therefore, on the relative strength of written guarantees."

Thomas Eagleton Seagull asked, "How will I know what a correct decision is when I have to make one?"

"Ah," said the Spirit of Permissiveness, "but you have already started on that course simply by wanting to become human. That's what makes you different from other seagulls—your dissatisfaction with being one yourself. You have made a value judgment. You've placed a higher value on being human. So whenever you are faced with a choice, you must base it on what you consider the best values."

"Comparison shopping is a good method," added the Spirit of Productivity. "You can really make a fine art out of being a consumer. Just wait till you discover the pleasure to be derived from the creative act of making a purchase."

"No, no," interjected the Spirit of Permissiveness. "I'm not referring to goods and services. I'm referring to goods and evils. Abstract principles to live by. Nothing tangible. The earth is *covered* with tangible rubbish."

"Litter," announced the Spirit of Productivity, "is the feces of an affluent society."

"No shit," replied the Spirit of Permissiveness.

Thomas Eagleton Seagull woke up suddenly and took it as an omen. "No shit," he said to himself. He kept repeating the phrase over and over again. "No shit. No shit. No shit." The more he continued, the better it felt. He alternated the accent. First: "*No* shit. *No*

247

shit. *No* shit." Then: "No *shit*. No *shit*. No *shit*." Now he changed the rhythm: "No-shit. No-shit-no. Shit-no. Shit-no. Shit-no." The corresponding change of order gave him an intensified giddiness. As if to further escape the dilemma posed by his dual visitation, he began to spout the words together faster and faster—"Noshitnoshit-noshitnoshitnoshitnoshitnoshitno..."—until finally they blended into one flowing stream of noshitness.

What a delirious accomplishment, to have a personal mantra before you were even a person.

Chapter 5

The next morning, two men who had been watching him for days placed a metal band around his leg while he was meditating on the beach. He had been chosen.

One of the ornithologists left his binoculars there by accident, and Thomas Eagleton Seagull had an experience in astral projection. He looked into the binoculars and saw *himself* magnified.

For the first time, he thought of the webbing between his claws as ugly. Back at the county dump, he pecked off a pair of booties from a big broken doll that had been thrown away, and he began wearing them on his own embarrassing feet.

That night he had a vision. He preferred to think of it as a nightmare. The Essence of Insecurity arrived to tell him that the only thing he had to fear was not being *accepted* as human.

"You've been observed talking to yourself a lot. That's a no-no," the Essence of Insecurity

248

harangued him. "And just smell your wingpits. *Peeeyiu-uuuu!* What are you going to do when you get *arms*? A human being's armpits are supposed to be charmpits. Your breath isn't so attractive, either. And then there's the matter of your crotch. *Yecchhh!* Furthermore, you have half a hemorrhoid hanging in there. What are you trying to do, get your name into the *Guinness Book of World Weirdoes*? And I hate to bring this up, but nobody is *ever* going to like you as long as you're constipated!"

"No shit," muttered Thomas Eagleton Seagull. "No shit, no shit, no shit," he continued, refocusing his attention until the Essence of Insecurity disappeared. But as soon as he became aware of achieving that control he lost it. Now a waiter he hadn't summoned brought him a tray with a giant fortune cookie on it.

With his beak, he pulled out a strip of Gospel. His fortune said: SUCCESS IS A PROCESS YOU REALIZE. That confused him, but the strip didn't end there. He pulled further, and there was another: EVERY MOMENT IS A REINCARNATION OF YOURSELF. He didn't understand what that meant, either. He pulled still more, as though he were a stockbroker with a ticker tape, and the message was: EVERY MOMENT IS A PARODY OF YOURSELF. He just didn't know when to stop. The next one said: ANY DISCIPLINE THAT IS NOT FUN IS SLAVERY. He was disturbed because he couldn't tell whether these messages were aimed at a seagull or a human being. He pulled the tape once again and it said: THOU SHALT NOT GOOSE A NURSING MOTHER. He tried noshitting for a while—but this time without paying attention to his attention—and, indeed, the break-through that he had been waiting for came.

Thomas Eagleton Seagull couldn't help but notice that the metal band that had been placed around his leg was now developing blurry numbers in a circle around the vague outline of a rodent wearing short pants and with outstretched arms.

It was a quarter to three when he looked at his embryonic Mickey Mouse watch and shouted, "The stigmata!"

He was on his way to being grounded at last.

Chapter 6

He had gone to say goodbye to Molly Salami Seagull. She asked, "Don't you have any feeling of loyalty to your species?"

"Do you call it loyal," he responded, "for our flock to dine luxuriously here at the county dump while thousands upon thousands of our fellow birds are dying each year of botulism by the sea? As a seagull, I can't do anything about that. As a human, I promise to investigate it thoroughly."

"Remember your promise," she called out as he flew off to the beach to begin building sand castles once again, only with more and more speed, so that by late morning he was able to fashion an exquisite fortress and then destroy it himself even before the waves could wash it away.

He knew now that he was ready. For his last meal as a seagull he nibbled away at a mushroom that was growing out of some cow dung in the pasture.

250

They came in broad daylight, two redeemers in human form, Language and Behavior. In awe, he watched them take away the sign that said COUNTY DUMP and replace it with one that said REFUSE DISPOSAL SITE.

He eavesdropped on their conversation.

"What are we going to do about *sonic boom*?" asked Language.

"I've checked with the Air Force about that," replied Behavior. "They are instituting a public relations campaign called The Sounds of Freedom."

"No shit," said Thomas Eagleton Seagull. He began to repeat it over and over to himself, so rapidly this time that at the point where his consciousness overran the speed of light, he started to hear a ringing in his ears and he blacked out.

When he came to, he could still hear the ringing in his ears. He opened his eyes and saw that it was a telephone ringing. Instinctively, he reached to pick it up and said, "Hello."

"Is this Thomas Eagleton Seagull?"

"Speaking," he said, unzipping and zipping his fly for the first time in his life.

Abruptly, he realized he was a man! He had actually achieved humanhood!

Yes, he was now a grown-up person, but he was still wearing baby booties. He removed them in a panic to see if his feet were still webbed.

They started unwebbing right there in front of his startled eyes, while the booties turned into

Thom McAn loafers with a pair of shiny pennies staring back up at him.

Not only that, but a voice on the other end of the phone was inviting him to be Potential Second-Best Human Being. He was so excited that he lost his equilibrium and said, "Quack-quack!"

"What was that?" asked the voice on the other end of the phone. "I'm afraid we have a poor connection."

"I said, 'I'm flabbergasted!'"

Then another voice got on the other end of the phone and told him to prepare an acceptance speech. "Oh, and there's just one other thing," the voice added. "Do you have any old skeletons rattling around in your closet?"

Filled with elation, Thomas Eagleton Seagull had to get himself centered. He looked at his wristwatch and said, "No shit" into the telephone.

The voice on the other end said, "Good," and hung up.

Chapter 7

"It was all over in a matter of minutes. No further investigation was made into Eagleton's medical history. Senator McGovern asked for someone to get Senator Eagleton on the phone. While he was in the other room talking to Eagleton, Mrs. McGovern walked into the room. She leaned over to me and whispered, 'Who is it?' I told her Eagleton.

"'That's not possible,' she cried, hurrying from the room to find her husband. But it was too late. McGovern had already asked Eagleton and he had accepted. Frank Mankiewicz was on the phone talking to him and McGovern was in one of the bedrooms where she

found him. I never did find out what had caused that uncharacteristic outburst by Mrs. McGovern. Throughout the campaign, her political judgment was frequently the best."
—Pierre Salinger
Life magazine

"So this is humanity," he thought, pushing the button marked LOBBY in the hotel elevator. He had decided to take a stroll outside while the writers were working on his acceptance speech.

Through the glass doors leading to the street, he could see a man wearing a magnificent uniform. "Must be somebody very special," he thought, striding through the lobby. "I'll find out."

As if by telepathy, the man in the magnificent uniform opened the door for him and said, "Good afternoon, sir," with such respect that he must already have known he was addressing one who had been selected as Potential Second-Best Human Being.

"How did you know?" asked Thomas Eagleton Seagull.

"I'm the doorperson, sir. It's my job to know."

"How did you get to be a doorperson?"

"Through reincarnation, sir. In past lives, I've always been dependent on others. But I struggled to be righteous, and now others are finally dependent on me. I am a living symbol of protection against burglary. I am also the embodiment of small talk. Nevertheless, between the lines of football plays and barometer readings, by my mere presence I am able to communicate, on some level of consciousness—throughout the year no matter what month or season—an appreciation of that holy day when we celebrate the birth of That Great Doorperson in the Sky."

It was like suddenly being thrust into a spiritual wonderland. In a daze, Thomas Eagleton Seagull wandered by the swimming pool. It was filled with milk and white sugar. Poolside, a parent was speaking words of encouragement to a child practicing the backstroke.

"Harder," cheered the parent. "Try harder. Don't you want to grow up and bear witness to the electric shaver?"

It was a minor miracle, turning anachronism into clairvoyance, much like turning swords into plowshares, or a felony into a misdemeanor.

Several blocks away, a street-corner speaker was insisting: "The reason they're against gay liberation is that if we come out of the closet, then they can't blackmail us."

"You people are disgusting!" yelled a heckler. "All homosexuals should be given vasectomies!"

"Now that," mused Thomas Eagleton Seagull, "would be conspicuous consumption."

He was amazed at his immediate grasp of economic theory.

As if to test his own programming, he asked himself, "Is there ever a spiritual basis for conspicuous consumption?"

And he answered himself, "Yes, if a Jewish grandmother owns two sets of false teeth, one for meat and one for dairy."

Here he was, all prepared to be an after-dinner speaker, although he had yet to eat his first dinner in this new body.

He walked along, buzzing with awareness of his novel condition. Now, as a human, he realized in retrospect that as a seagull watching television through a picture window, he had misinterpreted the true nature of the Deity.

"God is Packaging," he whispered to a passing senior citizen.

Chapter 8

The park in the city of the Human Being Convention had been transformed into a veritable sideshow of proselytization.

He was observing a tug-of-war between a group of Rosicrucians and a group of Theosophists—they were not using a rope—when he was offered a marijuana cigarette by a long-haired fellow. Thomas Eagleton Seagull was so high on life that he forgot this was illegal.

He flashed on a sense memory: that time he ate those seeds out of somebody's garbage in the county dump and got a pleasantly dizzy feeling afterward.

Now a woman was telling him, "Don't hepburn that joint."

Since he seemed open, she explained that her movement was concerned with female roles in this society.

"I was jilling off in bed the other night," she said, "and I realized that I was using *myself* as a sex object."

He was busy coughing, so she continued:

"But it's more than just that. My entire lifestyle is limited by my finances. If my employer paid me what I deserve, regardless of my gender, I wouldn't have to come home every day to a crummy apartment with cuntroaches crawling all over the kitchen."

As they walked along they passed a Sufi leader wrestling with his conscience, a Subudite changing her name and her mind, and a Freemason in judicial robes paving a path to purgatory.

"It's discouraging," she said. "Even the *I Ching* talks about the superior man."

"I feel a great deal of compassion for your plight," said Thomas Eagleton Seagull, "but what are you doing to improve the situation?"

"Personally, I'm trying to break into organized crime," she replied. "They run civilization from a male-supremacist orientation. And we have to overthrow that hierarchy, because the power filters all the way down to the control of local police stations. When I become Ms. Big, the first thing I'm going to do is put a stop to undercover cops committing rape."

They passed an assemblage of youthful zealots singing what sounded to his stoned ears like an obscene chant, perhaps the plaint of the wife of an impotent Hindu priest:

Hurry, Krishna! Hurry, Krishna! Krishna, Krishna!
Hurry, hurry! . . .

"At least they've broken up the nuclear family," said his new friend.

Chapter 9

It was during his first press conference that Thomas Eagleton Seagull almost slipped up about his past. The questions and answers had been proceeding smoothly. Then a reporter for *Speck* magazine spoke up:

"Sir, I'd like to call your attention to the issue of overpopulation. Recently, a prominent researcher, Dr. Max Feelbetter, in order to focus public attention on this crisis, took his own life by setting out to sea on a raft constructed entirely of Q-Tips. Now, my question is, sir, what specific remedy do you offer that would be an effective safeguard against, well, too many people?"

The combination of the hot klieg lights and the image of his old ocean momentarily befuddled Thomas Eagleton Seagull, and the response he gave shoved him right off the evolutionary ladder:

"Well, we've always devoured each other's young as if they were those of another species."

He was referring to the way gulls preyed upon eggs and chicks in his colony. There was an awkward silence among the reporters, and then that was replaced by awkward laughter. He must have been making a sardonic joke.

The *Speck* correspondent persisted: "Sir, your allusion to *A Modest Proposal* by Jonathan Swift is appreciated as comic relief, but birth control and abortion are nonetheless serious matters."

"Of course they are," said the Potential Second-Best Human Being, recovering from his fleeting lapse. "But this is a predicament that should be left up to the individual states. Otherwise, we would be guilty of unwarranted infringement upon the separation of powers guaranteed by our Constitution...."

Chapter 10

"What's your sign?" the waitress asked as she handed him a menu.

"I don't have one," he answered.

"Well, when were you born? I mean, if you might become our Second-Best Human Being, I would certainly be curious to know more about the direction of your karma."

"What's karma?"

It was Thomas Eagleton Seagull's karma that he should not understand the concept of karma.

The restaurant was uncrowded, and the waitress was able to continue their discussion between tables. She discovered that he could verbalize quite skillfully about social issues, from crime in the streets of America to drugs in the cadavers from Vietnam, but that he attributed a lack of will to the perpetrators and victims alike.

He wanted to give his own astounding advancement as an example of strong will, but this revelation was a luxury he could not afford.

"Do you mean to say," he asked, "that suffering people are merely helpless instruments of bad karma?"

"Why make moral judgments? I've traveled in many foreign countries. Once in Egypt I met a starving man. He was in pitiful shape. But I realized that suffering people serve a higher purpose by reminding those of us who are more fortunate not to complain. So I was torn between the impulse to feed him and the impulse not to interfere with his destiny."

"And which did you do?"

"I was about to give him a piece of bread and a taste of cider from my flask when he prevented me. He said that it would be an act of charity on my part to refuse his request for food, because if he were to die on the road to Mecca, he would become a martyr. So when he begged again with his outstretched hand, I knew it was only a test of my resistance."

The waitress observed that Thomas Eagleton Sea-gull was eating his dessert—a slice of pumpkin pie—by starting at the crusty base of its isosceles triangle. This was another slip-up, in the guise of an idiosyncrasy.

"Tipping is good karma," she said as she gave him his check.

Chapter 11

There was a line of seekers waiting for an audience with the Six-Week-Old Guru, who would answer only one question per person. A Baby-Talk Translator stood by to give the gurgles a more articulate form.

It was legend that the infant's emerging ego had been baptized at the altar of excess chromosome damage so that it had absolute empathy with whomever.

Eventually, Thomas Eagleton Seagull's turn came to ask a question. He had pondered it carefully. Now he looked into the carriage and spoke: "Is there free will?"

The Six-Week-Old Guru stared up at his Mickey Mouse watch and gurgled.

The Baby-Talk Translator translated: "It's four-thirty-three, time for the moon to go into Capricorn."

"Is that the answer to my question?"

"No," replied the Baby-Talk Translator. "You forgot to say 'Your Perfection' first."

"Oh, I'm terribly sorry." He addressed the infant again. "Your Perfection, is there free will?"

The Six-Week-Old Guru goo-gahed something in return, which translated as "I can't decide," and spit up pabulum all over a new saffron bib.

Thomas Eagleton Seagull regurgitated on himself at the very moment that a reporter from *Speck* magazine was taking a leak and checking it out. He was investigating a tip that the newly selected Potential Second-Best Human Being had actually been a seagull.

The reporter's horror over what he discovered by simple research was overshadowed only by his joy at being the one chosen to carry the torch for his magazine's slogan: "Ye shall know the truth, and the truth shall make ye Silly Putty!"

When the news broke, Thomas Eagleton Seagull tried to understand the basis of his anxiety. After all, he had originally wanted just to be human, not the Second-Best Human Being, let alone Potential, so what difference should it make to him now that his background presented a possible obstacle to that goal?

Yet it bothered him. Didn't other humans appreciate the energy he had harnessed so positively to transcend seagullhood?

Besides, it was a matter of public gossip that the

man who was presently the Best Human Being had himself been a turtle. More important, he continued to exhibit outrageous symptoms of turtle consciousness. Why was everybody ignoring *that* so readily?

But then a story was published that Thomas Eagleton Seagull had once been guilty of drunk flying. It didn't matter that such gossip was unprovable. The stench of vomit still clung to his aura.

Was this to be his fulfillment of the human dream?

Chapter 12

He came down gradually from the euphoria of his temporary status. The weight of prejudice against his previous incarnation was eventually deemed by leading editorial columnists to be too great for Thomas Eagleton Seagull to continue being regarded as Potential Second-Best Human Being.

Paradoxically, he was welcomed as a hero wherever he went after he had been banished from official consideration.

He received several offers to do commercials—for Hartz Mountain birdseed, for Trans World Airlines, for Alioto's Seafood Restaurant—but he declined them all.

He refused to consider a publisher's $1,000,000 contract to write a book called *The Sensuous Seagull.*

He turned down a professorial post in the Department of Applied Anthropomorphism at Stanford University. "I'd rather teach by example," he explained.

However, he was approached by the Survival of Will (SOW) Frozen Sperm Bank with a request he chose to accept. This was a worldwide organization based in Las Vegas that specialized in selective breeding for the future.

"We believe that competing ideologies are all subordinate to the strength of the will itself," expounded the director. "And so we invite men from science, industry, the arts, government, communications—we invite men who have in common the proven will to achieve, no matter what, to sow their seed in our laboratories, to preserve that mysterious force in their genes that will result in the ultimate triumph of the will—"

"Wait." Thomas Eagleton Seagull recalled his encounter with the woman he had met in the park. "Don't you have any frozen ovum too? I mean for the sake of equality."

"No way," replied the director. "That would require gestation to take place outside the womb. We must draw the line *some*where."

Thomas Eagleton Seagull had an impulse to say, "Let's just forget the whole thing," but he didn't want to offend the director, who went on:

"Naturally, we don't want to play God. But inasmuch as fifty percent of the spermatozoa die off in the freezing process, there is, in effect, a biological selection as well as our own admittedly fallible screening procedure."

"I do have one reservation," interjected Thomas Eagleton Seagull. "I would not want any offspring of mine, no matter how strong-willed, to be subjected to ostracism because of having been sired by me."

"Not to worry," the director reassured him. "You

see, we have concluded that pride can function as a *diversion* from exercising one's will. And, of course, being ashamed of one's specific ancestry works the other side of that same coin. Consequently, we mix all our donors' semen into one big frozen *superior* collective unconscious, to allow for an even *further* elimination of the weak. Thus, you can never be sure if it is *your* specific spermatozoon that will do the fertilizing. This method is our corollary to the military-firing-squad protocol that always includes one rifle loaded with blanks, so that each member can live with the possibility that his was not the fatal trigger. Conversely, no SOW descendants of yours will ever know for certain that there was a seagull in their past."

Chapter 13

The Survival of Will Frozen Sperm Bank had an exclusive contract with Soulmate Temporaries to provide those individuals who participated in the program as Receivers of fresh semen in the company condoms.

In the Waterbed Room at the Sperm Bank, Cleo, the partner assigned to Thomas Eagleton Seagull, had a surprise for him. She donned a seagull costume after they were both naked.

Cleo managed to smile seductively; she had been promised a huge bonus by the director of the Sperm Bank for the extremely specialized performance that would be required of her.

After a while, Thomas Eagleton Seagull began repeating her name: "Cleo...Cleo...Cleo..." Certain of his readiness, she assumed her position. She squatted down on hands and knees. The ruffle of her lifting tail enticed him into a strange kind of intoxication. He started moving his neck as though he were wearing an invisible stereo headset.

Situating himself behind her, he raised his bent arms outward till they reached shoulder level. Then, the rasping voice of his alter ego intoned a familiar cadence—"No shit, no shit, no shit, no shit, *no shit, no shit, no shit, no shit,* NO SHIT, NO SHIT, NO SHIT, NO SHIT, *NO SHIT!*"— as he mounted her.

She kept rubbing the back of her seagull head against his chest, occasionally turning around and tweaking the hair around his nipples with her beak.

Just before climaxing, she yelled out: "I'm fucking Thomas Eagleton Seagull!"

In return, he screeched: "I'm fucking Molly Salami Seagull!"

And he ejaculated in the process, going, "Hwa...hwa...hwa."

Having hypnotized himself into a lump of no-thought, he fell off Cleo.

When he regained consciousness, she was gone. He felt relieved at being left alone, because now he could comb his hair. He didn't feel comfortable doing that in front of anybody.

A tinge of regret seared his nude body as he remembered preening his feathers once. For an instant he wished he could unwind, back to that time, the Mickey Mouse watch he had never removed from his wrist.

Chapter 14

The next day, a Creature with Two Heads paid him a surprise visit. One head was Reality and the other was Paranoia. Each was a virtuoso ventriloquist, so it was impossible to tell which was speaking. Sometimes one head would be saying something and the other would suddenly continue in mid-sentence.

"Tell me," said the Creature. "What do you think is the greatest difference you have found between being a seagull and being a human?"

"I have a soul now."

"No, no, you've always had a soul. What you have now that you didn't have then is a reputation. An immortal reputation. Your soul is how you spend your passion. But your reputation is the image others have of you regardless of the administration of your soul." He began setting up a motion-picture projector. "And now I want to show you a little movie."

The film must have been taken through a one-way mirror at the Sperm Bank, for there on the screen was Thomas Eagleton Seagull's copulation scene of the day before.

"What do you plan to do with this film?"

"Oh, nothing special. We simply keep them all in vaults. We are supplied by Soulmate Temporaries not only with ravishing women such as Cleo, but also with homosexual men, sadomasochists, coprophiliacs, plus an assortment of wild and domesticated animals." The Creature held out an imaginary fan of playing cards. "Pick a perversion, any perversion. One might say that our films are a form of control insurance, along with nonsexual exploits such as bribery, embezzlement, smuggling. Whatever. But unless you plan to rock the proverbial boat, you really don't have anything to worry about."

Thomas Eagleton Seagull had never been so depressed. He felt trapped as a human and just wanted to escape.

"Why do you want to control people?" he asked.

"It's the only way we can stay in power. Regulation of the educational system is the fundamental target on our agenda. You see, we have an actual timetable for seizing total control, as measured by the grand scale of our pyramid structure: Provocateurs, Informers and Entrappers Tactical Yardstick—PIETY." The Creature brought out an immense organizational chart to illustrate his scenario. "Now cheer up," he said. "The past doesn't exist anymore, except in our vaults. Nor will the present seem so bleak in the future. So try to have your retrospect in advance, and you'll be content."

Despite the source, this advice worked. In fact, when a rock group called the Blind Munchies produced a hit record utilizing the soundtrack of his Sperm Bank film, Thomas Eagleton Seagull might even have regretted his anonymity, save for the secret royalties—a sort of consolation prize from the Creature with Two Heads—which helped support his family.

He had acquired a wife and two children. It was an enigma to him that he was afraid to tell them what it was he was protecting them from, especially since if he told them, then he would no longer be afraid that they would find out.

What kind of world was this, where strangers knew more about you than your family?

Chapter 15

He could hardly believe that he was being interviewed on the *Tonight* show.

Ed McMahon had just finished doing a commercial for a vibrator to be used only for the prevention of insomnia, called Dil-Doze.

Now Johnny Carson was saying, "Hey, somebody told me that you went to a sperm bank...."

A spasm of terror scattered itself throughout Thomas Eagleton Seagull's body. He knew that on this program they sometimes showed surprise film footage. But were they *now* going to present him and Cleo engaged in coitus for millions of unseen viewers? Was this the logical extension of spectator conversation?

"Well, Johnny, that's true, yes," he began to answer. His hesitation was surrounded by a slightly tense silence. "Now, I'm not trying to skirt the question," he wanted to say, "but can we talk about that another time? You could even show the film that was taken at the sperm bank. I've talked it over with my loved ones, and although we hadn't really thought in terms of network television, that would be a calculated risk based on our decision. But right now, Johnny, I'd rather share with you and your viewing audience an esoteric experience I had this morning. I drove from my hotel down to the beach at Malibu, and I was listening to the ocean. It has so many different tonal levels and rhythms. This used to be our music, you know. Anyway, after a while, I heard a Voice. 'I am Your Own Computer,' it said. 'I am the sum total of all the information that has been fed to Me.' I asked, 'Do all human beings have a Computer like You?' 'Everybody has His Own Computer, but each is unique. You are the only one who has a Computer just like Me, because each individually franchised Computer has amassed different information on which its conclusions are based. I, in turn, give you information all the time, even when you don't consult Me, but sometimes you are being insidiously fed by other Computers and you begin to substitute Them for Me. And when you do that, you, in turn, affect still *other* people's Computers. You must pay attention to Your Own Computer. But you, Thomas Eagleton Seagull, who came into this world totally innocent yet totally articulate, who fed Me a variety of new information joyously, already you have begun to ignore Me. When you told the interviewer from *Speck* magazine that you had to become Potential Second-Best Human Being for the sake of your son, I was saying to you, "What about your *daughter*?" But did you listen to Me? Oh, no. And just what do you think that did to *Her* Own Computer? We feed on Ourselves too, you understand. Whenever you desensitize anyone else's Computer, you automatically limit the associative powers of Your Own. So. Now that you have found out the Horn of Plenty is filled with the seeds of extortion, do you realize that they must have known from the beginning that you had been a seagull? That they knew you would be another diversion to their advantage?' Well, Johnny, I was shocked, to say the least. I wondered aloud, 'But what would be their motivation?' My Own Computer responded, 'Survival of the fittest reputations. When you were a sea–gull, you never asked why, you just did what you had to do. But you see, the ones who have something on *you*, well, *others* have something on *them.* The fear of public humiliation is a heavy burden. And the threat of prison is a shroud of domination. Moreover, for those who have already been there, the possibility of parole revocation pro-vides the soldiers of PIETY necessary to manipulate a state of division and conquest. You know you are dealing with experts in disseminating false propaganda, to make people suspicious, not only of simulated skyjackers and serial snipers, but also of each other, until they welcome repression. You must be kind to each other's Computers. You have a responsibility to be careful of what informa-tion you feed someone else's Computer. And feel free to call on Your Own Computer whenever you want a real look-see beyond the data.' And the Voice just disappeared, Johnny. Now, I'm not a preacher or anything like that, but I do feel a deep loyalty to my species...."

That's what he *wanted* to say, but apparently he did-n't want to say it strongly enough.

Instead, all he said was: "Well, Johnny, that's true, yes—I went to a sperm bank the other day and they could-n't even freeze it."

The studio audience gave him a standing ovation.

"They really love you," said Johnny Carson. "You're a great guest."

"No, they're only applauding for their own perception."

And they applauded him for saying *that*.

He gazed longingly at the package that Johnny Carson had to hold up on a pedestal. He felt so ashamed. What had happened to his freedom of will? As a seagull, he had never found it necessary to rationalize his behavior. But now he knew that if he were to say what he believed, they would have booed him. They would have accused him of spreading paranoia. They would have thought he was crazy.

Although he had been a human being for only a few months, Thomas Eagleton Seagull had already absorbed, as if by osmosis, the basic method of survival in his new environment.

He had learned how to fake sanity.

Chapter 16

The problem of predestination was weighing heavily on his mind. He sought out an Ancient Indian Sage who told him that there was indeed a Divine Plan—spontaneity.

"When you leave here," the Sage predicted, "you will immediately have a confrontation with a stranger. As a sacrifice to the Omnipotent Presence, you will give that stranger your wristwatch. Do you agree to carry out this prophecy of your own volition?"

"Gosh, I don't know. This would be the first night I slept without my watch on."

"You must have faith in faith."

"Okay, I'll do it!"

270

As soon as he got outside, a young man pursued

him much in the manner of a dope peddler. "Hey, mister," he murmured in a clandestine fashion. "Do you want Eternity?"

"I beg your pardon?"

"You have to atone for your sins."

"I don't have any sins."

"You cannot live with the Lord forever if you won't confess your sins now. How can you petition for forgiveness if you pretend you have nothing to forgive?"

"I'm not pretending. I just can't think of any sins."

"*That's* a sin."

Thomas Eagleton Seagull thought back. He had once been a seagull, but that wasn't a sin, it was just a skeleton in his closet. He had smoked marijuana, but that wasn't a sin, it was just against the law. He had withheld testimony on the Johnny Carson show, but that wasn't a sin, it was just a compromise. And then he thought of something.

"Does adultery count as a sin if you do it in a sperm bank?"

"Yes, yes, and unless you embrace Christ as your personal savior, you're going to burn in Hell!"

Whereupon Thomas Eagleton Seagull decided *not* to give his watch to this Jesus enthusiast.

He returned to the Ancient Indian Sage and related to him what had happened.

"Ah, good," was the response. "You are already an excellent student. Already you have mastered the technique of accepting your predestined will. Now, what is your next goal?"

"To avoid disappointment."

"Then you must give up all desires, including your desire to remain desireless. For passions of the spirit require more selfishness to sustain than passions of the flesh. To accept celibacy as a discipline necessary to attain enlightenment is to deny Nature. And to consider enlightenment as a finite stage in your development is to deny the possibility of further growth. Enlightenment is coming. Or to put it another way, enlightenment is *not* coming." He sighed deeply. "Have you not understood the way to maintain a balance between involvement and detachment? You must get in touch with your higher self."

And so it was that Thomas Eagleton Seagull decided to become a product.

Briefly he savored the implications of developing the power to inspire orgasmic release in others without even being conscious himself. That was certainly something to anticipate. He would never be disappointed again.

He realized that to reach such a level he would eventually have to surrender his will entirely. When he was a seagull, he was able to become a human being only through the dedicated exercise of his will. In the process, he had learned that his will existed only in relation to his lack of will.

"Surrendering my will," he prodded himself, "is itself going to be a continuing act of the will."

Thomas Eagleton Seagull looked at his Mickey Mouse watch to see what time it was. Then he gave it to the Ancient Indian Sage and said, "Infinity now!"

I Just Got Back from an Orgy

1968

Not an ordinary orgy, mind you. This one was being filmed. The way that came about was, this professional underground cinematographer, Peter Gessner, whose *Time of the Locust* told about Vietnam the way it is, had advertised in the *Village Voice* for backers for a movie he's been working on recently, telling about the East Village the way it is. He describes the project as a "nonexploitative film on the death of a hippie." It is turning out to be a documentary on the evolution from flower power to thorn warfare.

There were no takers.

So Peter decided to film this orgy sequence and use it as a selling point even if the juicy parts will have to be omitted in the final print. I was invited to attend. There are certain fringe benefits in every job. Some employees steal postage stamps; others use the boss's telephone; still others get invited to orgies.

There were several takers.

The first orgy I ever went to was a publicity party in New York City for a book about a courtesan, *Messalina*, published by Lyle Stuart. There were a lot of grapes, and a lady who got completely undressed and all the men laughed when she sat down to play the piano. That was more or less the peak of the afternoon's festivities. Things are pretty bad when you can't get laid at an orgy.

Then there was a more intimate—and more struc-
tured—session that took place at the Oakland, California,
home of Maxine Serett, author of *The Housewife's Hand-
book on Selective Promiscuity*. (In an obscenity trial, the
medical director and chief psychiatrist of the County Court
of Philadelphia had testified that the book could lead to
masturbation.) Some of those attending knew each other
from previous sessions of Maxine's Workshop in Advanced
Sensuality, an evolutionary process of which this "orgy" was
just another installment. I was there as a journalist.

Everybody was sitting on the floor. An ice-breaker
game was played. People separated into male-female
couples. One would have to confront the other—possibly a stranger till that moment—"Tell me why you would
not want to make out with me." And the other person
would have to respond. That question would be asked
again and again, with a different answer required each
time, until all possibilities had been exhausted. Then it
would be the other person's turn to do the asking.

Maxine saw me taking notes. "Come on, Paul," she
said. "Visiting reporters included."

A young woman smiled at me and said, "I'm available." So we played the game.

"Tell me," I said, "why you would not want to make
out with me."

"I can't think of any reasons."

I blushed, leered and chortled all at once. Then I
asked again. This time she mentioned something about
 her husband, who was elsewhere in the room asking the same question of another girl.

Every guest was given the opportunity to eliminate from a list of all the guests those with whom he or she preferred not to be grouped. Half a dozen mats; one group to a mat; four or five persons constitute a group. Coed, of course. As opposed to your standard orgy where everybody is supposed to do each other simultaneously, in this case the ritual is such that only one person in a group is chosen to be done simultaneously by all the others in that group. To the accompaniment, incidentally, of classical recordings.

Then, in a game of Musical Mats, the groups get reorganized a few times, and each time it becomes the turn of someone who has not yet been done, to indeed get done. A girl involved in doing somebody else's toes was watching the action on a different mat. I asked her if she was voyeuristically inclined. "No," she replied, "it's just that you feel very isolated doing toes." On another mat a fellow who was being done all over by four individuals—two of each gender—suddenly sat up and said, "Hey, I have to know whether a guy or a girl is doing that"—referring to his genital area—"so I know whether I'm enjoying it or not."

Later, there is a nude coffee break, and people perform the usual ballet to avoid touching each other's bodies. It is perhaps a trifle paradoxical for a male who a few moments ago was on a mat deliberately applying Vaseline to a female's nipples to say "excuse me" now because he has accidentally brushed against her buttocks in the kitchen.

But let us return to that orgy I just got back from.

Eighteen of us have gathered for the Lower East Side party at an Upper East Side apartment. We smoke pot to the sound of Big Brother and the Holding Company. We blow pretty plastic bubbles to the background of Judy Collins. We dance to the foreground of Country Joe and the Fish. We hold a mock funeral for Cardinal Spellman, and the American flag is flown at half-mast in mourning for the separation of church and state.

All the while, the cameras roll.

And then, like a play within a play, we are shown a pornographic film. In color, yet. It's a pair of girls engaging in delights of the flesh. I once asked Dr. Albert Ellis why he thought men fantasize about being with lesbians. "Because for a male," he said, "it's like getting two for the price of one."

The film would probably fall under the legal definition of obscenity as delineated by the Supreme Court, because it would be judged as intending to arouse the prurient interest of the viewer and as having no socially redeeming qualities. I disagree with the Supreme Court because I think that the arousal of prurient interest is, *in and of itself*, a socially redeeming quality.

It may be sad if words and images sometimes serve as a substitute for the real thing, but that's the risk of democracy.

Ideally, there would be stag films shown on a television channel. If you recoil at this idea, where is your compassion? Can't you envision an enticing

276

Statue of Liberty writhing in ecstasy as she beckons: "Give me your lonely, your horny...."

Which would you rather—that your child witness on TV a couple making love or a Marine setting fire to a Vietnamese peasant family's hut with his cigarette lighter? Which would you find easier to explain? If a soldier is shown on the news killing what he has deemed to be his enemy and he utters profanities in the process, would you leave in the death-making but bleep out the dirty words?

Can you accept the notion that a pornographic film has educational aspects? People do learn style from the media. In *Search For the Lost Self*, a documentary about emotionally disturbed children, there is one kid who goes into a fantastic verbal rage, then stops suddenly as if following a script with stage directions reading *Aside*, and says with an unknowing smile, "By the way, that's how they do it in soap operas."

So it is that people can learn technique from an obscene movie in which they witness other people doing the things that they can't do in soap operas.

Do you know that at the Kinsey Institute they have been doing exactly that? Couples who have been experiencing difficulty in relating sexually—and relating *generally*; you can't separate one from the other—watch these films together, and identify, and verbalize. And they have been helped.

Oh, if only Bonnie and Clyde had been given such an opportunity. I don't know how the creators of their screenplay knew Clyde was impotent unless maybe Bonnie wrote poetry about it in the underground press of that day.

I had heard all about the gory ending of that flick and how it was such a letdown because you'd built up this crazy empathy with Bonnie and Clyde. When I finally saw it, I did so with an emotional reservation, because I didn't want to get involved. That way I couldn't get hurt.

An attractive redhead at the orgy stripped and stood on the bed in front of the movie screen, and Gessner's *Time of the Locust* was superimposed upon her undulating body. What do you look at? Her breasts? Her vulva? The film?

A few people begin decorating her with Day-Glo paints.

What does it mean to watch frightening scenes of war fleeting across a multicolored girl with whom you'd like to make love? Does mixed media make you more detached or more involved? Do you think of napalm when you kiss? Do you fantasize about antipersonnel steel-pellet bombs when you caress?

The United States has suppressed for over two decades Japanese films showing horrendous aftereffects of the 1945 atomic bombing of Hiroshima. The Japanese government has more than once asked that restrictions on the film be lifted, but the U.S. government has refused because it might damage U.S.-Japanese relations.

It is called, in Japan, *The Film of Illusion*, because it isn't supposed to exist. It was taken by Tokyo University scientists who rushed to Hiroshima soon after the bombing. They were in the midst of filming when U.S. officials arrived and confiscated the film.

Ironically, the American authorities were just as determined to finish the documentary as were the Japanese, and used the same Japanese cameramen who had shot the original footage.

United States policy has opposed distribution of the film, however, because it shows in gruesome detail blast effects and the impact of the bomb on a densely populated area. Three-fifths of the city of 343,000 were obliterated.

Will this be the New Pornography, then?

Will the final scene in *Bonnie and Clyde* someday be banned in retrospect while the previous intimations of fellatio remain uncensored?

In San Francisco the Sexual Freedom League invited me to their New Year's Eve Orgy. Naturally, I accepted. It was for couples only. My date had guests that evening, so we took a cab—the driver gave her a rose, which she in turn gave to me—and after we were admitted to the orgy site, she left me there.

It was a large theatrical studio, with 150 people freeform dancing in the nude. Behind the closed curtains on the stage were 15 small mattresses for those who wished to screw.

I sat on a chair, conspicuous because I was fully dressed, sniffing my rose like a voyeuristic pervert.

As Tim Leary points out, any six people with a lawyer can start a new religion, but any four members of the Sexual Freedom League can start a new "circle." So far there is the Peace Circle, the Kama Sutra Circle, the Eroticism in the Arts Circle and the Horny Men's Discussion Circle, which concluded at one meeting that a good place to meet girls would be the local laundromat.

You don't have to be a circle jerk to love horniness, and so on New Year's Eve a few independents could be found backstage, playing with themselves as they ogled couples playing with each other.

Out front, some males were being frustrated by females who didn't think it should be assumed that they'd automatically have intercourse with their dance partners of the moment. I asked one girl if this wasn't cockteasing.

"No," she replied, "it's okay to hug when you're dancing close, but if a guy starts to kiss me or put his tongue in my ear, I tell him not to. Or if he begins to get an erection, then I tell him we'd better stop dancing. It's only fair. You have to draw the line somewhere."

At eleven o'clock a league official announced that somebody was smoking an illegal substance, and since the orgy, albeit legal, was particularly vulnerable to a police visit, the smoker was endangering the other guests and would he kindly leave.

And three-quarters of the party split.

Midnight arrived, but kissing didn't appear to be part of the anti-tradition.

280 I was undressed by this time, and later a girl started stroking my knee. Not knowing quite what would be appropriate to say under the circumstances, I said, "You're very neighborly."

At two o'clock in the morning we went backstage. If sex has become casual, the drug experience is now treated the way sex once was. You don't usually take LSD on your first date.

Before the Great Pentagon Demonstration, there was a demonstration of LACE, a combination of LSD and DMSO that was absorbed by skin and served as a hallucinatory aphrodisiac. An orgy was staged at the home of Abbie and Anita Hoffman for the benefit of reporters, to show how the drug works. Plans were to spray LACE on the military police in Washington. Now a few couples sprayed it on each other, and although they had met only shortly before, they undressed and started to fuck as though they were not being observed.

One of the couples, who met for the first time at this orgy, subsequently began living together, and they plan to get married. A truly romantic story, revealing a certain aspect of the human condition. On one occasion I attended an orgy with Lenny Bruce. When it was over, he had become obsessed with one particular girl and kept saying to her, "I have to see you alone."

Could it be that the need for love is so strong that a man might go to an orgy in the hope of finding Miss Right?

The Parts Left Out of the Kennedy Book

1967

An executive in the publishing industry, who obviously must remain anonymous, has made available to The Realist *a photostatic copy of the original manuscript of William Manchester's book,* The Death of a President.

Those passages printed here were marked for deletion months before Harper & Row sold the serialization rights to Look *magazine; hence they do not appear even in the "complete" version published by the German magazine* Stern.

In the summer of 1960 the Democratic National Convention in Los Angeles was the scene of a political visitation of the alleged sins of the father upon the son. Lyndon Johnson found himself battling a young, handsome, charming and witty adversary, John F. Kennedy, for the presidential nomination.

The Texan, understandably anxious, allowed his strategy to descend to a strange campaign tactic. He attacked his opponent on the grounds that his father, Joseph P. Kennedy, was a Nazi sympathizer during the time he was United States ambassador to Great Britain, from 1938 to 1940. The senior Kennedy had predicted that Germany would win the war and therefore had urged President Franklin D. Roosevelt to withhold aid to England. Now Johnson found himself fighting pragmatism with pragmatism. It did not work; he lost the nomination.

Ironically, the vicissitudes of regional bloc voting forced Kennedy into selecting Johnson as his running mate. Jack rationalized the feasibility of the situation, but Jackie was unable to forgive Johnson. Her attitude toward him expressed itself as a recurrent paroxysm of barely controlled scorn.

It was common knowledge in Washington social circles that the Chief Executive was something of a ladies' man. His staff included a Secret Service agent, referred to by the code name Dentist, whose duties consisted mainly of escorting to and from a rendezvous site, either in the District of Columbia or while traveling, the models, actresses and other strikingly attractive females chosen by the President for his not-at-all-infrequent trysts. "Get me that," he had said of a certain former Dallas beauty contest winner when plans for his campaign tour were first being discussed. That particular aspect of the itinerary was adjusted, of course, when Mrs. Kennedy decided to accompany her husband.

She was aware of his philandering, but would cover up her dismay by joking, "It runs in the family." The story had gotten back to her about the late Marilyn Monroe using the telephone in the bathroom of her Hollywood home to make a long-distance call to *New York Post* gossip columnist Sidney Skolsky.

"Sid, you won't believe this," she had whispered, "but the attorney general of our country is waiting for me in my bed this very minute—I just had to tell you."

It is difficult to ascertain where on the continuum of Lyndon Johnson's personality innocent boorishness ends and deliberate sadism begins. To have summoned then-Secretary of the Treasury Douglas Dillon for a conference wherein he, the new President, sat defecating as he spoke, might charitably be an example of the former; but to challenge under the same circumstances Senator J. William Fulbright for his opposition to administration policy in Vietnam is considered by insiders to be a frightening instance of the latter. The more Jacqueline Kennedy has tried to erase the crudeness of her husband's successor from her mind, the more it has impinged upon her memories and reinforced her resentment of him.

"It's beyond style," she would confide to friends. "Jack had style, but this is beyond style."

When Arthur Schlesinger Jr. related to her an incident he had witnessed firsthand—Lyndon Johnson had actually placed his penis over the edge of the yacht, bragging to onlookers, "Watch it touch bottom!"—Mrs. Kennedy could not help but shiver with disgust. Capitol Hill reporters have long known of Mr. Johnson's boasts about his six-o'clock-in-the-morning forays with Lady Bird and of his bursts of phallic exhibitionism, whether on a boat, at the swimming pool or in the lavatory.

Apropos of this tendency, Drew Pearson's assistant, Jack Anderson, has remarked: "When Lyndon announces there's going to be a joint session of Congress, everybody cringes."

It is true that Mrs. Kennedy withstood the pressures of scandal, ranging from the woman who picketed the White House carrying a blown-up photograph supposedly of Jack Kennedy sneaking away from the home of Jackie's press secretary, Pamela Turnure, to the *Blauvelt Family Genealogy* that claimed on page 884, under Eleventh Generation, that one Durie Malcolm had "married, third, John F. Kennedy, son of Joseph P. Kennedy, one-time ambassador to England." But the infidelities themselves gnawed away at her—as indeed they would gnaw away at *any* wife in this culture—until finally Jackie left in exasperation. Her father-in-law offered her one million dollars to reconcile. She came back, not for the money but because she sincerely believed that the nation needed Jack Kennedy, and she didn't want to bear the burden of possibly causing him to lose enough public favor to forestall his winning the presidency.

Consequently, she was destined to bear a quite different burden, with great ambivalence—the paradox of fame. She enjoyed playing her role to the hilt, but complained, "Can't they get it into their heads that there's a difference between being the First Lady and being Elizabeth Taylor?" Even after she became First Widow, the movie magazines would not—or could not—leave her alone. Probably the most bizarre invasion of her privacy occurred in *Photoplay*, which asked the question, "Too Soon for Love?" then proceeded to print a coupon that readers were requested to answer and send in. They had a multiple choice: "Should Jackie (1) Devote her life exclusively to her children and the memory of her husband? (2) Begin to date, privately or publicly, and eventually remarry? (3) Marry right away?"

Mrs. Kennedy fumed. "Why don't they give them some *more* decisions to make for me? Some *real* ones. Should I live in occasional sin? Should I use a diaphragm or take the pill? Should I keep it in the medicine cabinet or the bureau drawer?" But she would never lose her dignity in public; her faith in her own image ran too deep.

American leaders tend to have schizophrenic approaches toward one another. They want to expose each other's human frailties at the same time that they do *not* want to remove their fellow emperors' clothes. Bobby Kennedy privately abhors Lyndon Johnson, but publicly calls him "great, and I mean that in every sense of the word." Johnson has referred to Bobby as "that little shit" in private, but continues to laud him for the media.

Gore Vidal has no such restraint. On a television program in London, he explained why Jacqueline Kennedy will never relate to Lyndon Johnson. During that tense flight from Dallas to Washington after the assassination, she inadvertently walked in on Johnson as he was standing over the casket of his predecessor and chuckling. This disclosure was the talk of London, but did not reach these shores.

Of course, President Johnson is often given to inappropriate responses—witness the puzzled timing of his smile when he speaks of grave matters—but we must also assume that Mrs. Kennedy had been traumatized that day and her perception was likely to have been colored by the tragedy. This state of shock must have underlain an incident on Air Force One that this writer conceives to be delirium, but which Mrs. Kennedy insists she actually saw.

"I'm telling you this for the historical record," she said, "so that people a hundred years from now will know what I had to go through."

She corroborated Gore Vidal's story about Lyndon Johnson, continuing: "That man was crouching over the corpse, no longer chuckling but breathing hard and moving his body rhythmically. At first I thought he must be performing some mysterious symbolic rite he'd learned from Mexicans or Indians as a boy. And then I realized—there is only one way to say this—he was literally fucking my husband in the throat. In the bullet wound in the front of his throat. He reached a climax and dismounted. I froze. The next thing I remember, he was being sworn in as the new President."

[*Handwritten marginal notes: 1. Check with Rankin— did secret autopsy show semen in throat wound? 2. Is this simply necrophilia or was LBJ trying to change entry wound from grassy knoll into exit wound from Book Depository by enlarging it?*]

The glaze lifted from Jacqueline Kennedy's eyes.

"I don't believe that Lyndon Johnson had anything to do with a conspiracy, but I do know this—my husband taught me about the nuances of power—if Jack were miraculously to come back to life and suddenly appear in front of Johnson, the first thing Johnson would do now is kill him." She smiled sardonically, adding, "Unless Bobby beat him to it."

Postscript:

When Gore Vidal learned that "The Parts Left Out of the Kennedy Book" would be reprinted in this collection, he sent me the following letter:

Dear Paul,

You remain forever my role model, but... I do wish you'd get that story straight. I never said a word on British TV about LBJ chuckling, etc. I did chat with [conspiracy researcher] Mark Lane *before* I went on. He was spinning theories. I recalled that someone—Goodwin? [Richard Goodwin, a speechwriter for Robert Kennedy who was heavily involved with Jacqueline Kennedy's efforts to censure the Harper & Row book]—had told me that Jackie had gone back to the presidential suite on the plane to find him [Lyndon Johnson], alone, chuckling. That's it. The coffin was in the luggage compartment and anyone who got in there would have been frozen to death. Anyway, (1) I never went public with this story, but Mark Lane had me in headlines as having got it from Jackie—all untrue; (2) If it was Goodwin who told me, he is, as source, permanently tainted.

Buona fortuna,
Gore

REPORT OBSCENE MAIL TO YOUR POSTMASTER
—official stamp cancellation

Opening shot: The American Eagle symbol. Its *E Pluribus Unum* motto fades into the title of this screenplay.

Cut to: A bed. Mom and Dad carry on a dialogue for us to hear while the camera shows them from all possible angles in a parody of the beginning of *Hiroshima, Mon Amour.*

Mom: Honey?

Dad: Yes, dear?

Mom: Could I ask you something?

Dad: Of course.

Mom: Well—it's just that—you don't seem to have your heart in your foreplay tonight.

Dad: You mean it's not going to be a meaningful experience again?

Mom: It's never a meaningful experience anymore. It's just a ritual we go through each time.

Dad: I'm sorry but—do you realize how heavily committed we are?

Mom: Darling, that's what marriage is all about. Total commitment.

Dad: No, no, no—I'm talking about how heavily committed we are in Vietnam.

Mom: Oh, all you ever care about is what's going on in the world. Don't you ever care about my feelings?

Dad: Are you aware that we now have 750,000 troops over there?

Mom: I don't care if the whole American Army is over there.

Dad: You heard what the president said on television. That we should all of us not go to bed any night without asking whether we have done everything we could do that day to win the struggle in Vietnam.

Mom: I'm sure he didn't mean that literally, dear.

Dad: Well, I take it literally. I can't help it. I want to do something.

Mom: They already are doing something.

Dad: It's always they. Never we. I want to feel involved in the world situation.

Mom: I'm going to tell you something, sweetheart, and I want you to listen carefully. I'm getting sick and tired of a marital relationship that has to serve as a barometer of international tension.

Dad: Oh, come now, it can't be as bad as all that.

Mom: Oh, yes, it can. The day they built the Berlin Wall, a barrier went up between us.

Dad: I couldn't help it. I was suffering from universal guilt.

Mom: Nonsense. You were suffering from a severe case of unrequited nationalism.

Dad: Sometimes you talk like a Commie sympathizer.

Mom: And then there was Korea. The day they crossed the 38th Parallel you became impotent.

Dad: It was only temporary. I regained my virility.

Cut to: Close-up of a toaster. Immediately following the words "my virility" in previous scene, two slices of toast pop up. Mom's hand reaches for them. The family—Mom, Dad and college-age Son—are having breakfast. Dad is reading the newspaper. Son is trying to get his attention.

Son: Say, Dad?

Dad: (Camera behind him shows him underlining with a pen certain lines in an editorial.) Just a minute, son. (He writes, "That's so true!" in the margin.) Yes, what is it?

Son: I was thinking about what the president said on television last night about Vietnam—

Dad: And you felt you wanted to participate in some way?

Son: No, I don't want to kill any Vietnamese.

Mom: And you certainly don't want any Vietnamese to kill you.

Dad: Look, you don't have to kill anybody directly. I have a friend of a friend in the Defense Department. What with your ROTC credits, I think we might be able to get you into their special Military Adviser training program.

Son: Dad, what I'm trying to say is that as far as participation goes, I mean where I—me—where I could really do something concrete...well, what I was thinking of was that horrible danger lurking only 90 miles from our own shores.

Mom: You mean Cuba?

Son: No, Mississippi. I'd like to go there this summer.

Dad: But son, it's dangerous down there.

Son: I know that, but I've been doing a lot of soul-searching, and Dad...Mom...I—I've decided to become a voter registration worker in the South.

Mom: Oh, God, how have we failed!

Dad: Now you listen to me, you have no business going to Mississippi—

Son: But Dad—

Mom: Oh, God, where did we go wrong!

Dad: Don't but-Dad me. If you were really concerned about voting rights, you'd want to go to Vietnam and do something about insuring free elections there.

Mom: All right, that's enough—please, no arguments this morning. (To Dad:) Anyway, you've got to get to the office. (To Son:) And if you don't hurry you'll be late for classes.

Son: And what are your plans, Mom?

Mom: I think today I'm going to report some obscene mail to the postmaster. (Doorbell rings. Mom answers door. It's the Mailman. He gives her mail. She looks through the mail.) Ah, yes, here's some more of it now. (Looks at what appears to be a photo.) Uchh, disgusting!

Son: Can I see them, Mom?

Mom: Certainly not. They're obscene photographs. (Heads for telephone.) I'd better make an appointment right now. (Begins dialing.)

 Cut to: A telephone ringing. The Postmaster picks

it up, brings it to his mouth. As he speaks, camera moves back to show him sitting at his desk.

Postmaster: Postmaster speaking...yes, ma'am, yes... two o'clock this afternoon would be fine...oh, ma'am?...please be sure to bring the obscene mail with you...swell...I'll see you then...thank you... goodbye. (Hangs up. Then licks his chops and rubs his hands together.)

Cut to: Attractive, college-age Girl, talking to Son on campus.

Girl: I just don't want to get involved.
Son: Look, I'm not asking you to marry me...I'm not even asking you to go steady. All I want you to do is go on one lousy picket line with me.

Cut to: Dad's office. He presses buzzer of intercom. Secretary's voice says "Yes, sir?"

Dad: After you finish typing out those sales orders, I'd like you to do a little research for me. I want you to check into the height of the average Vietcong.

Cut to: Postmaster's office. Mom enters. He has the window shades down. Candlelight. Soft music on the phonograph.

Postmaster: Did you bring the obscene mail?

Mom: Yes.

Postmaster: You show me yours and I'll show you mine....

Cut to:

  Girl: I just don't want to get involved, that's all.

Cut to:

  Dad: You say the average height of a Vietcong gook is four feet, seven inches—are you sure?

Cut to: Mom and Postmaster dancing.

Cut to:

  Girl: Can't I just meet you at the movies after the demonstration?

Cut to:

  Dad: I have a sneaking suspicion that some of these so-called Vietcong I've seen on the news are actually Red Chinese soldiers.

Cut to:

Postmaster: Would you like to play Post Office?

Cut to:

  Girl: Look, I'll print your placard for you, but that's as far as I go.

296 Cut to:

Dad: They must be smuggling them in through Hanoi.

Cut to: Postmaster and Mom necking furiously on his desk.

Cut to:
Girl: I told you, I don't go all the way.
Cut to: Close-up of a strange man's face. He is a Rapist. He is talking to his Victim, a sweet little old lady.

Rapist: I'm going to rape you.
Victim: You just want me for my body.

Cut to: Son, nuzzling Girl's ear and mumbling into it at the same time.

Son: Please, you don't even have to carry a sign or anything. I just want you to be with me.

Cut to:
Rapist: Promise me you won't scream.
Victim: Oh, yes I will. (Screams.) Help! Criminal assault! Criminal assault! Help! Help! I'm being criminally assaulted! Help! (She keeps this up, and a crowd gathers around them, being careful not to interfere.)
Rapist: I'll still respect you when we're finished.
Victim: Years from now...when you talk about this...be kind.

Cut to: Dad, walking along the street, muttering to himself.

Dad: We're too soft on Communism, too soft, too soft....

Cut to:
Postmaster, teasing: You're giving me a hard time.

Cut to:
Girl, talking to Son: You can do whatever you want. I won't
protest.
Son: I know you've demonstrated with other guys.

Cut to: Victim. Her dress has been torn off. She is wearing old-fashioned pantaloons. Dad walks by and joins the
crowd watching. He speaks to a Man in the crowd.

Dad: Excuse me, what's going on here?
Man: Rape in progress.

(We now have a series of quick cuts, back and forth,
between Postmaster and Mom, between Son and Girl,
between Rapist and Victim—and the reaction on Dad's
face. His strain is clearly visible. We hear his inner voice
each time we return to the scene of the rape.)

Dad's Voice: Why is everybody just standing around and
watching?...This is different from Vietnam—there's
a perfect chance for personal involvement
here....Nobody else is doing anything about it, why
don't you?...You've been waiting all your life for an
opportunity like this....Go ahead....Go on....Go
on....Now!

(Dad surges through the crowd and pounces on the Victim, pummeling her madly and ripping at her undergarments. The crowd applauds and yells its encouragement to him. The crowd suddenly turns into cheering spectators in a baseball stadium, where the attack is now taking place at second base. The noise of the onlookers gets louder and louder, reaches a fantastic pitch, and then...)

Cut to: Close-up of Mom, in the kitchen.

Mom: Dinner's ready.

(Dad goes into the bathroom and washes his hands. As he is about to dry them, we see two towels on the rack. One is inscribed US and the other is inscribed THEM. At this point Son appears in the bathroom doorway. The frame freezes, as at the end of *The 400 Blows*. During this scene we hear the same music to which Postmaster and Mom had been dancing. We hear it faintly at first, but it rises to a crescendo at the freeze. We never find out which towel Dad reaches for.)

How I Spent My First Acid Trip

1965

I'm 33 years old, don't look a night over 23, and I blush with the innocence of a 13-year-old. For, with one recent exception, I've never been high.

Since I don't like the taste of alcohol, I don't drink, so I've never been drunk. I've tried marijuana maybe a dozen times, but always without success, either because I have a psychological resistance to pot or because I don't smoke regular cigarettes and consequently I'm not the least bit proficient at inhaling.

Then along came LSD. Escape was just a swallow away.

On Monday, April 19, I took my first trip, off on a borrowed Psychedelic Jargon—but the unreality of this dream might be more clearly understood within the context of the preceding weekend's reality.

Friday, April 16: I was in Toronto, taping a segment of the Canadian Broadcasting System's controversial TV program *This Hour Has Seven Days.* In my capacity as the atheist/humanist/existentialist from America, I protested in vain the demerits of Christianity with three clergymen, all pleasantly smug in the schizophrenic rationalizations of their vestried interest.

Saturday, April 17: In Washington, D.C., I was marching in front of the White House to protest again the war in Vietnam. Later, thousands of us gathered to hear speeches. Joan Baez sang "With God on Our Side" in nonviolent sarcasm—*Time* magazine called the lyrics tasteless—and a CCNY student's placard summed up the schizophrenia: *If God Were On Our Side, He'd Puke!*

Sunday, April 18: While the Easter parade was taking place elsewhere in New York City, I was with a group of gays picketing across the street from UN headquarters to protest the persecution of gays in Cuba. There were those who feared this conflict would split the left, and they didn't know whether their first loyalty should be to their sexual preference or their politics.

My LSD experience began in an upstairs room at the research mansion in Millbrook, New York, with a solid hour of what was described as "cosmic laughter" by my guide, Michael Hollingshead, the British rascal who had first turned on Tim Leary. The more I laughed, the more I tried to think of depressing things—specifically, the atrocities being committed in Vietnam—and the more uproarious my laughter became.

All that peristalsis was bound to have its effect. I laughed so much I threw up. The nearest outlet was a window, but my hands seemed absolutely unable to open it. Hollingshead opened the window with ease, and I stuck my head out. But was this a guillotine? Was my guide also to be my executioner? Such a fantasy occurred to me, but I trusted him and concentrated instead on the beautiful colors of my vomit.

On the stereo, the Beatles were singing the soundtrack of *A Hard Day's Night*. I started crying—for false joy, it turned out.

My wife, Jeanne, and I had seen that film. At this point we were temporarily separated, but I began to have reverse paranoia—that she was doing nice things for me behind my back—and I had a psychic hallucination that she had not only helped *plan* for that particular album to be played but, moreover, in doing so she must have collaborated with a guy she considered an asshole, in order to please me. What a fantastic thing to do! She had always complained of my association with assholes, yet now she had obviously worked *with* the one who had arranged for this acid trip.

Filled with gratitude, I felt compelled to call her up, but I held back because I also convinced myself that she had *planned* for me to call her up *against my will*. So I figured I would call her up but I would also assure her that I was calling of my own free will. I argued with myself about this for a while, as the dial on the downstairs pay phone became the inanimate object of my megalomania and changed into Dali's limp clock in "The Persistence of Memory."

I sat there immobilized, unable to call until I could rationalize that as long as I *knew* she had programmed this telephone call, and as long as I went through the *process* of deciding to call, it would be acceptable to my warped sense of independence.

The coin slot was all squiggly and vibrating, though. How was I ever going to get a dime in that? But then I took out a dime, and it was all squiggly and vibrating. My dime fit into that coin slot perfectly. I called collect, and the operator asked my name.

"Ringo Starr," I answered.

303

"Do you really want me to say that?"

I was amazed at my calm, logical response: "Of course, operator. It's a private joke between us, and it's the only way she'll accept a collect call."

That wasn't true, but when the operator told Jeanne that there was a collect call from Ringo Starr, she accepted it immediately. I explained why I was calling.

"Paul," she said, "you're telling me you love me for something I didn't *do*." And I had been so sure I'd *communed* with her....

Back upstairs, while I fed myself raisins during an imaginary orgy, Siobhan McKenna, reading from *Finnegan's Wake*—a record chosen by Hollingshead—mentioned raisins. I interpreted this coincidence as Fate.

LSD was fun. I could easily take it once a week, or once a month, or once a year, but if I never take it again I'll still be happy. Napalm is burning someone to death in Vietnam this very minute, but I'm alive, and that's really what I was laughing at—the oneness of tragedy and absurdity.

The climactic message I got while tripping was: IT'S VERY FUNNY! I felt an obligation to share this with all *Realist* readers in one giant headline with nothing else on the front cover. But no, I couldn't do that. I debated the matter, finally concluding that even though I lived by this universal truth, I would not jeopardize the publication by flaunting such a secret.

"Well, the least you can do," my lunar self said, "is inform your readers that no matter how serious anything in *The Realist* may ever appear, you will always be there between the lines saying IT'S VERY FUNNY!"

Okay, but I thought they already knew that.

When I told my mother about taking LSD she was quite concerned.

"It could lead to marijuana," she said.

Life Goes to a Cease-fire

1964

"On the island of Cyprus, Greek and Turkish Cypriots continued to kill each other despite all efforts to keep them apart.
Learning that a force of Greek policemen had laid siege to [a
village], a party of correspondents and photographers, wearing
mufti and including a team from *Life*, rushed to the scene. Suddenly they found themselves squarely in the line of fire and dived
into a ditch.

"Unwilling to stay pinned down, the journalists launched an
unorthodox assault of their own. [A *Time-Life* correspondent]
abruptly stood up in full view of combatants on both sides and
started waving his handkerchief as a flag of truce. His colleagues followed suit and the bunch of them, waving handker-
chiefs, started marching up and down no-man's-land. The
astonished enemies held their fire, and for two hours there was
a shaky peace in this torn Cyprus village."

—*Life* magazine

Photographer: Say, fella! (Waves handkerchief.) I wonder if I could get a picture of you for the folks back
home?

Cypriot: Okay, I guess so. (Poses, still in trench, holding rifle sheepishly.)

Photographer: Watch the birdie, now. (Click!)

Cypriot: Hey, do you think I could have an extra copy for
my wife?

Photographer: Why not? I'll be here for another week, and as soon as I get the negatives back, you can have your choice.

Cypriot: Why do you risk your life like this? I don't understand. How can you take such an awful chance?

Photographer: Apparently our presence brings about a sort of unofficial cease-fire.

Cypriot: You mean nobody wants to kill an innocent bystander, is that it?

Photographer: Yeah, you might put it that way. I suppose my camera just doesn't represent a threat.

Cypriot: Hey, I've got an idea. (Climbs out of trench.) Let me take a picture of you, all right? (As he is about to exchange his rifle for the camera, a shot rings out, and the Cypriot falls to the ground, mortally wounded.)

Photographer: You shouldn't have come out like that. (Takes his picture again.) Anything I can do?

Cypriot: What really bothers me (struggles to talk) is that somewhere in Hollywood there is an actress (coughs) who will be furious (gasps for breath) that I've taken her place on the cover of *Life* magazine (dies).

An Obituary for Lenny Bruce

1964

When I started to write a piece about the problems Lenny Bruce was having, I found myself alluding to him in the past tense, and I realized that it was as if he were already dead. His work was his life, and he couldn't get work. Following his obscenity arrest, club owners were afraid to hire him under threat of losing their liquor license. So, two years before Lenny apparently committed suicide with an overdose of morphine, I wrote this obituary, with his permission.

Lenny's FBI files, which I obtained through the Freedom of Information Act, indicate that shortly before his death, he visited the San Francisco office of the FBI and asked them to investigate a conspiracy by law enforcement officials to silence him. A former assistant district attorney in New York has since admitted that this was an accurate assessment. He stated:

"I feel terrible about Lenny Bruce. He was prosecuted because of his words. He didn't harm anybody, he didn't commit an assault, he didn't steal, he didn't engage in conduct that directly harmed someone else. It was the only thing I did in [District Attorney Frank] Hogan's office that I'm really ashamed of. We drove him into poverty and bankruptcy and then murdered him. We used the law to kill him."

My premature obituary evoked inquiries from newspapers, magazines, wire services, foreign publications, radio and TV. "What's the meaning of it?" asked one editor. "There's a lot of excitement at the city desk."

"That's the meaning of it," I replied.

A TV producer in Chicago who reads six newspapers a day assumed that the story of Lenny Bruce's death must have been suppressed. Many individuals simply assumed that they had missed the news in their daily papers. Some, upon learning the truth, resented my having caused them to waste an emotion.

"This way," I told Lenny, "when you really die, my reaction will be pure. I won't have to think, on some level of consciousness, 'Oh, shit, now I'll have to write an obituary.' "

"There's just one thing you're overlooking, Paul."

"What's that?"

"I may outlive you."

Four years after Lenny's death in 1966, the New York Court of Appeals upheld a lower court's reversal of the guilty verdict.

Lenny Bruce and John F. Kennedy had something in common. They were both great cocksmen. I couldn't help thinking, among the other thoughts one has at the death of a friend, that there must have been a special throb of mourning among all the ladies who had been limited partners in the countless less-than-one-night-stands of comedian and President alike.

Lenny once told me that the role of a comedian was to make the audience laugh "at a minimum of, on the average, once every fifteen seconds—or let's be liberal to escape the hue and cry of the injured, and say one laugh every twenty-five seconds...."

More and more, though, he began to get so serious during performances that it was obvious he wasn't even *hoping* to get a laugh every 15 to 25 seconds. I asked him about this apparent inconsistency with his previous definition of the comedian's role.

"Yes, but I'm changing," he replied.

"What do you mean?"

"I'm not a comedian. I'm Lenny Bruce."

Often an audience would assume he was trying to be funny. For example, when Gary Cooper died in 1961, Bruce was touched by the *New York Daily News* headline, "The Last Roundup," and he shared this with the audience. They laughed, of course. And when he happened to hear on the radio a rock 'n' roll song, "(There Is a Rose in) Spanish Harlem," he bought the record and came onstage with a phonograph and he played it. "Listen to these lyrics," he told the audience. "This is like a Puerto Rican *Porgy and Bess*." They laughed, of course.

At this stage of his career, he would still utter only euphemisms like *frigging* once in a while. It was fun being with Lenny Bruce in those days. In a Minneapolis museum, he improvised a treatise on the symbolism of a piece of abstract sculpture; it was actually a fire extinguisher. In Milwaukee, we decided to have Chinese food one afternoon. We got into a cab, and I asked the driver if he knew of a good Chinese restaurant. Lenny told him, "Take us to where all the Chinese truck drivers go."

In Milwaukee, three plainclothes policemen went into his dressing room, kicked a musician out and told Bruce he was not to talk about politics or religion or sex, or they'd yank him right off the stage. The night

311

before, a group of 28 Catholics had signed a complaint about his act, which they'd gone to see voluntarily. Lenny was scared. He toned down his performance slightly. One of the cops was even smiling at some of the material. They told him later that he shouldn't say "son of a bitch" in his impression of a white-collar drunk.

I asked him why he didn't take any legal action.

"Nah, they'd just say I was trying to get publicity. You know: 'Say anything you want about me, but be sure to spell my name right.' "

They spelled his name right in Philadelphia. He was arrested on a phony narcotics charge. The case was dismissed, but a prominent judge attempted a $10,000 shakedown, and Bruce's idealistic image of Spencer Tracy was shattered. That was the start of his legal career.

There was a time when Lenny read a lot, from Jean-Paul Sartre's study of anti-Semitism to the latest girlie magazine. From city to city he carried in his suitcase a double-volume unabridged dictionary. But in his dying days he carried around law books instead. And he wasn't as much fun to be with anymore.

I remember I was on my way to his hotel in San Francisco, and I passed a barbershop in Chinatown where a sort of Asian Nairobi Trio was inside making music, like a jazzed-up version of "Bei Mir Bist Du Schoen" with violin, guitar and bass fiddle. The owner let me in, whispered that he wouldn't give me a haircut, and I sat down and listened. It was one of those rare and precious moments.

I told Lenny about it, observing that there was a time he would have stopped in that barber shop and listened, and he would have dug that scene with all his soul. But no more. He was too involved with his court cases. So there was no more digging of the scene outside himself.

"But," he reminded me, "I'm fighting for ten years of my life."

He was right. These punishments can become abstractions quickly enough for the rest of us, but 10 years of compulsory rehabilitation was 10 years of his life, and maybe that prospect could somehow interfere with one's freeform style of living.

A few years before, I had overheard the following conversation in a Milwaukee nightclub:

"Nobody knows where Lenny Bruce is staying."

"He's staying at the YMCA."

"What does he do there?"

"They say he reads a lot."

"He's gonna read himself right out of a job."

In a way this was an accurate prediction, because Lenny found that novelists didn't have to say *frig* or *fug* any more. He began to want the same privilege of non-restriction. His point of view was the same onstage and off, and he wanted to talk to his friends in the nightclub with the same freedom of vocabulary he could exercise in the living room.

But Lenny wasn't exactly like a book. He finally realized that. "If a book is obscene in Georgia," he observed, "it'll be obscene in Bellmore, Long Island. No, it doesn't work that way. Fortunately, the law is not a punishment instrument. It always protects. If the book is obscene in Georgia, and the book is not obscene in Bellmore, Long Island, the Supreme Court don't make no never mind, because the police can arrest you every day no matter what you say because they found that what you say is erratic. One day you say 'Pray for Chessman' and next day you say 'Lynch Gilligan.' "

And, it's safe to speculate, Lenny's "obscenity" was a convenient rationalization to arrest him for saying such things as "Cardinal Spellman looks like Shirley Temple."

Lenny fantasized the following courtroom dialogue (although the first line was borrowed from reality):

Prosecutor: Your honor, this man made a mockery of the Church, not just the Catholic Church, but the Lutheran Church—the Church itself—he made a vulgar and obscene mockery.

Judge: Any lesbian that's found guilty of rape, no matter how good a tough-looking bitch she is, one of the elements of rape will be that there's penetration, and if there is none, the bench says "Fuck you, counsel."

Prosecutor: Your honor, I've never heard such language in the court in my life.

Judge: The use of foul and coarse language will not constitute obscenity if it is used as a realistic portrayal, and Cardinal Spellman is modeling for a Barbie Doll. He looks like he's made out of celluloid to me....

The real courtroom was just as absurd.

In New York, an expert witness for the prosecution, Ernest van den Haag, who writes for *National Review* and teaches a course at the New School titled "The Crisis of the Individual," was testifying about contemporary community standards and said that he's made a study of nightclubs although he hasn't been inside one for 20 years.

Defense attorney Ephraim London conceded that Judge Murtagh might never have visited a prostitute to gain his knowledge of that field, and Judge Phipps pointed out "so the record will be clear" that London was referring to Murtagh's book about prostitution, *Cast the First Stone*.

Not being a whore, however, Lenny Bruce didn't arouse enough sympathy from those two on the three-judge panel to acquit him. His monologues, they stated, contained anecdotes and reflections that were obscene. They listed the following examples, quoted verbatim from their decision:

1. Eleanor Roosevelt and her display of "tits."

2 Jacqueline Kennedy "hauling ass" at the moment of the late President's assassination.

3. St. Paul giving up "fucking."

4. An accident victim—who lost a foot in the accident—who made sexual advances to a nurse, while in the ambulance taking him to the hospital.

5. Uncle Willie discussing the "apples" of a 12-year-old girl.

6. Seemingly sexual intimacy with a chicken.

7. "Pissing in the sink" and "pissing" from a building's ledge.

8. The verb "to come," with its obvious reference to sexual orgasm.

9. The reunited couple discussing adulteries

315

committed during their separation, and the suggestion of a wife's denial of infidelity, even when
discovered by her husband.

10. "Shoving" a funnel of hot lead "up one's ass."

11. The story dealing with the masked man,
Tonto, and an unnatural sex act.

12. Mildred Babe [Didrikson] Zaharias and the
"dyke profile of 1939."

The court further stated, "The dominant theme of the performances appealed to the prurient interest"—later con-
tradicting this by saying that "the monologues were not
erotic. They were not lust-inciting, but while they did not
arouse sex, they insulted sex and debased it."

The judges added that "the performances were lacking in 'redeeming social importance' " and that "the monologues contained little or no literary or artistic merit. They
were merely a device to enable Bruce to exploit the use
of obscene language. They were devoid of any cohe-
siveness. They were a series of unconnected items that
contain little of social significance. They were chaotic,
haphazard, and inartful." If Lenny Bruce has gone to Hell,
the devil will have been replaced by an art critic wearing
black judicial robes.

The law states that to be obscene, material must be
utterly without any redeeming social importance. Therefore, if *one single person* felt that Bruce's performances
had *the slightest bit* of redeeming social importance—and

there were several who so testified—then he
should have been found not guilty.

If I ever end up in court on anything, I'll probably get a haircut, wear a white shirt and tie, and swear on the Bible, because I don't have the guts to be as consistent as Lenny was—in faded blue denims and long sideburns, calling the oath a farce. He always wanted to win purely on the basis of the law, and so he was willing to risk losing purely on the basis of prejudice by judge or jury. For a sub-theme of Bruce's work had always been that people get indignant over the wrong issues.

During one of the performances for which he was arrested, he made that point thusly: "If a titty is bloodied and maimed, it's clean; but if the titty is pretty it's dirty. And that's why you never find any atrocity photos at obscenity trials, with distended stomachs and ripped-up breasts...." In the course of that same performance, he also said, "Query: If a tape recording is my voice, are they using me to testify against myself, since it's my voice that would indict me?"

Lenny asked me, "Can you imagine them playing *that* in court?" This was months later, in his dingy hotel room, cluttered with tapes and transcripts and photostats and law journals and briefs.

"I love the law," he said.

Only his love had developed into an obsession. Once, when he was teasing his eight-year-old daughter, Kitty, by pretending not to believe what she was telling him, she said, "Daddy, you'd believe me if it was on tape."

As more and more nightclub owners became more and more afraid to hire him, he devoted more and more of his time and energy to the law. When he finally did get a weekend booking in Monterey, he remarked, "I feel like it's taking me away from my work."

He would let almost nothing interrupt his practice, not even sleeping or eating. He turned down an invitation to be on the Les Crane show. He refused to be the subject of a *New Yorker* profile. He wouldn't give Lillian Ross even 15 minutes of his time.

Lenny Bruce's formal education never went beyond grammar school, but he became something of a legal genius. His research uncovered an amendment to New York's statute 1140a, under which he was arrested, which *excluded from arrest* in an indecent performance: stagehands, spectators and—here was the fulcrum of his defense—*actors*. The law, signed by then-Governor Franklin Roosevelt in 1931, had been misapplied to him.

"Ignoring the mandate of Franklin D. Roosevelt," observed Lenny the Lawyer, "is a great deal more offensive than saying that Eleanor had lovely nay-nays."

And so he spent Thanksgiving Day looking for a judge to help him. He still had dreams of Lewis Stone from the old Andy Hardy movies. "If I win," he asked me, "what do I win?" He answered himself: "The right to work." He had borrowed $5000 to advertise "five performances only," and then the theater owner refused to open the premises for the first show on Thanksgiving Eve.

Lenny could still make fun of his predicament. "I was thinking of going on welfare," he commented.

Onstage he would have mumbled through boredom some old bits, he would have created some new material (on his bed there was a clipping about how

318

Philadelphia officials had declared that anyone wearing blackface in the Mummers parade this year would be ineligible for a prize), but mostly he would have lectured about law enforcement and courtroom procedures and statutory subtleties. He had always talked about his environment, and it was just that encounters with the law had increasingly *become* his environment.

Outside the court, he was Lenny the Hermit, confining himself to his home in Hollywood Hills, with a barbed-wire fence but an open gate, visited by friends, hangers-on and peace officers harassing him as they stood near the unused pool. His mother would bring over his daughter. Lenny would have been up all night with his legal conflicts, stopping only to eat some grapes and work on landscaping his garden even though rain was pouring down hard and he would end up all muddy ("But if I go to jail, I want to have it finished")—and then in the morning he would take a shower with his daughter. He didn't want her to grow up thinking there was something dirty about the human body.

On a rare occasion, he left his house to be in the audience at my "Evening with a Self-Styled Phony" at the Steve Allen Playhouse. During the question-and-answer session following my ramblings, he asked me to clarify what I had said about empathizing with people with perversions. So I gave as a for-instance the time in a subway when I let myself get aroused by an elderly lady whose buttocks were unavoidably rubbing against me. Lenny called out, "You're sick!" The audience howled, I said "Thank you, Mr. President," and that ended *that* show.

319

In New York, the judges ordered him to undergo a psychiatric examination before they passed sentence. "Watch," Lenny told me, chuckling but also with genuine terror, "they're gonna say I have a persecution complex."

The first issue of *The Realist* quoted Malcolm Muggeridge, former editor of *Punch*, the British humor magazine: "As I see it, the only pleasure of living is that every joke should be made, every thought expressed, every line of investigation, irrespective of its direction, pursued to the uttermost limits that human ingenuity, courage and understanding can take it. The moment that limits are set...then the flavor is gone." More than anyone else I've ever known, Lenny Bruce lived up to that ideal. But now the flavor will never be the same, for he is gone.

When the newspaper called me up at three o'clock that cold December morning for a statement, I simply said, "It was God's will."

1964

It seems there was this lady who purchased a bottle of Coca-Cola from the vending machine in the cafeteria where she worked. After drinking from the bottle, she discovered a dead mouse in it. Several witnesses testified that the mouse was unquestionably in the bottle when it came from the vending machine and before the lady started drinking from it. Of course, if they were really her friends, they would have told her up front, wouldn't they have?

Anyway, she—and for a reason that must surely go under the heading of Mental Anguish by Association, her husband also—brought a lawsuit (*Trembly et al. vs. Coca-Cola Bottling Co.*, 138 N.Y.S. 2d 332, if you *must* know) based upon negligence and breach of warranty.

The defense claimed that the question of breach of warranty should not have been introduced into the case. After all, when did Coca-Cola ever *guarantee* not to have dead mice in their bottles? Certainly the Fatty Arbuckle case had set a precedent in that area.

As for the charge of negligence, the defense depended on testimony concerning its washing, rinsing and filling operations, indicating that its standards were comparable to those employed by other similar bottling companies.

The court held that such evidence of adherence to established and accepted washing and inspecting practices was admissible but not necessarily conclusive, since that procedure did not eliminate the possibility of human or mechanical failure in the discovery of foreign substances.

In other words, there shouldn't have been a dead mouse in the Coca-Cola bottle, notwithstanding the fact that other bottling companies could have had dead mice in their bottles if they really wanted to.

Well, the jury decided in favor of the plaintiffs, and the lady and her husband won a lot of money.

Now, the question is, at what point did her disdain for the past turn to anticipation of the future? Or did those two disparate emotions exist simultaneously right from the start? Does the threshold of pleasure really teeter on a continuum of ego-involvement?

What I'm getting at is, when Richard Nixon was asked for a statement about the murder of Lee Harvey Oswald following the assassination of John F. Kennedy—and he said, "Two rights don't make a wrong; I mean..."—was it a Freudian slip to which any significance could justifiably be attached?

And when Governor Nelson Rockefeller declared a 30-day moratorium on political speeches, that was a political speech. Otherwise, he wouldn't have had to bother announcing it.

Jack Kennedy probably would have been reelected to the presidency in 1964—for the wrong reason: glamour.

322

Reporters loved to gossip about the voluptuous movie stars with whom he was always supposed to be having affairs. On one occasion there was joking speculation as to whom Barry Goldwater would be carrying on with, were he to be elected. Helen Hayes? Irene Dunne?

Now Lyndon Johnson is President. Who will be his mistress—Judy Canova?

I know this is in questionable taste, but you know that won't stop me. The assassination of a president has already degenerated to the questioning of a stripper named Jada who had worked for Jack Ruby. "I don't know what his politics are," she said. "He never discussed that with me." Is it in questionable taste to wonder about the relationships between Ruby's strippers and Dallas policemen?

Lenny Bruce says he knows comedians who have worked for Ruby. They report that he has a tattoo of a vagina on his upper arm, and when he makes a muscle it opens and closes.

During his lifetime John F. Kennedy provided the inspiration for a candy bar called Vigah. The commercialization of his death was merely its chocolate-covered extension. Grownups have *their* Beatles too.

One post-assassination manufacturer had this special note in his ad: "Volume Buyers—Organization Fund-Raising Chairmen—Write or Wire for Fast Information." All purchases are voluntary, though, and if there be any criticism of the sellers, it must apply equally to the buyers. That includes the more than 400 persons (at last count) who have requested photostatic copies of President Kennedy's will at the going rate of $100.

An ad for the Hilton Hotels in *Time* magazine was "dedicated to the hope of a new world of friendship symbolized by the eternal flame lighted at Arlington November 25, 1963." How long *is* an eternity? On December 10, the eternal flame was accidentally extinguished by some holy water. That's the trouble with automation. If only a way could be found to enlist an infinite army of sacrificial Buddhist monks to serve as an ever-overlapping eternal flame.

Within minutes after the word flashed that President Kennedy had been shot, all four Nike missile stations that surround the Dallas-Fort Worth area were called to an emergency "one-minute" alert. All that was lacking was the placing of a warhead atop the missile, which would have taken about 15 seconds. (During the Cuban crisis, the Nike bases in Texas were top priority and were on a *five*-minute standby.)

I was scheduled to speak at a gathering sponsored by the Committee to Aid the Monroe Defendants on Saturday night, November 23, the day after the assassination, and the invitations promised: "Laugh with Paul Krassner...." It wasn't easy.

Since this was a left-of-center group who had first assumed that the assassin was a right-winger, I started out by asking, "Aren't you sorry it turned out to one of your nuts instead of one of theirs?"

 Apparently, the FBI also believed it was a right-winger, for within an hour after the shooting, they went to H. L. Hunt and advised him to get out of Dallas, fast. Under an assumed name he took American Airlines flight 42 to New York, for a shopping trip. (Announcements over the loudspeaker at the airport in Dallas still refer to Kennedy Airport as Idlewild.)

But pity the poor FBI. People kept calling them and telling them what they had *dreamed* during the nights preceding and following the assassination.

When the time came for comments about the assassination, though, everybody got into the act—each and every ax-grinder—from the *American Jewish Examiner* ("American Jewry Grievously Weeps for Adored, Martyred President") to *White Citizens Awake* ("Our beloved President was assassinated by Marxist Lee Oswald who was silenced by a Jew, Jacob Rubinstein, before he could expose that Communism is Jewish"); from the *National Informer* ("Did Castro Order Death of Kennedy?") to the John Birch Society's full-page ad ("We believe that the President of the United States has been murdered by a Communist within the United States....Nor is it in character for the Communists to rest on this success. Instead, we can expect them to use the shock, grief and confusion of the American people, resulting from the assassination of our President, as an opportunity for pushing their own plans faster") with a coupon at the bottom; from the Advance Youth Organization ("Build a living memorial to President Kennedy....Picket U.S. Steel") to Robert Moses's statement on November 22 ("The World's Fair had counted confidently on the international leadership, support and encouragement of President

Kennedy. We shall have to go on without his support but with his inspiration ever in mind").

Coda: In the Los Angeles *Herald-Dispatch*, a Negro weekly, Waldo Phillips claimed that Kennedy was "shot at his own request." The motivation? "Medical reports had indicated that he had less than 90 days to live due to an intensified terminal malign spinal cancer." Why not die a martyr?

Jack Kennedy would have appreciated that. He had a sense of the absurd. Once in the White House, he doodled on a piece of scrap paper—along with the usual geometric designs—*The President of the United States*.

And it would have amused him to know that the Chamber of Commerce in Evanston, Illinois, has voted not to name anything after him.

According to Hearst correspondent Ruth Montgomery, readers have been calling newspaper offices with the suggestion that Jackie Kennedy be nominated for Vice President because they were impressed by her "superb dignity" (as opposed to what AP described as Christine Keeler's "stony composure").

Variety's obituary inadvertently summed it up: "President Kennedy is a loss to America and the world but, since partisans and individuals alike inevitably see matters in their own reflection, Show Business is especially the loser as a result of the still unbelievable tragedy."

And in the excitement of his sorrow, one man reached the sublime. Jack Ruby, journalistically returning to the crime of his scene, explained in a syndi-cated apologia: "Suddenly there was a great commotion. Out of there walked Oswald. He was about ten feet from me. He came out all of a sudden with a smirky, defiant, cursing, vicious Communist expression on his face."

When Oswald was reported to have boasted to his wife that he was the sniper who took a shot at General Edwin Walker in Dallas last spring, Walker himself had no comment on the investigation. He did have comments about the Kennedy assassination. "There are no gaps," he told a Canadian interviewer. "Oswald admitted being a Communist....How can you say it isn't clear as day? You are all brainwashed."

He also asserted that Jack Ruby was a member of the American Civil Liberties Union—which, he added, is Red-tainted. However, defense attorney Melvin Belli points out: "Everyone who knows me will tell you I am strongly anti-Communist. I took this case only after I made certain Jack Ruby had no Communist leanings or con-nections."

Actually, Jack Ruby is capitalism personified. A cou-ple of years ago, there was an article in *Adam*, a raunchy girlie magazine, about Amateur Night for strippers at Ruby's nightclub:

"Amateur Night proved an immediate hit with the Carousel's audiences. Many times the erotic enthusiasm of the spectators seemed exceeded only by the impish delight of the amateur performers—hot and breathless from the experience of baring their bodies for the first time before an audience....The wild cheers of Amateur

Night spectators indicate they feel they're getting their $2 worth—which is the cover charge. Many of the luckier males get an added bonus when the girls—who are encouraged by the club to mix with the customers—accept an invitation to have a drink. The club serves beer and setups, with most of the customers bringing their own bottles. The club caters to large stag groups, especially college students and oil or cattle conventioneers. Most of the amateurs 'pack' the audience with an admiring throng of their boyfriends to cheer for them. 'In fact,' manager Ruby observed, 'many of the girls perform at Amateur Night under the urging of their boyfriends who claim they see a lot more of them on our stage than they do on a date.' "

Thus spake the avenger of our president. Alleged avenger. When I wrote that Ruby "allegedly" shot Oswald, I asked, parenthetically, "How's that for fairness?" *The New York Times* accepted the torch; a Texas-datelined story stated: "Oswald was allegedly shot by Ruby." (The *Times* wasn't as objective in reporting that Pope Paul visited the site where Jesus performed his first miracle. Allegedly performed, *New York Times*, baby.)

But it was a real TV first. And for those who slept late that Sunday morning, the scene was repeated over and over throughout the day and evening in glorious slow motion. Even children who were jaded from watching *Divorce Court* all week sat there like refugees from a Keane portrait.

Let us, however, postulate this hypothesis: Instead of Ruby, one of his amateur strippers goes to the basement of the Dallas city jail. She sees Oswald and his smirky Communist expression. In a flashing moment of Christian compassion, she throws off all her clothes and runs to Oswald, embracing him with loving forgiveness.

Would the live TV cameras remain focused?

Would the kinescope be shown again and again?

Would parents permit their children to watch?

Would Colpix issue an LP comparable to the album it *has* issued: *Four Days That Shocked the World*, including "Lee Harvey Oswald—actual voice—denial of guilt," statements by the Dallas cops and best of all, a track devoted to an "on-the-spot report from basement of the Dallas jail at the moment Oswald is shot by Jack Ruby."

Doesn't that grab you by the decibels?

The only thing missing is Pearl Bailey calling out, "One more time!"

In Chicago, radio stations have received a record, a musical tribute to John F. Kennedy titled *God's Game of Checkers*. It was accompanied by a press release stating that Jack Ruby was mailed the first copy of this "controversial phonograph record" and that his attorneys are expected to play the record in the courtroom "as the high point of the defense." The song lyrics, rendered in hootenanny style, tell of a cowboy watching on TV the grief of the late president's young son at the funeral.

And, finally, the Kennedy funeral was reviewed in *Casket and Sunnyside* ("The Authority of the Funeral Service Industry Since 1871"):

"All during the funeral period there were members of the armed forces participating in the ceremonies and rituals in Washington and all over the world including the ships at sea. Salutes were fired periodically—not at an enemy but to honor the death of the Commander in Chief. While this was being done there was the trust that God would not permit anything else to overwhelm the nation during the funeral period. The same trust was shared by the heads of other nations who left their lands to be present for the funeral.... At the same time that the nation mourned the death of the President and accorded him a funeral appropriate to his place and rank in our society, it is to be understood and appreciated that his accused assassin, Lee Oswald, was also accorded a funeral and burial. These two events serve not only to remind us of the oneness of our society but compel us to recognize that there is a dignity to all men regardless of their accomplishments or their crimes. November 25, 1963, was the day the world stood still. On that day this nation buried President Kennedy, Officer Tippit and accused assassin Oswald. In doing so this country saw its unity under God and reaffirmed the dignity of man."

The assassination of President Kennedy will change the course of history, but for all of us—if only because he is dead and we are alive—the occurrence was in the end just one more dead mouse in a Coke bottle.

Castro and the Kennedy Convertible

1961

SCENE I

Castro: You are going to attack Cuba.

Kennedy: We are not going to attack Cuba.

Castro: Why do you say that?

Kennedy: Because it would be immoral for us to play the role of an aggressor nation.

SCENE II

Castro: We have put down the invasion that you were behind.

Kennedy: We were not behind the invasion.

Castro: Why do you say that?

Kennedy: Because if we were behind the invasion it would have been successful.

SCENE III

Castro: Now the truth is out—you were behind the invasion.

Kennedy: No matter that it was unsuccessful.

Castro: Why do you say that?

Kennedy: Because it is better to have lied and attacked than never to have been President at all.

1961

As the opening credits roll across the screen, the voice of Fabian is heard, singing Steve Allen's lovely lyrics to Dimitri Tiomkin's haunting melody, "Psychita's Theme."

> Cling to me, my darling nymphet
> Like I'm a rock, and you're a limpet,
> Your charm could fill the missile gap, li'l Psychita,
> Oh-oh-oh-oh-oh
> You are even sweeter than apple ci-eeder,
> Oh-oh-oh-oh-oh
> So tell me, dearest one, no matter what
> The weather,
> That clouds up above
> Won't darken our love,
> And we'll have a lifetime of puberty,
> Together.

The scene: An aerial view of a highway. Pan to neon sign reading "Mom and Dad's Motel." Cut to motel office. Mom and Dad, played by Robert and Loretta Young, are sitting and talking.

Mom: Ever since they built that new highway a year ago, our business has been falling off something awful.

Dad: And we can't always depend on Humbert Shmumbert in Cabin 5. Do you realize he's been our only guest for the entire past year? Let's face it, he's not going to stay at our motel forever. What happens to us when he decides to go?

Mom: Well, frankly, dear, I'll breathe a sign of relief. I don't like all the time our daughter has been spending with Mr. Shmumbert. It's not right. It's not healthy.

Dad: You're worried about Humbert Shmumbert? Why, that harmless fellow is no more lecherous than I am. And besides, Psychita's only a child. What could a middle-age man possibly see in her?

Cut to: Full view of exterior of cabin. Close-up of door, showing number 5. Cut to interior. Music: "Psychita's Theme." Psychita stands in front of a rumpled bed, wearing only panties, a half-slip and a brassiere. She is 13, going on 14.

Psychita: Humbert, will you please come help me fasten this darned old bra?

Humbert Shmumbert, played by Oscar Levant, enters from bathroom, buttoning his shirt. He is 47, going on 48.

Humbert: I don't see why you have to wear one of these things anyway. (Helping her.) Your breast-buds have barely begun to grow.

Psychita: I know, but Mom saw this advertisement for Teenform, and it says, "The understanding mother buys her daughter's first bra now, whether or not she needs it physically." It's supposed to give me poise or something. It even expands as I develop. The ad says they sell it at all "understanding stores."

Humbert: Alas, the trend along Madison Avenue is becoming increasingly anthropomorphic.

Psychita: Oh, stop showing off all the time with those big words, willya, please.

Humbert: God, I just adore you to pieces when you become perturbed like that.

Psychita: You can let go of my brassiere now. I have to do my algebra homework.

Fade in to highway scene. Cars rolling along. Close in on car being driven by beautiful woman, Janet Victim, played by Tony Curtis. Close-up of the seat next to her, empty except for a paper bag stuffed with $40,000. Janet's thoughts can be heard as she makes driving grimaces.

Janet's voice: I'm a thief, that's what I am. If only I could tell somebody and unburden my conscience. But how could anyone ever sympathize with a common ordinary thief? Why, they might just as well—they might just as well identify with—with a pedophiliac! (Starts to rain.) Hmmmm, it's starting to rain. I'd better pull up at a motel for the night.

Cut to Mom and Dad's Motel. Janet's car pulls up. Cut to interior of motel office. Dad is reading the paper. Mom is sewing. Psychita is doing her algebra homework. Humbert is twiddling his thumbs. Janet Victim enters.

Janet: Oh, hello there. I wonder if I could have a room for tonight.

Mom: Surely. Just sign the book there.

Close-up of Janet's hand signing registry book: "Janet Pseudonym, Thief River Falls, Minn."

Mom: Nasty night for driving.

Psychita: Two x equals y plus one.

Humbert: I'll help you with your luggage (looks at registry book), Miss Pseudonym.

Janet: Oh—yes. Thank you.

Humbert takes her suitcase. Janet carries the paper bag full of money herself. Cut to exterior shot, showing Psychita standing on motel office porch, as Humbert and Janet enter cabin. Close in on door, showing number 4. Cut to interior of Cabin 4.

Janet: I would like very much to confide in you, Mr. Shmumbert.

Humbert: Call me Humbert. Tell me, do you have any photographs of yourself when you were a little girl—perhaps at the age of 12?

Janet: No, I'm sorry, I don't. Listen, I've stolen some money.

Humbert: Oh, that's too bad. You don't happen to have
a younger sister, do you?

Janet: No, I'm sorry, I don't. I think it's forty thousand dollars.

Humbert: Perchance you have some young female
cousins?

Janet: No, I'm sorry, I don't. Would you help me count the
money, please?

Cut to exterior of motel office. Psychita is still standing
on the porch. Cut to interior. Mom is still sewing, and Dad
is still reading. Close in on clock above the desk. As if to
indicate the passage of time, the hands move from eight
o'clock to nine o'clock within two seconds.

Dad: There goes that crazy clock acting up again.

Mom: Yes, we really ought to have it fixed one of these
days.

Cut to exterior of motel office. Follow direction of Psychita's eyes to Cabin 4, as Humbert leaves it and returns
to his own cabin. Cut to close-up of Psychita's face. Her
eyes harden with anger. Through tight lips, she speaks.

Psychita: Why, that no-good, two-timing, dirty-rotten, dou-
ble-crossing fink!

Cut to interior of Cabin 4. Janet is just stepping into the
shower. She smiles when she sees what brand of
soap is there. She lathers herself up, smiling a

337

toothy smile all the while. Suddenly the shower curtain parts. Standing there is Psychita, large butcher knife in hand. Music: "Psychita's Theme." Janet stops smiling.

Psychita: For the first time in your life, feel really dead.

Psychita wields the weapon over and over again. Camera achieves montage-in-motion effect by a series of quick cuts: to knife, to Janet's arm, to knife, to look of horror on Janet's face, to knife, to Janet's chest—very important in this scene to show all that violence but no nipples.

Cut to interior of motel office. Mom and Dad are sitting and talking.

Dad: Nothing exciting ever happens around here.
Mom: Why don't you see if there's anything good on TV?
Dad: I guess I'll go put on one of those stupid family situation comedies—but you never see *them* watching television.

A moment after Dad exits, Psychita walks in, unnoticed by Mom. She stands there, dripping blood.

Psychita: Mom, I have to talk to you. Something has just happened that is going to change my whole life.
Mom: Why, of course, dear. I feel sorry for girls who can't go to their mothers for a frank talk. Thank goodness you and I have never been embarrassed with

338

each other. I can make it all sound so simple and easy and natural that you'll get over your nervousness in a hurry. You'll feel sure, secure, safe. Nothing can show, no one can know. I'll tell you the nicer way.

Psychita: I know all that jazz, Mom. No odor, no chafing, no binding. "Don't be an outsider," the Tampax ad says. But what I'm trying to tell you is—

Humbert bursts into the room.

Humbert: You must call the police! Right away! Someone has murdered Janet Pseudonym. Someone...(sees Psychita, dripping blood)—Psychita! You? How? Why?

Psychita: Big man, you always use such big words, now look at you. I did it because of you, ya big lug. I saw how long you were in her cabin.

Humbert: But we were only counting the money she'd stolen. Forty thousand dollars in singles takes a lot of time to count. It's not as if we were doing anything wrong, Psychita.

Fade in on the office of Dr. Listen, a world-renowned psychiatrist, played by Sal Mineo. Mom and Dad sit in rapt attention as he speaks.

Dr. Listen: The money was returned to Janet Victim's employer, and Humbert Shmumbert is in prison on two counts: one, for impairing the morals of a minor; two, by withholding information from the police, as an accessory to an embezzler. But I'm sure that what you're really interested in hearing about is Psychita. As you know, she's been committed here at State Hospital for an indefinite period of time, depending on our final prognosis. We've tested her in every possible way, from the Stanford-Binet to the Rorschach, from the Multiphasic Personality Inventory to the Thematic Apperception Pictures, from sensorymotor coordination to encephalographic examination, from hypnosis to sodium pentothal. Basically, this is what we've uncovered. As in the case of any teenager, Psychita became a product of her culture, which is essentially an imbroglio of romantically oriented phantasmagoria.

Mom and Dad: Yes, Doctor.

Dr. Listen: Her world was built of concepts derived not only from the two of you in your role as parents, but she also most definitely internalized quite deeply the values imparted to her by movies, advice-to-the-lovelorn columns, popular fiction, magazine articles, window displays, tabloid newspapers and so on *ad infinitum*. Our civilization, through its various media of mass communication, does everything it can to imbue its members—and teenagers are of course the most susceptible—with one of society's pivotal paradoxes: that lust in and of itself is bad, but that it becomes automatically transformed into love concomitantly with the act of marriage.

Mom and Dad: Of course, Doctor.

Dr. Listen: Now then, the average teenage girl is able to accept this inconsistency by getting involved with the details of vicariousness—wearing lipstick, for example—but Psychita's environment, you must realize, also included the motel you both operate. A motel by its very nature is dedicated, to a very large extent, to the promulgation in actuality of the loveless lust that Psychita's peers were able to rationalize through lustless (or puppy) love.

Mom and Dad: Go on, Doctor.

Dr. Listen: When Humbert Shmumbert happened to come along, Psychita was psychologically ready for him. She was also, unfortunately, keenly fitted to satisfy his particular perversion. For an entire year, then, they carried on a glorious—albeit aberrant—affair. And then Janet Victim entered the picture. Psychita became, literally, insanely jealous. Her schizophrenic environment that I have described, combined with a predisposition resulting from certain hereditary factors, led her almost inevitably to commit her crime of passion.

Mom and Dad: Certain hereditary factors, Doctor?

Dr. Listen: Ah, yes. When you first adopted Psychita, it was thought advisable not to reveal to you the truth about her medical history. Now, however, the story can—nay, must—be told. Fifteen years ago, a psychotic by the name of Normal Bates was committed to this very institution. I shan't go into the details of his particular split personality.

Suffice it to say that Normal had a classic Oedipus complex. Whether or not we accept the orthodox Freudian doctrine of universality is immaterial, for most of us do not kill our rival-fathers. To all intents and purposes, though, Normal Bates did exactly that. He killed his mother—a divorcée—and her lover. The guilt and anguish he felt as a consequence of committing matricide toppled Normal over the brink to the insanity toward which he had been heading all along. In order to convince himself, so to speak, that he had not killed his mother, he became her. Not constantly, mind you. Sometimes, he was himself. Other times, he was her. And still other times he was, simultaneously, both himself and his mother.

Mom and Dad: But what does all this have to do with Psychita, Doctor?

Dr. Listen: You see, in some of the lower forms of life, there appears to be a gradual anatomical combining of the sexes. This is true, for example, in the ostracods, a group of shellfish that actually reproduce their species by the process of self-impregnation. But this of course becomes rarer and rarer as we ascend the evolutionary scale. Nevertheless, it was discovered during a routine physical checkup of Normal Bates that he had a certain type of tumor known as the arrhenoblastoma, so named because it contains blastodermic cells. The blastoderm is one of the basic membranes in an unborn child, from which all the organs of the fetal body develop. Now, even though Normal Bates's actual mother was dead, her personality remained alive in one half of his mind while—logically enough—in the other half of his mind Normal's Oedipal desires likewise remained alive. And although it has been a well-kept secret all these years, one night he shattered medical history.

Mom and Dad: You mean?

Dr. Listen: Yes. Normal Bates was a functional hermaphrodite. He was Psychita's father and mother, both. He was also, as it were, her brother.

Fade in on a room in State Hospital, empty except for Psychita, sitting on a chair and smiling wanly. She is holding a middle-age-man doll. As the camera moves further and further away, her thoughts are still audible, accompanied by slow, muted music.

Psychita's voice: So they think they're getting even by keeping me here till I'm an adult, huh? Oh, sure, I'll miss living a normal teenage life. I'll miss exerting a strong influence on family purchases from furniture to automobiles as well as commanding a sizable amount of disposable income on my own. I'll miss being a member of a group that saved the movie industry, that buys 90% of all the single records sold and half the albums, that spends more on clothes than the average for the total population, that spends $300 million a year on cosmetics alone. Yes, I'll miss being part of the

343

$10 billion teenage market. But I'll have the last laugh, society, because you haven't gained an inmate, you've lost a consumer.

The strains of "Psychita's Theme" become louder and louder, drowning out the sound of a childlike giggle.

1961

And now, class, we shall take up a sociological phenomenon that took place back in the Twentieth Century—the Freedom Riders.

In May of the year 1961, there began attempts to eliminate bus-station racial barriers. Violence resulted. Unfortunately, it was Mother's Day, and most of the police force was off-duty.

Schools were started to teach prospective Freedom Riders the principles of passive resistance. Simultaneously, other schools were started to teach the principles of mob rule.

Historical evidence indicates that waiting rooms had signs reading WHITE INTRASTATE PASSENGERS and NEGRO INTRASTATE PASSENGERS. You see, the courts had outlawed enforced segregation only among *interstate* bus passengers. Thus a new race made its appearance in the South—the interstate Negro. Obviously, the interstate Negro was far superior to the intrastate Negro.

At any rate, United States marshals were sent to straighten things out. Fortunately, the CIA was not behind this invasion—no need to remind you of the Cuban fiasco, although one student here, who shall remain nameless, described the Cuban fiasco in a mid-semester examination as a small foreign sports car.

Despite this racial blot on our national conscience, the Attorney General of that day, one Robert Kennedy, assured the world that in 40 years there might well be a Negro elected President of the country. And, of course, in the year 2000, an interstate Negro was indeed voted into that high office.

While on the way to Washington, however, he was arrested in Jackson, Mississippi, for using an intrastate white urinal.

1958

This is a diaphragm. Women use it when they don't want to have a baby. That is very immoral. Why, you ask? Because it is artificial, that's why. But never fear. There are other methods to prevent conception. They are very moral. Why, you ask? Because they are natural, that's why.

This is big brother's pajama bottoms. He had a nocturnal emission last night. What a shame. It woke him up. But see the semen stain. It has millions of dead sperms. They were killed the natural way.

This is big sister's sanitary napkin. It doesn't look very sanitary any more, does it? There is an ovum somewhere in that bloody mess. But it will never be fertilized. It will be flushed down the toilet bowl. That's the natural way too.

This is a baby. It was born dead. Every day in the USA, 136,000 infants are stillborn or die within a month. Now suppose their Mommies and Daddies had interfered artificially with the process of procreation. God's purpose would never have been achieved. Just think what a tragedy that would've been. But as least some of the dead babies were baptized. That's the natural way.

This is a special calendar. It marks off menstrual periods. That's for the rhythm method of not having babies. A husband and wife are in bed. They don't want to have a baby yet. They start to make love. Then they get out of bed. Because they have to look at the calendar. The calendar says that the time is fertile. So they don't continue making love. Unless they'd like to gamble on having an unwanted baby. That's the natural way.

This is a husband and wife who *do* want to have a baby. But the calendar says that the time is sterile. Lucky for them they have a calendar. It saves them from having unnecessary intercourse. So they stop making love. Because one thing would lead to another. Ask advice-to-the-lovelorn columnist Dorothy Dix. She should know. She tried it once with her colleague, Dr. Crane. Just to prove her theory. Later she had to write to his Worry Clinic. She was worried because she missed her period. She missed it very much.

This is a confessional booth. There is a screen in the middle. The person on one side is a priest. The person on the other side is a confessor. He is confessing that he has had evil thoughts. The priest tells him that to have an evil thought is evil. It is just as evil as committing the evil act that the evil thought is about. Priests never have evil thoughts themselves. They don't have to. They have an ample supply of other people's evil thoughts to draw upon.

This is the husband and wife again. The ones who don't want to have a baby yet. Now the calendar says that the time is sterile. How convenient. Now they can make love without stopping. And without worrying. But they are good, consistent Catholics. And so they are worrying. Because they know that evil thoughts are evil Their evil thought is to have intercourse but to avoid having a baby. They can't be sure they won't have a baby—that's why

the rhythm system is moral—but the *intention* is there. Tomorrow they will go to confession.

A Child's Primer on Telethons

1958

See the tired man. He has been up all night. He is running a telethon. He wants the people to send money. It is for leukemia. That is a disease. Little children like you can catch it. Evil.

See the sexy girl. She is a singer. She doesn't know whether the telethon is for leukemia or dystrophy or gonorrhea. Her agent got her the booking. She needs the exposure. Notice her cleavage.

See the handsome man. He *does* know that it's for leukemia. You can tell. He is singing a calypso melody. Listen to the lyrics. Give-your-money, he sings, to-leukemia. Give-your-money...to-leukemia. Listen to the audience applaud. He is very talented.

See the sincere politician. He is running for reelection in November. He is against leukemia. He is willing to take an oath against it. That proves he is against it.

See the wealthy businessman. He is making a donation. He wants his company's name mentioned. Then we can buy his product. Then he will make profits. Then he can make another donation next year. Splendid.

See the little boy. He has leukemia. Too bad for him. The nice lady is holding him up to the TV camera. Aren't you glad it's not you? But wouldn't you like to be on television? Maybe you can fall down a well.

See the pretty scorecard. It tells how much money they get. They want a million dollars. Uncle Sam has many million dollars. He cuts medical research funds by more than seven million dollars. Why? He needs the money for more important things.

See the mushroom cloud. That costs lots of money. It has loads of particles. They cause leukemia. Money might help to find a cure. That is why we have telethons. See the tired man.